East European Perspectives on European Security and Cooperation

edited by
Robert R. King
Robert W. Dean

The Praeger Special Studies program—
utilizing the most modern and efficient book
production techniques and a selective
worldwide distribution network—makes
available to the academic, government, and
business communities significant, timely
research in U.S. and international economic, social, and political development.

East European Perspectives on European Security and Cooperation

Praeger Publishers   New York   Washington   London

Library of Congress Cataloging in Publication Data

King, Robert R
    East European perspectives on European security
and cooperation.

    (Praeger special studies in international politics
and government)
    1. Europe, Eastern—National security.   2. Europe,
Eastern—Foreign relations.   3. World politics—
1965-   I. Dean, Robert W., joint author.
II. Title.
UA646.8.K53   327.47   73-15188
ISBN 0-275-28788-2

PRAEGER PUBLISHERS
111 Fourth Avenue, New York, N.Y. 10003, U.S.A.
5, Cromwell Place, London SW7 2JL, England

Published in the United States of America in 1974
by Praeger Publishers, Inc.

© 1974 by Praeger Publishers, Inc.

Printed in the United States of America

Eastern Europe has entered a period of transition. Many of the dogmas associated with the cold-war confrontation have been dispelled as the result of the evolving Soviet-American policy of détente. Rigid and hesitant patterns of East-West interaction have given way on both sides to a vigorous search for possible areas of cooperation, most importantly in the realm of expanded economic links. Although a certain degree of caution is called for in projecting the final outcome, the prospect of broader and deeper ties has nevertheless introduced the need to adapt both foreign and domestic policies in order to exploit détente. For Eastern Europe, readjusting foreign policy toward the West to take advantage of economic and political opportunities has been counterbalanced by measures to control the impact of détente at home. How this evolving process, which is generally designated as European security, has influenced the policies and perceptions of each of the countries in the Warsaw Pact and Yugoslavia is the subject of this book.

The editors wish to thank the Research and Analysis Division of Radio Free Europe and its director, J. F. Brown, for assistance in the preparation of this volume. Unity Evans carefully and methodically edited the manuscript, and Maria Hofheinz cheerfully typed the final draft. A number of the contributors to this volume are associated with Radio Free Europe. The views set forth in the various essays and in the volume as a whole, however, are those of the editors and contributors, and do not necessarily reflect the opinions or policies of Radio Free Europe.

CONTENTS

Chapter   Page

LIST OF ABBREVIATIONS

ADN   Allgemeiner Deutscher Nachrichtendienst (German Press Agency, the official East German news service)

Agerpres   Agentia Romana de Presa (Rumanian Press Agency, the official Rumanian news service)

agitprop   agitation and propaganda (usually a reference to ideological activity carried out under the direction of communist parties)

APA   Austria Presse-Agentur (Austrian Press Agency)

BBC   British Broadcasting Corporation

BTA   Bulgarska Telegrafna Agentsia (Bulgarian Telegraph Agency, the official Bulgarian news service)

CC   Central Committee

CDU   Christlich-Demokratische Union (Christian Democratic Union, a West German political party)

Ceteka   Ceskoslovenska Tiskova Kancelar (Czechoslovak Press Agency, the official Czechoslovak news service)

Comecon   Council for Mutual Economic Assistance

CPCS   Communist Party of Czechoslovakia

CPSU   Communist Party of the Soviet Union

CSCE   Conference on Security and Cooperation in Europe

CSSR   Czechoslovak Socialist Republic

CSU   Christlich-Soziale Union (Christian Social Union, a West German political party)

DDR   Deutsche Demokratische Republik (German Democratic Republic)

DM   Deutsche Mark (the West German monetary unit)

dpa	Deutsche Presse-Agentur (German Press Agency, a West German news service)
ECE	Economic Commission for Europe
EEC	European Economic Community
FRG	Federal Republic of Germany
GATT	General Agreement on Tariffs and Trade
GDR	German Democratic Republic
GFR	German Federal Republic (a formulation used by certain communist countries to designate West Germany)
HSWP	Hungarian Socialist Workers' Party (the Hungarian communist party)
IMF	International Monetary Fund
MBFR	Mutual and Balanced Force Reductions
MFN	most-favored nation
MFR	Mutual Force Reductions
MTI	Magyar Tavirati Iroda (Hungarian Telegraphic Agency, the official Hungarian news service)
NATO	North Atlantic Treaty Organization
NEM	New Economic Mechanism (in Hungary)
PAP	Polska Agencja Prasowa (Polish Press Agency, the official Polish news service)
PRC	People's Republic of China
RSR	Rumanian Socialist Republic
SACEUR	Supreme Allied Commander, Europe
SALT	Strategic Arms Limitation Talks

SED   Sozialistische Einheitspartei Deutschlands
           (Socialist Unity Party of Germany, the East Ger-
           man communist party)

UNCTAD   United Nations Conference on Trade and Develop-
           ment

INTRODUCTION
Robert W. Dean
Robert R. King

In his testimony before the Senate Foreign Relations Committee, Secretary of State designate Henry Kissinger observed that many of the countries of Eastern Europe had "advocated a European security conference precisely because they believe it gives them a greater possibility to develop their national identities, and in several of these countries it has led not to a change in the governmental structure but to a greater, what we would call liberalization within the governmental structure." With two important changes Kissinger's comment could serve as the point of departure for this volume. First, the focus must be expanded from the formal conference to the whole process of détente which it symbolizes and may accelerate; second, "adaptation" must be substituted for "liberalization." In ratifying the European status quo, the security conference may create the conditions for altering some of the more rigid rules that have determined patterns of interaction between East and West, as well as some of those that have governed domestic development in Eastern Europe for some 25 years. There is little in the visible process of détente, however, that guarantees (or for that matter excludes) liberalization in either the domestic or the foreign policies of the East European states. But that circumstances relevant to both are in a period of change is hardly open to question.

It is the uncertainty about the dimensions of this change and the ambiguity of the "European security" concept itself that warrant a closer look at the issue from the perspective of the individual East European states, as well as a discussion of related military, economic, and ideological variables.

THE EVOLUTION OF THE IDEA

Several definitions of "European security" are possible. In the more constricted sense it means the Soviet-inspired proposal for a multilateral conference of European states, which, as initially conceived, would not have dealt with the fundamental issues at the root of European insecurity—the German question, including Berlin, and the confrontation of opposing military blocs. But the call for

such a conference became a standing feature of Soviet and
Warsaw Pact policies toward Western Europe.

In the broader sense "European security" encompasses
the whole question of the nature of future relationships
among European states. This definition would include the
entire complex of. Soviet policy toward Europe and American-
European relations, the conference being only one aspect
of these wider issues. It is, however, the conference itself that has come to be the focus and forum for the re-
examination of East-West relations in Europe. The original
concept of a gathering that would produce a declaration on
the principles of interstate relations and a mutual pledge
of nonaggression was expanded to include economic, technological, and cultural relations, and, at the insistence of
the United States and other members of the North Atlantic
alliance, mutual military force reductions. Expanding the
conference agenda and dovetailing it with concurrent military discussions have tended to give the question a predominant position in contemporary European foreign policies.

The holding of a European conference, as opposed to
a four-power meeting, was initially proposed by Soviet Foreign Minister Vyacheslav Molotov in 1954, but the true gen-
esis of the conference was the suggestion made at the United
Nations by Polish Foreign Minister Adam Rapacki in December
1964. After that the proposal was taken up on various occasions, but it was at the Bucharest meeting of the Political Consultative Committee of the Warsaw Pact in June 1966
that it was treated as a matter of importance and urgency.
American involvement in Vietnam and the limitation of
French participation in NATO appeared to presage a decline
in American influence in Europe, which might be encouraged
and exploited by a Soviet policy of détente. At the same
time the Soviet Union viewed a security conference as a
vehicle for gaining recognition and consolidation of its
hegemony over Eastern Europe. This recognition seemed particularly important in light of the opposition from Rumania
and other East European states in the months preceding the
Bucharest meeting to Soviet efforts to strengthen the Warsaw Pact.

The next step in the Soviet campaign was the Karlovy
Vary (Czechoslovakia) conference of European communist parties in April 1967, which reiterated the call for a conference and at the same time launched a program to promote
the dissolution of NATO. This aggressive campaign against
American influence, however, encountered problems that reduced its momentum. Rumania, which refused even to send a
representative to Karlovy Vary, had defied the Pact policy

of a joint posture toward West Germany and precipitated a
crisis within the organization by establishing diplomatic
relations with Bonn three months before the Czechoslovak
conference. The Middle East crisis of 1967 refocused Soviet attention outside Europe, and events in Czechoslovakia
preoccupied Moscow during 1968. European security was, for
a time, in abeyance.

Despite the trauma of the invasion of Czechoslovakia,
Soviet European policy did not undergo any significant al-
teration. Seven months after the invasion the leaders of
the Warsaw Pact countries issued a message to all European
states, one of the major points of which was the convening
of a conference on European security. The so-called Budapest Appeal was less specific than the earlier Bucharest
and Karlovy Vary documents, but it was considerably more
moderate in tone and reflected an interest in serious negotiation rather than propaganda. Although the conference
itself was still over four years away, the Budapest meeting was followed by concrete steps to improve East-West relations, which had been demanded by the West European states
before they would agree to participate in a multilateral
gathering. In May 1969 Polish party leader Wladyslaw Gomulka departed from the earlier collective Warsaw Pact approach and suggested bilateral negotiations with West Germany on recognition of the western frontiers of Poland.
In October of the same year the new Brandt-Scheel coalition
government in Bonn announced its willingness to discuss unresolved questions with the Warsaw Pact states. Meetings
of the foreign ministers of the Warsaw Pact states in
Prague in October and of the party leaders in Moscow in
December paved the way for improving bilateral relations
with the Federal Republic. In August 1970 a Soviet-West
German nonaggression treaty was signed, and a similar agreement between Bonn and Warsaw, clearly accepting the Oder-
Neisse border, was signed in December of the same year.
The four-power agreement on the status of Berlin, upon
which the Western states insisted before agreeing to a
conference, was concluded in September 1971.

Although the United States and the NATO countries insisted that certain concrete steps, in particular the Berlin agreement, must precede the convocation of a security
conference, the major obstacle was their determination to
link the conference with measures to reduce military forces
in Europe. The United States has all along been the primary advocate of force-reduction negotiations. In the
face of growing demands for cuts in the number of American
troops stationed abroad, Washington has favored mutual

force reduction, coupling American troop withdrawals with similar Soviet moves, to prevent weakening the Western military posture. At the NATO meeting in Reykjavik in June 1968, the proposal for Mutual and Balanced Force Reductions (MBFR) talks was formulated. (France, incidentally, never has associated itself with the scheme.) The Soviet Union and its allies revealed little interest in force reduction talks. By 1970 it had become clear that Western participation in a security conference depended upon them, but it was only in the spring of 1971 that Soviet party leader Leonid Brezhnev indicated a willingness to negotiate on military cuts. During the visit of Presidential Assistant Kissinger to Moscow in September 1972 it was agreed that preparatory talks for a security conference would begin in Helsinki in November and that preliminary discussions on force reductions would begin in January 1973.

At the Prague conference of the foreign ministers of the Warsaw Pact states in January 1972, the East European states proposed that the agenda of the conference include three items: (1) agreement upon a system of obligations by European states that would exclude the use or threat of force in interstate relations, and agreement to observe principles of international conduct, including noninterference in internal affairs and respect for sovereignty; (2) expansion of economic, technological, scientific, and cultural exchanges among the states of Europe; (3) creation of a permanent representative body of the states participating in the conference, whose aim would be to further European security and cooperation. The NATO states' proposed agenda included provisions similar to the first and second Warsaw Pact points, but it also insisted that the conference should adopt measures to encourage the freer movement of people, ideas, and information, as well as cooperation in cultural, economic, technological, scientific, and environmental protection fields.

During the preliminary discussions from November 1972 until June 1973 the groundwork was laid for the conference itself, the first stage of which took place in Helsinki in July 1973 at foreign-minister level. During this phase, which lasted just over one week, the various participants made known their positions on the questions of inter-European relations and approved the decisions taken during the preparatory phase. The second stage of the conference opened in Geneva in September 1973 at specialist level, and three commissions were established, broken down into various subcommittees. The first commission was instituted to draft a statement of principles to govern international

conduct and propose "confidence-building measures," which
would include such steps as advance notification of military maneuvers. The second commission was to deal with
trade, industrial cooperation, science and technology, environmental problems, and other economic issues. The third
was to present proposals on the freer movement of individuals and groups, expanded dissemination of information,
broadened cultural exchanges, and educational cooperation.
The third and last phase of the security conference will
presumably approve the results achieved at Geneva. The
level of representation at this final stage and its timing
will undoubtedly depend on the progress made during the
second stage; it will probably take place in late 1974.
      The relationship between the security conference and
the force reduction talks is complicated, but sluggishness
in Vienna could undoubtedly retard progress in Geneva and
Helsinki. Five months of force reduction negotiations in
Vienna (January to June 1973) produced few concrete results
and left most important issues undecided. Resumed in October 1973, the talks have shown little promise of early
results. Although the Soviet Union prefers to reject any
link between them and the Conference on Security and Cooperation in Europe (CSCE), the United States and its NATO
allies have consistently reiterated that they run in parallel. With the growing domestic pressure to reduce American forces in Europe, the United States may well make
progress in Vienna a more explicit condition for the success of the security conference.

A PERIOD OF TRANSITION AND
NEW PRIORITIES

      The Warsaw Pact governments have approached the idea
of European security and a European security "system" with
a characteristic penchant for generalization. This has
been an asset in projecting a common profile as well as
a self-evident case for the conference. There can be little doubt that a genuine convergence of interests exists
among the East European states in the conference as a vehicle for the ratification of the political-territorial
status quo. Beyond this the consensus is less credible.
A host of essentially national priorities and heterogeneous
considerations exist that impinge upon the attitudes of
the respective political elites. Such factors as the differing levels of development, dissimilar styles of leadership, and the diverse relationships of political elites to

their respective populations mean that each will approach
the longer-term prospects of European security with a variety of expectations and objectives. The subject of this
book is therefore less the conference itself than the possible consequences for Eastern Europe of the détente process
associated with it.

The broad hypothesis on which this book is based is
that Eastern Europe is in a period of transition or readjustment in which the former East-West equilibrium based
on a balance of tensions has been, if not eliminated, then
considerably altered. In the West German contractual acceptance of the political separateness of the GDR and of
Poland's claim to the Western Territories, the penultimate
step toward recognition of two major East European security
goals has been achieved. This, as well as the multilateral
confirmation of the status quo that the CSCE is expected
to produce, has introduced what might be termed a period
of new priorities in Eastern Europe. This is as true for
Poland, where interests long held in check by more fundamental objectives have now moved center stage, as it is
for Yugoslavia, where the Soviet-American détente requires
the readjustment of a nonalignment policy during a period
of domestic instability intensified by the imminence of
Marshal Tito's departure.

The ramifications for the communist portion of Europe
in this period are of course only one side of the equation.
Formal acceptance of the status quo, paradoxically enough,
introduces a new measure of ambiguity into the entire European setting. The reference points of national policy have
changed--to what extent and with what longer-term effects
it is impossible to say--and states on either side of the
European divide must confront the thorny problems of adaptation. For the NATO countries the reduction of tensions
has rendered the common creed of Soviet hostility toward
the West less believable in the view of many. The unanimity
that would provide a meaningful platform for alliance policy in the future has thus far proved elusive, and the
specter of dislocations like that which erupted between
Washington and Bonn during the Middle East war has become
ever more real. The Kremlin is hardly burdened with the
task of seeking a voluntary consensus within the Soviet
sphere. But inasmuch as East-West agreements have removed
some of the more compelling reasons for the marriage of
Soviet-East European interests, they introduce a new element of uncertainty into intrabloc relations. With the
burning questions of East-West division resolved, the Soviet role is less that of ultimate guarantor of basic East

European claims than that of an arbiter of the terms and
modes of peaceful engagement.

In the five years since the Czechoslovak reformist ex- ✓
periment was aborted by the Soviet Union, the Western approach to Eastern Europe has undergone a fundamental change.
Western policy has now turned away from the assumption that
an evident, if inchoate, East European desire for greater
independence from Moscow was capable of acceleration and
exploitation, and that therein lay opportunities for enhancing Western security, and has accepted the premise
that, at least in the short term, the real opportunity,
indeed, the only opportunity, for reordering political and
social relations in Europe in the interests of general
European security lies in negotiations with the USSR. To
phase it somewhat differently, the West recognizes that the
road to a new modus vivendi with the states of Eastern Europe runs of necessity through Moscow.

Conventional, as well as official, wisdom seems now to
be governed by the proposition that as Soviet security is
enhanced (specifically by mitigating the perceived potential military threat and eliminating prospective areas of
conflict such as uncertainty over borders), as confrontation within the European system is decreased and cooperation expanded, Moscow will be inclined to permit its East
European client states greater freedom. Within the expanded
limits of Soviet tolerance their prerogatives in internal
and external affairs will be liberalized. So, too, Western
recognition of the permanence of political and territorial
realities in East Europe will diminish the psychological
and strategic insecurity of the regimes themselves and remove any lingering hesitancy over greater interaction with
the West. The earlier inclination toward isolation and
self-containment bred by the ambiguity of Western intentions
will be greatly dissipated. This will be especially true
of East Germany, Czechoslovakia, and Poland.

Following this reasoning further, the longer-term, but
ineluctable, effect of such a European security settlement
would be to promote the definition and pursuit of political and economic objectives along more clearly discernible
national lines. The more fluid context of interstate relations in Europe resulting from Soviet-West German efforts
to reach a broad understanding, as well as the forward
movement toward the European security conference itself,
is already apparent.

As to what must be achieved at the conference, the
West is unanimous in pressing for solutions that would re-

duce the physical and moral distance between peoples and societies. Greater interaction at this level, the Western argument runs, is just as important as state-to-state accords in providing a bulwark of European security, in ameliorating mutual suspicion, and in creating a grid of human understanding. This of course seems a doubtful proposition to many in authority in Eastern Europe. A European settlement that results in increased contacts and more permeable borders could have a corrosive effect on the fabric of stability in some East European societies. These prospects perforce generate pressures that encourage each country to consider how, within the framework of an ongoing détente, it will secure, extend, and protect its own interests. For all of them an emergent European security settlement presents both opportunities and dangers, and it is such considerations that, official rhetoric notwithstanding, are likely to have an individuating effect.

In Eastern Europe these developments have given rise to both conformist and divergent pressures. For the German Democratic Republic the departures from past practices involved in a policy of détente perhaps spell greater uncertainty, and therefore ambivalence, than for others. The East German leadership has found itself obliged to reach an accommodation with its Western counterpart in order to secure the keystone of its policy: formal recognition of its sovereignty and independence. At the same time it is forced to wrestle with the fact that such a gain, accomplished in the broader framework of a European security settlement, will aggravate the difficulty of maintaining and securing its own system and ideology. The danger of ideological infection has been heightened, and if the existing inflexibly orthodox system is to remain intact, new methods of immunization must be found. In such a setting, the GDR would be forced, as Peter Bender has put it, into new exercises in legitimacy. The policy of Abgrenzung (delimitation) has emerged as the GDR's first line of defense in the new situation.

The GDR stands at one end of the East European spectrum, followed closely by the Husak leadership of Czechoslovakia. On the other end are those countries where the gap between society and the party elite is by all indications less pronounced, where the regimes are psychologically and strategically more secure, and where there were no fundamental disputes similar to that between West Germany on the one hand and Poland, the GDR, and Czechoslovakia on the other. The prime example is Rumania, where the credibility and strength of Ceausescu's policy of autonomy from the

Soviet Union stems from the roots it has established in the public consciousness. In Hungary a similar correspondence between public policy and popular sentiment exists, the result of an inventive economic policy that has produced tangible benefits for the populace over the last five years and placed the Kadar regime on a more secure political footing internally. Such regimes, while not without observable strains, are perhaps less dependent on the need to preserve ideological purity as a domestic prop and hence might be more disposed to emphasize the gains of greater maneuverability vis-à-vis Moscow, which would advance their domestic priorities, as well as to avail themselves of the multilevel cooperation with the West that might result from the European security conference. Their natural interests, for example, in expanding cooperation in the Danubian area would seem a far more permissible undertaking from the point of view of the Soviets, who have been extremely reluctant to sanction any experiments in regionalism. In Poland the Gierek leadership's policy of industrial modernization and its commitment to improving the standard of living are predicated on a new European atmosphere that permits and encourages a more cooperative and activist policy toward the West.

Will the general acceptance of the European status quo contribute to limiting and redefining the future role of the Soviet Union in Eastern Europe, particularly with regard to crisis management? It is widely acknowledged that the Soviets were reluctant to intervene openly in Poland in December 1970 partly because the policy of cooperation with the West would have suffered a severe setback had they done so. It is a defensible hypothesis that, following a European security conference and taking into account the continuing benefits that it would presumably derive from a European settlement, the Kremlin would feel constrained to show an even greater restraint in Eastern Europe in order to preserve its stake in a settlement it worked so hard to bring about. Furthermore, if the Kremlin policy makers are in fact motivated by longer-range aspirations to extend Soviet influence in Western Europe, to "Finlandize" it, they can hardly afford a second violent Czechoslovak-type exercise in Eastern Europe to preempt "counterrevolution." The USSR, that is, will retain the ultima ratio of its hegemony, but it will face new restraints in exercising it. Any longer-term influence would certainly be vitiated by the use of force now or in the foreseeable future, a fact surely not lost on the Rumanian and Yugoslav leaderships in their enthusiasm for European security.

On the other hand, it is also clear that recognition of the status quo in Europe means recognition of Soviet power and influence in Eastern Europe, and its prerogatives in protecting both. The acknowledgment of Soviet power and influence as it stands today is the essence of the SALT and other East-West agreements concluded thus far, just as it will be the essence of any settlement reached at a European security conference or of any foreseeable evolution within the Soviet sphere.

At the same time, however, recognition of the status quo in its broadest outlines does not mean that a period of stasis will have begun in Europe. On the contrary, the expectations of both sides and of some individual states are that the new situation will create the basis for movement and political evolution in accord with their own interests. In a new situation in which military force becomes a less acceptable instrument, the maintenance of cohesion and stability in Eastern Europe becomes a key question for the Soviet Union. While it may be possible to codify relations between East and West in accordance with the principles of noninterference and renunciation of force, it is unlikely that the Soviet Union will in practice reorder its relations with the East European states on such a basis. The prospect of military intervention hardly accords with the principles that are ostensibly to be recognized as the ground rules of a new European order. Nevertheless, elaboration of the ideological thesis that the principles of socialist international relations differ qualitatively from those that govern relations among nonsocialist states provides a continuing a priori basis for intervention by force. The right to extinguish counterrevolution, the common obligation to defend "socialist sovereignty," and the device of multilateral action in preserving common socialist interests are in fact the doctrinal baggage of a Pax Sovieticus.

On the other hand, with Soviet security more assured the obligation to orthodoxy in domestic development might be less stringently enforced and patterns of divergence might seem less of a threat. Indeed, one might speculate that Moscow would be acting in its own interests in permitting a greater flexibility to East European regimes in solving their own particular domestic problems and in seeking a more genuine political, economic, and social equilibrium, one that corresponds more closely to specific national conditions. The limits will still be broadly defined by the Soviet Union but their tolerance will be expanded so that while diversity in Eastern Europe as a whole might be greater the stability achieved would be more genuine. Assuming that domestic development proceeds along these lines, the likelihood of internal disruption will diminish and with it the need for Soviet intervention. The signs of domestic diversity that now exist in the Warsaw Pact--in Hungary, Rumania, and Poland--are evidence of an incipient Soviet flexibility that the evolution of a European security settlement could encourage.

It should be stressed, however, that whatever new tolerance levels the process of détente may produce, experimentation and diversity are bound to have strict limits. Varying domestic patterns in Eastern Europe must not be confused with the surrender or diminution of Soviet control. What has been outlined above is the greater Soviet willingness to tolerate diversity--not a change in the real balance of Soviet-East European relationships in favor of the latter. It is to be assumed that East European leaderships are being advised by their Soviet mentor that the pace of détente must be matched by their ability to control its impact on their domestic stability and on their relations with Moscow. This means that even closer bonds and greater accommodation with Moscow are more than ever the essential condition for taking advantage of increased collaboration with the West in the national interest. These are evident in recent efforts toward coordination and synchronization in the area of ideology, in the acceleration of economic integration, and in the now annual institution of the Crimean conferences of party leaders of the Warsaw Pact.

The constant, then, in this multilevel and complex process of détente is Soviet determination to maintain hegemony undiluted and unchallenged. The essays that follow discuss which of the new pressures that can be distinguished in Eastern Europe are likely to interact with the changes in the region that are broadly associated with European security and the reduction of tensions.

East European Perspectives on European Security and Cooperation

SOVIET POLICY IN EASTERN EUROPE AND THE IMPACT OF DÉTENTE
J. F. Brown

Cohesion with viability has been the main Soviet aim in Eastern Europe since the death of Stalin. The definition of cohesion in this context is relatively easy: a situation where, in spite of local differences caused by differing local conditions, there is a general conformity of ideological, political, and economic policy, both domestic and foreign, as laid down by the Soviet Union in any particular period. By viability is meant a degree of confidence and efficiency, especially economic, in the East European states that would increasingly legitimize communist rule and correspondingly reduce the Soviet need for a preventive preoccupation with the region.

The Stalinist period in Eastern Europe--here defined as the period during which Stalin lived--was relatively brief. It was mainly devoted to a dual process of <u>Gleichschaltung</u>: at the national level through the imposition of leaderships trusted by Moscow; and at the domestic level through a revolutionary transformation that assumed earthquake dimensions at the time and later laid the foundation for future socialist development.

The cohesion, therefore, that came about under Stalin was of a very distinctive kind, one that achieved its revolutionary purpose but that could hardly last once the purpose was achieved. Viability was hardly relevant to it, since viability is essentially a postrevolutionary condition. Indeed, had Stalin lived beyond 1953, the system he created, successful though it was for the purposes of basic transformation, would have required modification in the new phases of consolidation and development. This job was left to his heirs.

There was no consistent Soviet policy in Eastern Europe for several years after Stalin's death. This was because of leadership divisions in Moscow and the paralysis in constructive thinking produced by the departure of a leader of Stalin's stature. True, important changes in policy, leadership, and atmosphere did occur in Eastern Europe very shortly after Stalin died, but they were nothing more than reflections of what was happening in the Soviet Union itself. They were reactions to Stalin rather than indications of how Moscow thought the East European states should be governed or their leaderships manipulated. The upheavals in Hungary and Poland in 1956 and the varying degrees of instability in other states as well were the result of the essential unviability of Stalin's system and of the failure to replace it by any new concept in the three years after his death.

This failure Nikita Khrushchev sought to redeem. Within a year after the Hungarian and Polish upheavals his leadership had been recognized; within two years it had been consolidated. In 1956 the seriousness of the task was evident; by 1958 he had the means to try to meet it.

His attempts and his only partial success are well known enough to observers of recent East European history and need not be covered in detail here. Against a theoretical background of newly enunciated principles of equality governing relations among socialist states, Khrushchev saw the two institutions of Warsaw Pact and Comecon, particularly the latter, as the instruments to weld a new, firm, and less brittle cohesion between the Soviet Union and the East European states and among the East European states themselves. But Khrushchev, much more than his predecessor and more than his successors, tended to stress the viability rather than the cohesive aspect of the Soviet aim. Whether he consciously believed that the greater the viability the greater the cohesion that would follow, whether he saw no unity, dialectical or otherwise, between the two, is difficult to say. But what is certain is that, directly in the Soviet Union and indirectly in Eastern Europe, he pursued policies and generated an atmosphere that broke the rigid frame of Stalinist conformity in quest of a viability that would make the communist system more operative and thus more attractive to its own citizens and to those laboring under other systems.

In Eastern Europe Khrushchev's attempt had a profound impact on both the national and domestic levels. The East European states were now able to assert if not their national identity then at least their distinctiveness to a degree impossible under Stalin. It was never intended, of course, to allow them anything more than a semblance of independence: any illusions on this account Khrushchev sought to dispel immediately. But still, he did much to foster a situation in which East European leaderships, the composition of several of which he helped change, developed some degree of autonomy and even of bargaining leverage in their relations with the Soviet Union. (In their relations with each other some were quite quick to show themselves legatees of traditional rivalries or prejudice.)

The autonomy that the East European states, or their leaderships, developed at the national level obviously enhanced the stimulus for change at the domestic level, especially when sweeping domestic change, set off by de-Stalinization, was promised in the Soviet Union itself. Among the many factors affecting the degree of domestic change, which varied greatly from state to state, perhaps the most important were the level of economic advancement, public pressure, and the degree of self-confidence of the ruling elite. Sometimes the very autonomy the various leaderships now enjoyed worked against serious domestic change, as in Rumania, in Czechoslovakia before 1962, or in Poland after 1958. But domestic needs, plus the innovative example of the Soviet Union, produced considerable domestic reform and experiment in Eastern Europe—important steps toward viability and the first faltering steps toward the legitimization of communist rule in Eastern Europe.

After the uneven process generally known as de-Stalinization in Eastern Europe the most noticeable, positive reform measures of the Khrushchev era were those affecting economic structure, planning, and policy. Practically every country was affected by them, and it was hardly coincidental that the great stimulus to economic reform in Eastern Europe in the 1960s was given by the Liberman proposals in the Soviet Union in 1962. Reform blueprints or series of single measures for greater economic efficiency subsequently appeared in the German Democratic Republic, Czechoslovakia, Hungary, and Bulgaria, and even the Polish and Rumanian leaders were constrained to make some efforts at piecemeal change.

These reform measures, again, an illustration of growing diversity, met with different fates in different countries. In the GDR and Hungary they were to achieve great success; in Czechoslovakia they were one ingredient that produced the heady mixture of the Prague Spring; in Bulgaria they were hardly given a chance to operate before they were withdrawn. But even more important than their degrees of success or failure were their potential effects on the political and social life of the countries involved. Even the most cautious of these reforms, because they broke with the old command system of economy, tended to encourage pluralism in other branches of the polity as well. This is what bold and perceptive reformers realized and sought to accelerate; it was also what perceptive and apprehensive party "apparatchiki" realized and sought to brake. Thus, some embryonic form of political life began to reemerge in countries like Czechoslovakia and Hungary, not to mention Yugoslavia, which was developing its own system in a completely different way. In these countries the existence of interest groups came not only to be recognized (they had always existed in all communist societies) but also to be quietly accepted, and as a result the role of the Communist party was either publicly or tacitly modified. Its leading role continued to be proclaimed, but no longer was it seen as directing every aspect of policy implementation. As the amount of leeway grew for the interaction between various interest groups, so the party tended to assume a more Olympian role, that of arbitrating issues between various interest groups and of setting the general policy and frame within which public life was to be conducted.

Khrushchev lost power in October 1964, but the developments that began in Eastern Europe during his period of rule continued for several years after it was terminated. In fact, the Khrushchev era in Eastern Europe ended in August 1968 rather than October 1964. The momentum of what had begun during his rule increased after it, and had he remained in power no one would have tried harder than he to check it. He had allowed to be set in motion forces that he appears to have seriously underestimated, among them East European nationalism and the threat to Communist party dominance by other political, economic, and social forces within some East European societies. Thus, forces that it was first considered could be harnessed for purposes of legitimizing communist rule, and even Soviet hegemony, were found to be so strong as to undermine the legitimacy they had been intended to strengthen. In the pursuit of viability, the goal of cohesion was made less attainable.

There were three outstanding examples of this: Albania, the leaders of which, from nationalistic considerations, took advantage of the Sino-Soviet dispute and threw off Soviet tutelage; and more important, Rumania and Czechoslovakia. In the former national autonomy developed into a nationalist Rumanian policy, repudiating Soviet hegemony through the skillful manipulation of various factors, of which the Sino-Soviet dispute was perhaps the most important; in the latter domestic reform rushed headlong toward a repudiation of all known variants of the communist system itself. Both processes took place during the Khrushchev era and were made possible by it; both accelerated after his departure.

This acceleration after October 1964 was facilitated by a number of factors, of which two were perhaps the most important. The first was that for over three years after Khrushchev's fall there was practically no Soviet policy toward Eastern Europe. There was, therefore, a hiatus similar to that which had occurred after Stalin's death. Not only was the new Soviet leadership relatively inexperienced in East European affairs; it was much more directly concerned with consolidating its power in the Soviet Union. Secondly, the serious consequences of what had been initiated in Eastern Europe during Khrushchev's rule could not quickly be realized or even foreseen. True, Rumania, after a brief period of cordiality, soon dashed any hopes the new Moscow leadership may have had of permanent quiescence with new manifestations of its independent spirit. But Rumania was isolated, the problem it presented capable of containment. The far more serious threat to the foundation of the Soviet and communist system in Eastern Europe, the transformation beginning in Czechoslovakia, did not become evident until early 1968. In December 1967 Brezhnev visited Prague for one day and left apparently reassured. Only in retrospect could he be blamed for lack of discernment.

The Soviet-led invasion of Czechoslovakia or, if pedantic precision is necessary, the formal removal of Alexander Dubcek in April 1969, marked the end of the Khrushchev era in Eastern Europe. It marked the beginning of a new period in which the relationship between cohesion and viability has been strongly tilted in favor of cohesion. The trauma of Czechoslovakia itself, the disruptive potential the Prague Spring had for other parts of Eastern Europe and possibly for the Soviet Union itself, convinced the Soviet leaders that the spirit of innovation and experimentation, of reformation, that had been abroad in Eastern Europe during the 1960s had to be terminated. They had condemned Khrushchev for "hare-brained scheming" immediately after his downfall in 1964. They had used the term then in relation to his domestic policy. Only four years later were they to realize that it may have had a relevance even more pressing for Eastern Europe.

The situation now demanded a counterreformation, the reinstitution of orthodoxy. The process as applied in Czechoslovakia is all too well known, but the "normalization" imposed by the Husak regime should not distract attention from the broader developments in Soviet-East European relations over the last five years.

Immediately after August 1968 there were many who feared that the crushing of the Czechoslovak experiment would lead to the imposition of a relationship between the Soviet Union and Eastern Europe akin to what had existed in Stalin's day. This, however, was not attempted. What has evolved is a far more sophisticated effort to promote cohesion through a comprehensive integrationist policy at every level. With the invasion of Czechoslovakia and its ideological buttress, the Brezhnev Doctrine, as reminders of its grim ultimate deterrent, the Soviet leadership embarked on this comprehensive policy designed eventually to create a situation in which the circumstances that led to the necessity for invasion would no longer arise.

Integration is usually a term associated with economics, and it is true that it is most often used in referring to the Soviet Union's continued efforts, through Comecon, to exploit its own and Eastern Europe's economic strength and potential. In this, of course, Brezhnev is carrying forward Khrushchev's policy. But, whereas Khrushchev precipitately sought integration through a supranational planning body--and failed--Brezhnev, with more realism and sophistication, seeks integration "from the bottom up" through a systematic interlocking of the basic elements of the East European economies with each other and, principally, with that of the Soviet Union. It is a long-range program, publicly admitted to be so. But an important start has already been made with the agreements of several East European governments, including the Rumanian, to invest in Soviet raw material industries. Presumably the ambition is that eventually the interlocking will be so complete as to make supranational planning the logical culmination of this process.

Economic integration, therefore, is still an essential part of the Soviet Union's plans, but its concept of integration goes further and wider. There is now much greater stress on political, cultural, and ideological integration as well. The apparently annual reunion of party leaders in the Crimea is simply the apex of a whole pyramid of the most varied types of meeting, at senior, intermediate, and junior levels of the various hierarchies, that are taking place constantly. It can be said almost without exaggeration that scarcely a day goes by without news of a meeting of some kind involving East European and Soviet officials claiming some expertise or other.

The aim of such exercises, often officially described as being held "to exchange experiences," is uniformity--to create conditions in Eastern Europe that will preclude the possibility, on both the national and the domestic levels, that divergencies will assume the disruptive dimensions they have occasionally had in the past.

This massive essay in directed consensus does not mean, of course, that Moscow now eschews pressure or control of a more direct kind on individual East European regimes to secure its hegemony. There was evidence of this in the removal of Ulbricht in 1971, in the pressure on Yugoslavia and Rumania in the summer of 1971. There is reason to suspect direct interference by Moscow through the Soviet embassy in Warsaw in certain aspects of Polish domestic policy. Certain of the personnel changes in Hungary and the shifts in policy emphasis made in March 1974 were due in some measure to Soviet direction. But, if the Soviet leaders have not suddenly become hidden persuaders (nor are ever likely to become such), they appear to see the future Soviet-East European interaction as one where direct pressure will be less needed than in the first generation of communist rule in Eastern Europe.

They have, in fact, shown considerable sophistication and restraint in recent East European situations requiring crisis-management techniques. Ulbricht's age and health were used as a lever to remove a serious impediment to Brezhnev's Westpolitik. The Soviet reaction to the Polish crisis in December 1970 was one of restraint, confidence in the new leader, Edward Gierek, and readiness to help defuse an explosive situation--a successful stance, as things turned out. Brezhnev's skillfully conceived and conducted visit to Belgrade in September 1971 and subsequent Soviet policy toward Yugoslavia have resulted in at least a partial rapprochement that puts Moscow in a better position than before to profit from any present or future Yugoslav instability.

Soviet policy toward Rumania and Hungary deserves special consideration, because each of these countries, in its own way, has presented challenges to Moscow's goal of stabilized uniformity. The Rumanian challenge, first ideologically formulated over 10 years ago in the April Declaration of 1964, has been on the national level, against Soviet hegemony. As long as Ceausescu survives it will remain--and the steps taken by him to institutionalize his

personal rule at the end of last March indicate his concern
at showing up his power still further. But since the summer of 1971 the Soviet leaders seem to have banked on the
possibility that this challenge can be reduced to the level
of a tolerable irritation through a series of diplomatic
maneuverings that, Ceausescu's globe-trotting notwithstanding, enhance Rumania's isolation, through Rumania's own
growing economic vulnerability and need, and through an increasing disenchantment among many sections of the Rumanian
population with the shortcomings of Ceausescu's rule.
Working on these assumptions, there would seem to be little
need for anything but the more indirect kinds of pressure
on Rumania. It is a policy that has certainly produced
results over the last three years. There has been little
serious strain between the two countries and, in its economic relations with the Soviet Union and Comecon, Bucharest
has probably shown greater cooperation than at any time
since the very beginning of the 1960s. But there is no
guarantee that this satisfactory calm--from the Soviet
point of view--will continue indefinitely. Indeed, by the
spring of 1974, there were already signs that it was being
disturbed. The CPSU, through its loyalist parties, had begun to serve notice that it favored the eventual convening
of a new world conference of communist parties. The Rumanian was among those parties making it quite clear that it
disapproved of the idea--at least, in the view of what were
apparently the Soviet intentions in wanting the conference.
One of these intentions was to take some measures against
the Chinese party. This ran directly contrary to the Rumanian party's oft proclaimed principles of mutual tolerance in interparty relations as well as to the Rumanian
state's persistence in maintaining its friendly links with
Peking. It is true that, since Ceausescu's ostentatious
visit to Peking in the summer of 1971, which caused serious
strain in Soviet-Rumanian relations, Bucharest has pursued
its friendship with China in considerably lower key. But
the intensification of Sino-Soviet polemics during 1973-74,
in which all other Soviet allies have fully joined, has
made the Rumanian policy even more anomalous. If Moscow
now seeks to enforce a commitment of support from all its
allies against China, then a renewed period of strain with
Rumania seems unavoidable.

The problem presented by Hungary has been quite different. Hungarian foreign policy has been virtually indis-
tinguishable from that of the Soviet Union, although there
is occasional evidence, as for example in economic relations with the West, of differences of view. Yet, the im-

plicit Hungarian challenge to the Soviet concept of what
Eastern Europe should look like was, for several years,
more serious than the Rumanian. This was because Hungarian
domestic policy, in the shape of the New Economic Mechanism,
was from its inception in 1968 until very recently a Khrushchevian anachronism. It embodied those dangers of economic
and social pluralism, of real political interaction, of institutional reform that burst out of control in Czechoslovakia and that, for several years now, the Soviet leaders
have been seeking to eliminate.

The Soviet attitude toward the Hungarian reform was
one of considerable restraint. In part it was a restraint
induced by a great deal of Hungarian skill and finesse,
particularly on the part of Kadar himself. The Hungarian
leadership not only supported Soviet foreign policy, it
constantly assured Moscow of the Hungarian party's control
over the situation and strongly rejected any notion that
its domestic policy be a model for others. It thus sought
to pre-empt any charge that Hungary was an agent of contam-
ination. In fact, from the very beginning Kadar used his
bargaining leverage with the Soviet leaders to good advantage. To many it seemed doubtful whether Hungary could
preceed with the implementation of its New Economic Mechanism after the crushing of the reform movement in Czechoslovakia in August 1968. There was considerable surprise
when the Hungarian leaders not only continued their reforms
but expanded them. In retrospect, of course, it seems that
Kadar was very well placed, vis-à-vis the Soviet leadership,
to do precisely what he did. He had supported Brezhnev in
an action the wisdom of which he doubted and that both knew
to be fraught with great risk. It succeeded; and the price
Kadar was asking for his services must hardly have seemed
too exorbitant to Brezhnev at the time.

It was only later, perhaps as late as 1972, when the
Soviet leadership evidently realized they may have been a
little too complacent about some of the implications of
Hungary's reforms. Its tactics then were to add its own
expressions of concern about the situation to the already
existing--and increasing--difficulties that the reforms were
facing in Hungary itself. These included certain purely
economic problems, such as investment "overheating," inflationary tendencies, and so on. But, far more important,
was the growing discontent of large sections of the working
class over what they (rightly) considered their own far too
small rewards from the prosperity the New Economic Mechanism
had brought society as a whole. Many conservatives inside
the Hungarian party itself appear to have sided with these

working class dissidents in an effort to slow down or change the course of the reforms. It was these two elements in Hungary, working together, plus the Soviet leadership, working, one assumes, independently for the most part, that have succeeded, not in destroying the Hungarian reform (nobody ever wanted that), but in pulling it back toward, if not yet inside, the bounds of what the Soviet Union apparently considers safe and acceptable. The first important step in the direction was taken at the Hungarian party central committee plenum in November 1972 (a visit by Brezhnev took place immediately afterward). The second was taken in March 1974, at the plenum that removed Reszo Nyers and several other leaders identified with reform and that emphatically reaffirmed the working class orientation and orthodox character of party policy that the November 1972 plenum had handed down. Since the plenum in March 1974, Hungarian politicians (including Kadar himself) and the communications media have sought to reassure the public that there will be no essential policy changes. No one expects the New Economic Mechanism to be scrapped overnight. But very few expect Hungary in the future to be quite so different from the rest of Eastern Europe as it was in the recent past. The Khrushchevian anachronism will gradually disappear.

This impressive revival of domestic conservatism in Eastern Europe could not, of course, have been achieved solely through Soviet manipulation. Moscow's post-1968 concept of cohesion found ready acceptance among the numerous officials in the East European communist parties threatened by the reform trend of the previous decade. If one of the main reasons for Khrushchev's fall was the opposition of the entrenched party apparat in the Soviet Union, then the distrust of Khrushchevism by large sections of the East European party apparats has been the main reason for their acceptance of the new Soviet policy. The reversion to orthodoxy, the counterreformation, has meant a shoring up of their power under the ideological rubric of reaffirming the leading role of the party. In fact, considerations of power have been the mainspring of the ideological offensive waged in Eastern Europe for the last five years. A deliberate effort has been made to "depoliticize" public life by "reideologizing" it. But one of the main aims and consequences of this effort--having little to do with ideology as such--has been the strengthening of the power and prerogatives of the ruling Communist party.

The process described above has been aimed at restoring cohesion or, more correctly, at creating a new kind of

cohesion between the Soviet Union and Eastern Europe. This
has been the main Soviet preoccupation for the last five
years. But essential to cohesion is public stability, a
truism that the Soviet and East European ruling parties
have frequently been taught by experience not to overlook.
No sooner had consolidation in Czechoslovakia appeared restored than the workers' riots in Poland broke out in December 1970. This upheaval not only led to a change of
leadership in Poland but also led to tremors of uncertainty
in other East European countries. The Polish temper was
mollified by a number of important material concessions
that have considerably raised the workers' standard of living. As for the rest of Eastern Europe, it appears that
Gierek's desperate actions in early 1971 gave a strong impetus to most governments, as well as to that of the Soviet
Union, to incorporate "consumerism" as a basic part of
their economic policies. In the GDR it had, in fact, become entrenched even before the Polish upheavals. But it
has now become a basic (and fairly successful) part of
the Husak regime's "normalization" policy in Czechoslovakia.
It was embraced in a typically massive way by Bulgaria at
the end of 1972. It had always been in the philosophy governing Hungary's New Economic Mechanism; in November 1972
it became an obvious weapon in Kadar's effort to divert
worker discontent.

But it would be a mistake to see this policy of consumerism in Eastern Europe as serving solely the negative
purpose of fending off trouble. It should also be seen as
serving the more positive purpose of regalvanizing economic
life, in other words, of re-creating viability to accompany
the re-created cohesion. There is almost a River Rouge,
capitalistic smack about some Soviet and East European
leaders in this context. The Polish leader, Gierek, for
example, seems genuinely to think that good living conditions and open, two-way communication between management
and the shop floor will at one and the same time appease
worker resentment, blunt any demands for institutional innovations like workers' councils, and generate conditions
for an efficient upsurge of production. Similar thinking
is to be found elsewhere in Eastern Europe as well as in
the highest echelons of the Soviet party.

It is hardly surprising that the advocates of this
(prevailing) philosophy of government have welcomed compu-
terization and other aspects of the scientific-technological revolution. They have not done this solely for the
increased economic efficiency this revolution might bring,

nor should their eagerness be taken simply as yet another
symptom of underdeveloped countries' grasping at the latest
supermodern straw. Their hope apparently is that centralized direction, armed with the new technology, can achieve
the same economic results, and even better ones than could
be achieved through decentralization and the various institutional changes characteristic of the economic reforms of
the 1960s and still characteristic of Hungary's NEM. The
manifold dangers inherent in those reforms could, therefore,
be avoided.

But, obviously, this completely new dimension in technological development--still only in its infancy in Eastern
Europe--reinforces more than ever the need for a large technical intelligentsia as the executor of economic policy.
This section of society has been growing steadily in Eastern Europe for the last 10 or 15 years. It is manifestly
the aim of the political leaderships to make it not only as
proficient but also as apolitical as possible. They have
been prepared to make material concessions to its members
and to bring increasing numbers of them into positions of
real responsibility in the governing economic hierarchy.
This has been a feature of East German policy for several
years now. The results there have been encouraging, and it
would seem that what has been adopted successfully in the
GDR is now being adopted more massively than before in the
rest of Eastern Europe. In a subtle way, therefore, and
probably unconsciously, the GDR, under Erich Honecker, is
becoming a model for Eastern Europe, something that it never
was under Ulbricht, despite the latter's claims for the
East German system when he was in power.

It remains now to discuss two external factors that
could affect Soviet-East European relations and the course
the Soviet Union wishes to take.

The first factor, Soviet rivalry with China, can be
dealt with briefly. In quite contrasting ways, Chinese
pressure influenced Soviet policy in Hungary and Poland in
1956; it also influenced Soviet efforts to re-create a formal edifice of socialist unity in 1957. Later, when the
Sino-Soviet conflict became an acknowledged reality, Albania broke with Moscow and accepted the tutelage of Peking
while Rumania adroitly manipulated the situation to en-
large its own area of autonomy. More recently, in the summer of 1971, when Soviet relations with both Yugoslavia and
Rumania appeared to deteriorate markedly, there was serious
speculation about the creation of a "Balkan triangle," com-
posed of Albania, Rumania, and Yugoslavia, looking to China
for protection. This speculation was soon dissipated, how-

ever, by the conciliatory change in Soviet policy toward
Belgrade and Bucharest and a realistic assessment in both
capitals of the very feasibility of any putative Chinese
protection against Soviet coercion.

For the foreseeable future it would appear that, whatever the possibilities that the Chinese may have a disruptive influence on the course of Soviet-East European relations, it will be on the national, rather than the domestic,
level. That is, it would be similar to the disruption already created by the Albanian and the Rumanian precedents.
It is not likely, however, that this would occur unless the
threat of military conflict between the Soviet Union and
China became so acute that any East European state so inclined could exploit the situation to extract concessions
from Moscow on the national level. If such a situation
did arise then Moscow would, in any case, have to decide
between a more coercive or a more relaxed policy in Eastern
Europe to keep would-be recalcitrants in line or to rally
support against China. This, however, is a scenario that,
though often envisaged in the West, is still not an actual-
ity in the East. It remains, therefore, speculative exercise rather than diplomatic analysis.

Chinese influence on internal developments in Eastern
Europe still lacks any dimension of seriousness. Apart
from the special case of Albania, the only demonstrable instance of regime domestic policy ever being influenced by
China was the Bulgarian "great leap forward" in 1958 and
its antecedent propaganda. Just how far Nicolae Ceausescu's
"mini-cultural revolution" was affected by what he saw in
China in 1971 is debatable, but the fact that this question
can even be raised shows the sparseness of ready examples
of Chinese influence on the East European domestic scene.

Not quite as miniscule, but so far still negligible,
has been Chinese influence on "nonofficial" elements in
East European societies. The dazzling militancy of Peking
has attracted some discontented older Communists and some
romantic younger intellectuals, both of whom see the socialist order as developed in Eastern Europe, not to mention
the Soviet Union, as a debasement rather than a fulfillment
of original revolutionary ideals. Such elements of discontent certainly exist and might well grow. But, with the
possible exception of the veteran dissidents in Bulgaria
in the first half of the 1960s, they have as yet had no
noticeable impact on the regimes they despise.

A far more potent threat to the stability of Soviet
order in Eastern Europe would be the prospect of détente in
general and a real European security and cooperation arrange-

ment in particular. This both the Soviet and the East European leaderships realized and have taken steps to forestall.

Their reasoning, especially the Soviet, was quite logical. Having been generally successful in restoring stability in Eastern Europe, the Soviets were understandably loath to see it cracked by fissures emanating from the West. Both the Soviet and all the Eastern European leaders are aware that any real interaction between the societies of Eastern and Western Europe would lead to a restlessness, a questioning of accepted norms, a widening of horizons, new standards of comparison—in fact, to a situation incomparably more fluid, unpredictable, and disruptive even than that prevailing in the 1960s. Indeed, any such interaction would endanger not only Soviet but also communist control in Eastern Europe, at least in the form and manner exercised up to now.

Knowledge of this has been behind the strenuous Soviet and East European attempts to resist Western proposals at both Helsinki and Geneva for a "freer flow" of information, people, and ideas. (Rumania has resisted the least; not because it is any less fearful of what the West proposes but mainly because of its dislike of acting en bloc with the rest of its nominal allies.) The contacts covered under "basket three" on the Helsinki and Geneva agendas that the Soviet and East European leaderships will tolerate are essentially those carefully conducted exchanges they have countenanced previously. They have even admitted their readiness to allow more of these. "Freer flow," in the Western sense, they want no part of.

But the Soviet Union has clearly shown that it is not prepared to take any chances even on the limited degree of genuine détente it would be prepared to allow. Since the preparatory meetings for the European security conference began, the Soviet leadership has accelerated those cohesive processes that had been taking place in Eastern Europe since August 1968. Indeed, so intensive have the Soviet moves been during this period that some observers have concluded that the drive for cohesion is a relatively new phenomenon prompted by Soviet fears of the impact of détente. What in fact these Soviet fears have done is to add a new dimension to a situation already existing for several years.

It hardly is surprising that what is in fact a new variation has been mistaken for a new theme. The evidence for the intensification of the drive for cohesion is indeed so great. Domestic propaganda in all the Soviet-allied Eastern European states proclaiming that détente actually means a sharpening of the ideological struggle against Western values has increased enormously since the beginning of 1973. So have the arguments justifying a rejection of the Western demands for a free flow of information, people, and ideas. During the same period there has been a considerable increase in the number of multilateral conferences held on ideological subjects. China and its sins have, of course, figured on the agenda of these conferences, but the most important item has usually been the need for a more efficient counter to Western ideological penetration. This was probably discussed at the Crimea informal summit meeting in July 1973, and it apparently dominated the meeting of central committee secretaries responsible for ideology the following December.

Indeed, there is enough evidence to indicate that, in both Eastern Europe and the Soviet Union so far, what détente--more correctly, the debate about it--has produced so far has been exactly the opposite of what was predicted by many in the West. In the Soviet Union there is clearly less scope for dissent than two years ago. In Eastern Europe the acceleration of the drive for cohesion has seriously affected the domestic situation in Hungary and has led to new drives for ideological conformity in all the Soviet-allied states. In all states it is the conservative rather than the reformist elements that appear even stronger. On the national level, though Rumania keeps up its uphill struggle for independence, the general trend has been for an even more strongly pronounced Soviet leadership.

There are at present few grounds for assuming that these tendencies will be reversed by any progress made in negotiations between East and West. Indeed, the evidence so far points to their being intensified. The Western predictions about evolution in the East made possible by détente seem to have been based on assumptions either that a "secure" Soviet Union would feel confident enough to relax its grip on its allies, or that the Soviet Union would somehow agree to the type of contacts between East and West that would set in motion once again the force for change in Eastern Europe. These predictions, based on one or the other assumption, may still be vindicated. But what all deliberations on détente have shown up to now is how insecure the Soviet Union feels itself in its relations with Eastern Europe and how insecure the Eastern European leaderships still feel in relations with many of their own people. And the signs are that this insecurity will continue. This is hardly the basis for an eventual relaxation, but talks for still greater efforts toward "comprehensive

multilateral integration." Détente, or the quest for it,
looks like it is leading to a tightening rather than an
easing of the Soviet grip on Eastern Europe.

CHAPTER

2

EUROPEAN COOPERATION
AND IDEOLOGICAL
CONFLICT
Charles Andras

Some Western Sovietologists have suggested that an increasingly consumer-oriented economic policy in the communist states and their expanding cooperation with the West
will gradually erode the primacy of Marxist-Leninist ideology and, ultimately, lead to a "deideologization" of policy.
Sufficient time has not yet elapsed to permit the authen-
ticity of this theory to be tested, but since the mid-1960s
pragmatic leaders, economic experts, managers, technicians,
and members of other similar groups have been playing an
increasingly important role in shaping the policies of the
socialist regimes. During the same period of time consumerism has spread and contacts with the West have multiplied
in all areas of interstate relations.

Despite these developments, however, the last few
years have witnessed an increase in ideological activity
and growing criticism of ideological relaxation in the party
and in society at large. An ideological campaign has been
launched the aim of which is to strengthen the influence
of Marxism-Leninism in the European communist states and
shelter these countries from the "harmful influence" of
the "bourgeois-capitalist-imperialist" West. Although one
can also see evidence of tentative effort to launch a counteroffensive in foreign countries against hostile Western
ideologies, the main concern of the ideologues is still the
home front, where it is necessary to invigorate the official
ideology and ensure that its influence dominates policy
making and public life.

It is not merely coincidental that the European communist states' ideological endeavors parallel their campaign to achieve détente, security, and cooperation in Europe. The implications are obvious: European unity is de-

sirable only to the extent that it does not undermine the
ideological monopoly of Marxism-Leninism and does not interfere with the "consolidation" of the socialist countries.
The current ideological crusade is not confined to the repetition of old Marxist-Leninist dogmas and slogans; it also
includes an effort to accommodate the official ideology to
the demands of the technological age. In a sense one can
speak of ideological "modernization" in this connection.
It is, of course, a cautious experiment the results of
which are limited and which leave many problems unresolved,
but the fact that the existence of a gap between ideology
and the requirements of the modern age has been directly or
indirectly admitted is not without significance.

The campaign was initiated and is led by the Soviet
Union, but the East European states, at least formally,
are cooperating in the drive to arouse a new Marxist-Leninist awareness within their communist parties and among their
populations and to reduce the influence of foreign ideologies. This is not to say that there are no differences in
tone, content, or emphasis. The most ardent supporter of
the Soviet Union is the German Democratic Republic (GDR),
which seems to be particularly concerned about the potential
ideological influence of its immediate Western neighbor,
the Federal Republic of Germany (FRG). Hence East Berlin
advocates an effective ideological frontier as a natural
corollary to European cooperation. Czechoslovakia has
probably produced the greatest volume of ideological rhetoric, all of it still strongly influenced by memories of
1968. In the last two years Hungary and Poland have also
stepped up the campaign for ideological vigilance, a move
that in Hungary is in sharp contrast with the relatively
open intellectual climate that still prevails there.

Among the Warsaw Pact states the only, although limited, exception is Rumania. The Ceausescu regime has conducted an elaborate program to strengthen the influence of
its Marxist-Leninist ideology without, however, reiterating
many of the bloc's favorite slogans about ideological unity
and without resorting to many of the methods adopted by
the other socialist regimes.*

---

*Within the context of this chapter general references
to the Warsaw Pact states or Eastern Europe do not always
apply to Rumania. Important divergences are specifically
noted, however.

18

THE IDEOLOGICAL FRONT

Before taking a closer look at the campaign itself, it might be well to examine the main considerations that generated the East European states' concern with the task of ideological consolidation. Several of these factors are of an internal or domestic nature; others are external and stem primarily from East-West cooperation. There is a continuous interaction between them, however, so that they frequently overlap and it is not easy to separate them. On the whole, they can be divided into four categories.

The first is that of indigenous ideological weaknesses on the domestic front, which are attributed to the fact that the process of building socialism has turned out to be more complex than originally anticipated. Nationalization of material resources and one-party rule have not ensured the victory of socialism in the ideological sphere. As a result, "remnants of the past" litter the ideological field and hamper the consolidation of Marxism-Leninism. Among such remnants the most frequently mentioned are petit-bourgeois attitudes, nationalism, and religious conviction. The revival and spread of the petit-bourgeois mentality are ascribed mainly to improved standards of living and the influx of Western consumerism. Nationalism is presented as a grave threat to the East European attempts at consolidation and unity. The "vitality of religious thinking" has astounded many ideological experts, and they have no universally accepted explanation for it; but all agree that it seriously hampers ideological work even among the younger generation. These relics of the past are components of the general bourgeois-capitalist Weltanschauung. Their ability to survive, it is stressed today, was underestimated by previous regimes; the correct approach is to accept them as obstacles on the road to socialism that can be removed only by patient ideological work, not by force.

Two other domestic factors exert an influence on the state of ideology in the socialist countries. One is the attitude of youth. Young people have no personal experience of the oppressive character of the defunct bourgeois-capitalist system in their homeland, nor did they participate in the heroic days of socialist liberation and construction. Therefore they show no particular concern about "imperialist-capitalist-revanchist" threats from abroad. The other factor is the existence in everyday life under socialism of the practices of moneygrubbing, speculation, corruption, and other forms of "vulgar materialism"--in short, practices linked with higher standards of living, petit-bourgeois

thinking, and the imitation of Western ways. Such things
(according to the growing volume of criticism, especially
in Hungary, Czechoslovakia, and the Soviet Union) are incompatible with the character of socialist man.

The second category of factors is that of ideological
divergences and splitting activities within the larger
Marxist-socialist family. What is meant here are the so-
called pseudo-Marxist and revisionist concepts of the Right
and the Left that challenge the ability of the orthodox
Marxist-Leninist (that is, Soviet) model of socialism to
deal with the problems of the modern age. They endorse
the national models of socialism and in this respect join
forces with the "imperialists" to split the unity of the
socialist community. The two most typical examples of re-
visionism are the Garaudy school on the Right, and Maoism
on the Left. Rightist trends are said to have resulted in
the Czechoslovak experiment of 1968. Indeed, it is striking to note the preoccupation of the orthodox ideologues
with the "reform misconceptions," "ideological distortions,"
and "treacherous revisionist activities" of the Prague
Spring. The Maoists, on the other hand, are accused of
such activities as stepping up their endeavors to split
the world communist movement, of interfering in the internal affairs of the socialist community, of fomenting a
spirit of nationalism and chauvinism, of lending support
to antisocialist forces in Europe, of spreading the concept
that the two superpowers are dividing the world into two
spheres of influence. But despite certain ideological con-
gruences the "New Left" that has emerged in the Marxist community of the West also gives rise to serious concern because of its criticism of socialist reality in the Warsaw
Pact states and its impact on the younger generation.*

In third place are the complexities of East-West contacts and European cooperation. Early in this decade the
East European governments began to realize that the various
sectors of East-West cooperation cannot be isolated from

---

*As one Hungarian expert put it, "Undoubtedly a good
many followers of the 'New Left' sincerely desire something
that differs from capitalist society, and this is a point
on which we might agree with them. What we must criticize
--in addition to the ideological differences in our views--
is their criticism of implemented socialism." (Bela Kopeczi,
first secretary of the Hungarian Academy of Sciences, "The
Ideology of the 'New Left,'" Tarsadalomtudomanyi Kozlemenyek,
nos. 1-2 [Budapest, 1973].)

each other and that political détente and economic cooperation can generate pressure for the broadening of human contacts, more tourism, cultural exchanges, and so forth.   In
Marxist-Leninist thinking, however, culture has an ideological function, and it is believed that unrestricted cultural cooperation can open the gates to ideological infil-
tration.   But the ideological element may complicate the
whole process in other ways as well.   For instance, political rapprochement with West Germany (in itself a constructive development) can also activate a potentially dangerous
ideological interest in West German social democracy and
in the European social democratic model in general.   In
the sphere of purely economic cooperation, imported Western
goods can foster consumerism or lead to comparisons between
the two opposing socioeconomic systems, to the detriment
of socialism.   The socialist regimes have come to realize
that a simple psychological factor, human curiosity about
foreign countries, cultures, and peoples, plays a major
role in keeping this cooperative mechanism going and that
it is not easy to suppress it or to channel it in an acceptable direction.

Obviously, it was in anticipation of such problems
that since the very beginning of the European security campaign the Warsaw Pact countries have shown little enthusiasm
for liberalized, let along unlimited, cultural cooperation
and exchanges between the two parts of the continent.
Their first proposals regarding European security did not
even mention culture; they were primarily concerned with
economic and technological-scientific cooperation.   Only
after the NATO countries had begun to urge a free--or, as
it is now called, freer--flow of people, ideas, and information did the socialist regimes put cultural cooperation
on the list.   They did so reluctantly and only under public
pressure, and their attitude has not changed to any great
degree.   In fact, they have even become more cautious and
in some cases have been explicitly hostile to the idea of
expanding cooperation beyond certain limits.

The fourth consideration is "Western interference."
The first three factors affect ideology in the Warsaw Pact
countries without actively involving the "capitalist-im-
perialist forces" in the West.   But the fourth--and in the
eyes of the East European countries the most dangerous--
is the West's allegedly organized, coordinated, purposeful
use of the new channels opening in East-West relations to
undermine the ideological unity of the socialist regimes
and to erode the influence of Marxist-Leninist ideology.
The theoretical foundation of the Western approach is said

to be the "diversionist" thesis that peaceful coexistence, which, in an era of détente and cooperation, should govern relations among states belonging to the opposing systems, is incompatible with ideological conflict and should therefore be extended to the field of ideology. But, say the East Europeans, this is only a pretext for stepping up the capitalist ideological campaign against the socialist states and amounts to interference in their internal affairs. The only purpose behind the proposal to permit a freer flow of peoples, ideas, and information is to facilitate and legalize the ideological penetration of the socialist countries. Therefore, the East European news media have concentrated their attacks on Western research institutes and newspapers and mainly such radio stations as Radio Free Europe, Radio Liberty, the British Broadcasting Corporation, the Deutsche Welle, and sometimes also the Voice of America. The activities of such stations, it is claimed, have nothing to do with ideological coexistence or cultural exchange; their real aim is to erode socialism from within; they foster a spirit of nationalism, of national communism; they attack the leading role of the working class, of the workers' party, in a socialist state; they oppose Marxist-Leninist ideology and all efforts to achieve socialist consolidation. And the ideological officials in the socialist countries have charged that what is offered by the West as material for cultural exchange has very little to do with real culture. It is alleged that Western books, films, plays, and other materials of cultural exchange are permeated by reaction, racism, chauvinism, militarism, sadism, brutality, pornography, and disdain for human life--and that, as a Soviet author sighed, "these 'ideas' are . . . inalienable elements in the "spiritual life' of a capitalist society."[1]

The catalog of the things that affect the state of ideology in the East European countries cannot be concluded without a short reference to a specifically Soviet phenomenon, the so-called dissident movement. Evidently this is treated by the Soviet regime as resulting from the connivance of hostile forces active in the ideological field. The emergence of the dissidents, their attempt to begin a dialogue with Western intellectuals, and the world-wide echoes their protests have aroused must have been among the major reasons that prompted the Soviet Union to take the lead in the current struggle to achieve greater ideological vigilance and more effective control over East-West contacts.

In analyzing the new situation created by the broadening of East-West contacts the East Europeans have drawn a number of conclusions: First, that East-West cooperation is such a complex operation, involving such a variety of forces and interests, that it is impossible to exclude from its channels the circulation of what can be called, in the broadest sense, the ideological and cultural element. Second, that the influx of harmful ideological-cultural ideas can undermine the influence of Marxism-Leninism in the socialist countries, mainly owing to the low level of ideological preparedness on the domestic front. Not only average citizens but even party members, it is said, can fall victim to foreign ideological influences and develop erroneous concepts about socialist intentions in the present stage of East-West relations. They can show, for instance, a certain willingness to accept Western interpretations of peaceful coexistence and to embrace theories about the existence of a real balance of power between East and West (thus underrating the real might of the Soviet Union); and at the other end of the spectrum some can even begin to doubt the socialist propriety of conducting business with capitalist firms. Third, that the trend toward broader contacts cannot be stopped without jeopardizing the success of the policy of détente. What they feel they can do, however, is to make East-West exchange as selective as possible and simultaneously combat Western influence on the domestic front more actively. Fourth, that East-West cooperation is not a one-way street, since it also increases socialism's chances to exert a stronger influence on world events and to transmit the Marxist-Leninist message to the outside world with more determination. All this, however, presupposes a more coordinated approach to ideological problems and general improvement of the socialist propaganda apparatus.[2]

On several of these points Rumania has been in agreement with the other Warsaw Pact states, but it would not subscribe--and this is an essential divergence--to the idea that a coordinated approach was needed or engage in any stepped-up anticapitalist propaganda or even in an offensive abroad.

PEACEFUL COEXISTENCE--THE SOVIET VERSION

The Warsaw Pact's "ideologically negative" experiments in broadening contacts with the West and the conclusions drawn from them have to a great extent determined the "pos-

23

tive" message and the main targets of the campaign. At
the center of interest lies the principle of peaceful coexistence, destined to be the cornerstone of East-West relations. Once the Marxist-Leninist concept of this principle is understood, all other ideological issues relevant to
East-West cooperation fit more easily into place. At least
this is the East Europeans' hope, and hence one of their
primary aims is to force acceptance of their own definition
of peaceful coexistence.

Peaceful coexistence, according to the East European
view, is a new historical continuation and even sharpening
of the class warfare and of the ideological conflict between
the two systems, a form that permits the avoidance of war,
the limitation of the arms race, and so on. Thus, peaceful coexistence does not include ideological coexistence,
nor does it mean sanctioning the capitalist social system.
Not even interstate agreements could achieve ideological
coexistence, since there can be no peace between opposing
ideologies. Consequently, Western efforts to extend peaceful coexistence to cover ideologies and class warfare are
inconsistent with the very nature of this concept and with
the realities of historical progress. Those who preach
the reconciliation of ideologies want to change the principle of peaceful coexistence into "a sort of Trojan horse,"
"to enforce the ideological capitulation of socialism."

However, from the Eastern viewpoint the very Western
sources that want to extend the scope of peaceful coexistence to include ideologies have in fact stepped up the
ideological campaign against the socialist countries and
have resorted to "illegal methods" of doing so. In this
context, the "freer flow" proposal is cited as a typical
example, which, if accepted in its original form, would
allegedly open the door to the ideological subversion of
the East mainly through radio programs and by misusing human contacts and other forms of cultural exchange. This
constitutes interference in the internal affairs of the socialist countries and resembles cold-war tactics.

The East Europeans also wish to emphasize that the
first achievements of the policy of peaceful coexistence--
the Ostvertraege, Nixon's commitment to the principle of
détente, Brezhnev's summit diplomacy, and the staging of
the Conference on Security and Cooperation in Europe--are
not the result (as many erroneously believe) of deep-going,
essential changes in the nature of capitalism, nor of a
balance-of-power situation between East and West. On the
contrary, the policy of peaceful coexistence is successful
because the international balance of power has changed to

the advantage of the socialist countries, thanks to their
consolidated power and consolidated actions.* They are now
in a position where they can impose their policy on the
West, which has thus been compelled to accept the rules
governing peaceful-coexistence diplomacy. Naturally the
economic factor, for instance, the critical energy situation in the United States, is said to have played a role
in forcing the West, and particularly Washington, to come
to terms with the Soviet Union.

At the same time, the East Europeans have warned that
the West's acceptance of contemporary realities should not
be regarded as final. As they see it, the reactionary
forces are still very strong, the political integrationists
have not given up their struggle in NATO, and the CSCE idea
has not yet won a complete victory over powerful antagonists treacherously encouraged by Chinese diplomacy.

Thus, in order to ensure the continuation of a policy
of peaceful coexistence, the socialist countries must maintain their strength, including military power. They cannot, of course, ignore the fact that East-West cooperation
is built on the prospect of mutually advantageous agreements, which are only possible if both sides are willing
to give up something. Agreements with the West, however,
have always to be judged from the long-term, historical
point of view. If they contribute to the "improvement of
socialist class objectives," if they "create more favorable
conditions for international class warfare," mutual concessions are always acceptable to Marxists-Leninists. But
under no circumstances can agreements with the bourgeois
governments impose obstacles to or limitations on the ideological struggle of the socialist regimes.

The Soviet bloc regimes have deemed it particularly
important to emphasize that the policy of peaceful coexistence is not an ad hoc undertaking or an "adventurist" experiment by the Soviet Union and its Warsaw Pact partners.
The key principles of this policy, it is said, were laid
down by Lenin himself, and it was he who put them into
practice for the first time in the foreign policy of the
young Soviet state. The 23rd Congress of the CPSU reaf-

---

*Several sources have claimed that behind the assump-
tion of a balance of power lies the "demagogic intention to
equate the imperialist and socialist armies." (Hartmut
Hehls and Heinrich Schmidt, "Friedliche Koexistenz und Klas-
senkampf," Deutsche Aussenpolitik, vol. 13, no. 5 [East
Berlin, 1973].)

firmed the validity of peaceful coexistence, and the 24th instructed the CC to "continue to apply the principle of peaceful coexistence in practice and to expand mutually advantageous links with the capitalist countries." The mandate of the CPSU was endorsed by other members of the Soviet bloc, and peaceful coexistence has thus become the common policy of the whole bloc in its relations with nonsocialist states, and above all with the West. The policy of peaceful coexistence is therefore the Leninist answer to the question of how to resolve many practical problems connected with East-West cooperation.[3]

No such historical reminiscences, however, mention that the doctrine of peaceful coexistence, among others, underwent severe modification in the Khrushchev era. It was not Lenin but Khrushchev who firmly stipulated that peaceful coexistence does not include ideology and that it is in fact another form of class warfare on an international scale.

SOCIALIST UNITY AND ALL-ROUND INTEGRATION

Peaceful coexistence, as conceived by the Soviet bloc, regulates the socialist states' external relations with the nonsocialist, primarily the so-called capitalist, world. Simultaneously it is also supposed to provide the socialist regimes with a protective umbrella against undesirable interference from abroad and to allow them to stabilize the position of Marxist-Leninist ideology at home so that it can eventually become more potent abroad. In these efforts the problem of socialist unity, a unity with emphasis on foreign policy and ideology, plays the cardinal role.

Officially, the discussion centers on the "unity of the community of socialist states." The phrase is rarely defined in precise geographical terms. In principle, it should include all 14 socialist states; in practice, however, it covers only the "core of the community," the Warsaw Pact or the "alliance of European socialist states."

Unity is not a newcomer to the Soviet bloc's propaganda vocabulary, but in the present context the stress is on a "higher order of unity," built on all-round socialist cooperation, and in the course of the ideological campaign socialist cooperation is not infrequently replaced by the more eloquent synonym "socialist integration."

The first voices to call for speeding up socialist cooperation were raised immediately after the occupation of Czechoslovakia in 1968, and their concern with consolidation was primarily military and ideological. Next, a two-phase program of socialist economic cooperation and integration, to be carried out within the framework of Comecon, was promulgated. Finally, since 1970, there has been an insistence on tight coordination of socialist foreign policy and a fresh interest in closer ideological cooperation. As the argument goes, it is through "greater unity" and deepening cooperation that the socialist community (in effect, the Warsaw Pact countries) can effectively increase its influence on world developments. "It must be borne in mind," a Soviet scholar admonished, "that on the [all-round] cohesion of the world socialist community depend the effectiveness of its struggle against imperialism and the forcefulness of its influence on the world revolutionary process."[4]

What, then, is meant by the consolidation and integration of socialist foreign policies? Soviet bloc ideologues profess that the "main law-governed patterns" of their creed apply not only to socialist construction in the domestic field but also to the foreign policies of the socialist states.[5] Consequently, foreign policy must be subject to common planning and execution. More concretely, the "fraternal socialist states" must draw up a common foreign policy program and implement it in the closest cooperation and unity. A high-ranking East German CC official justified a united socialist approach to foreign policy on three grounds: first, it ensures favorable conditions for consolidating the positions of socialism; second, it helps to repel the influence of imperialism and to check its aggressiveness; and, third, it contributes, in a spirit of proletarian internationalism, to the advancement of all revolutionary, anti-imperialist democratic movements and forces. To leave no doubt in anyone's mind, he summed up his argument thus: The coordination of foreign policy is designed "to do everything possible to maintain world peace, to change power relations . . . to the advantage of socialism in order to weaken the positions of imperialism and to speed up the revolutionary process throughout the world."[6]

The caretaker and coordinator of the bloc's European security campaign, the Political Consultative Committee of the Warsaw Pact, came to prominence as the principal integrator of the socialist countries' foreign policies. Each of its sessions was celebrated as a further step toward complete unification of planning and operation. But the committee's significance may be overshadowed by a comparative newcomer to the scene, the yearly meeting of Soviet bloc leaders in the Crimea. The publicity given to the

27

latest such gathering as supreme decision maker in matters of socialist foreign policy is unexampled, and there can be no doubt that the informal character of the Crimean summits suits Brezhnev's personal style of diplomacy to a T.

In his famous Alma Ata speech, the Soviet party leader disclosed that

> participants in the Crimea meeting [in July 1973] were unanimous in the opinion that at the present stage it is essential to improve considerably the standard of ideological cooperation among the fraternal countries and parties. A profound study must be made of each other's experiences, and of the joint struggle against bourgeois ideology.[7]

A few days later, a leading Czechoslovak party paper[8] gave two reasons for effecting closer coordination in the field of ideology. The first was the emergence of a new situation that favored "the spreading of ideas and truth about socialism and social construction, malevolently distorted by bourgeois propaganda." The second was that "the revival of international relations [had] activated anticommunist propaganda." This, it was said, operates in two ways: in the socialist world it attempts to infect the minds of the public with reactionary ideas, and in the "capitalist" world it tries to immunize the working people against the ideas of revolution and socialism.

All this indicates what the final goals of ideological consolidation must be: "To protect the building of socialism at home against the aggressive endeavors of imperialism," and to guide the ideological offensive abroad and thus speed up "the victory of socialism over capitalism."[9]

The working principles, methods, and instruments of ideological integration have never been clearly disclosed. Mention has been made of a "joint, collective analysis of the typical problems of our times,"[10] and of working out common solutions and putting them into practice in bilateral and multilateral projects. It is also intended to coordinate and consolidate research into the functioning of the "capitalist propaganda apparatus," and to study its methods of work and ideological distortions. The Czechoslovak source quoted above observed that "a number of practical issues suitable for closer cooperation among ideological sections and institutions of the fraternal parties and mass communication media" were on the agenda.

At this stage it is difficult to ascertain how many
of the early programmatic declarations and suggestions have
been put into practice. It is known, however, that since
the early 1970s the number of intrabloc "ideological" and
"cultural" conferences, bilateral as well as multilateral,
has sharply increased. Even the Rumanians have attended
several of them, although this does not necessarily mean
that they subscribed to everything agreed on by the other
delegations. Two or three research institutes (or at least
units) have been commissioned to study the ideological complexities of East-West relations and to "unmask the truth"
behind the "modernization of capitalism," and evidently
there is a somewhat greater degree of collaboration among
the socialist mass media. Moreover, in addition to the
existing bilateral friendship treaties, since 1971 a new
set of bilateral agreements has been concluded between members of the bloc, or more exactly between their ruling parties, pledging closer cooperation in the fields of ideology,
culture, and propaganda.

It is not without interest that the conclusion of the
agreements between the East European parties was openly
disclosed (although the texts were not published), while
the existence of similar agreements between the CPSU and
its East European partners has only been hinted at.[11] The
only party that does not appear on the list of ideological
confederates is the Rumanian, and the reason is obvious:
The Bucharest regime does not want to take an active part
in the bloc's ideological coordination and consolidation
campaign.

All this emphasis on consolidation and integration in
matters of foreign policy and ideology does not mean that
cooperation in other fields (primarily military and economic)
has been reduced, much less interrupted. Many such projects are by now well established (military integration, in
the technical sense, is almost complete), and they need to
be treated differently from the relatively new experiments
taking place in fields directly exposed to the effects of
East-West détente and to foreign influence. They certainly
exist, and are in the forefront of the regimes' attention.
For instance, the unusually strong support given by the
bloc media to Brezhnev's Westpolitik underlined the need
for further consolidation of military unity and for economic
ties among the socialist countries, as guarantees that the
bloc's beneficial influence on détente and peace would be
stabilized.

BUILDING SOCIALIST UNITY

The recurring trend toward greater socialist unity, with its intermediate stages of cooperation and integration, has posed for the regimes one of the most fundamental questions of all: how to build a tight, integrated socialist community in an era of increasing East-West détente and growing cultural contacts. More specifically: What should be the constitutional framework of this higher unity? What should be the legal status of its members? And what principles should regulate their relations with each other?

If a coherent, comprehensive philosophy regarding the building of socialist unity exists, it has not been published; it must be pieced together from various articles, studies, and documents of varying degrees of significance. The first blueprints for an integrated community (in practical terms that of the Warsaw Pact states) appeared in 1969, and very little progress has been made since then. The main features of these attempts are described below.

"Higher unity" is not defined merely as an arithmetic sum of component parts; it involves the fusion of interests, energies, and resources into "goal-oriented cooperation." It is a unity of a qualitatively higher kind, although it does not imply a supranational community. At this stage it would be premature to speak of a political merger resulting from the accelerated cooperation that exists, primarily in the economic sector. Certainly merger remains the final aim, but it can only come as the crown of a long historical process, which cannot be artificially speeded up. For the moment rapprochement is the immediate aim, and it is hoped that this will lead to mutual enrichment and the flowering of individual nations and to full realization of their sovereignty and equality within the framework of the socialist community.

The pressure for higher unity has brought into focus the questions of the Soviet Union's status in the community and of the relationship of its other members to Moscow. In the Stalinist period Soviet supremacy was openly imposed from above, and manifested itself in the "leading role of the Soviet Union." In the new era, however, after the Hungarian and Polish Octobers of 1956, the Czechoslovak Spring of 1968, the Sino-Soviet split, and the bitter controversies about polycentrism in the socialist movement, it was not possible simply to return to the former situation. The dilemma has been resolved by letting member states justify the privileged status of the Soviet Union in the socialist community.

Since 1969 a new Soviet Union has emerged on the screen of East European propaganda: a world power with multilateral obligations; a nuclear power with an invincible military potential, defensive as well as offensive; an economic giant with huge resources and a market of immense capacity; and a pioneer in industrial and technological revolution. This great country is also the land of Lenin; it has the richest experience in building socialism and communism and consequently provides the smaller members of the community with a model of how to proceed with the construction of their own socialist system and how to resolve the problems of modernization. All these qualities, the East European regimes have argued, invest the Soviet Union with special rights, privileges, and responsibilities in protecting their community and in promoting peace and progress; this is a role that no other socialist state can fill or even hope to share with the Soviet Union. To quote from a Hungarian commentary: "In its own national interest, a socialist country cannot do better than aim at close unity with the Soviet Union."[12]

The internal stability of this concept of unity is grounded in the principle of socialist (or proletarian) internationalism, in the dialectics of the "national" and "international," and in the single model of socialism. A large proportion of the regimes' propaganda is devoted to the eludication of these concepts and notions.

Socialist internationalism is supposed to govern the relations among socialist states, but it has been suspected by Western experts of being used as a cover for the so-called Brezhnev Doctrine, the concept of limited sovereignty. The communist leaders, including Brezhnev, and their ideological experts have resolutely denied the existence of any such doctrine and have described socialist internationalism as a new, higher version of international law reflecting a newly attained and more highly developed stage in the construction of socialism. It explicitly propounds the sovereignty and equality of all nations, they claim, but imbues these categories with a socialist class content. In this sense, "mutual support and solidarity in the struggle against imperialism and on behalf of socialism" is not an artificial doctrine imposed from above but a natural postulate of the class content of the socialist relationship.

The "national" and "international" relationship is a closely related subject. It involves the questions of how member states should build their common house, of how much of their national sovereignty can be sacrificed on the altar of socialist internationalism without damaging legiti-

31

mate national interests. In the Marxist-Leninist view, "national" and "international" are linked in a dialectical unity. The international can be realized only through the national and vice versa; socialist internationalism and integration lift national sovereignty and independence to a new, higher level. A small country integrated into a large socialist community has a greater standing in the world, a better setting for self-realization, than it would have in a state of lonely vegetation. On the other hand, in spite of a tightening unity the member states preserve their sovereignty and independence. This is extolled as one of the distinctive characteristics of socialist integration and contrasted with capitalist integration, in which the participants must, it is said, renounce their sovereign rights. Socialist sovereignty has, of course, a class content, which means that class solidarity takes precedence over other interests.

All these postulates set the stage for the justification of the concept of a single or universal model of socialism. This concept stipulates that the building of socialism is a standard process, regulated by laws that are generally valid and were first crystallized and tested in the social fabric of the Soviet Union. No country can claim to build socialism in the true Marxist-Leninist sense unless it adheres to the over-all pattern furnished by the Soviet Union (and the East European states). Local divergencies are indeed accepted, but should never be fundamental and should be resolved by striking a correct balance between the national and international, the particular and the general. The greatest sin committed by the Czechoslovak reformers was that they denied the raison d'etre of a universal model and rejected, one by one, its essential components, such as the dictatorship of the proletariat, the leading role of the Marxist-Leninist party, and a centrally planned economy.

While promoting the idea of socialist unity the regimes have also denounced its various opponents--revisionists of the Right and of the Left, nationalists, champions of the "third-road ideology," remnants of the old bourgeois classes, and so on, and their diverse supporters abroad. Actually, they charged, one of the chief purposes of the foreign propaganda directed against the socialist community is to undermine its unity. The forces hostile to socialism want to achieve this by permitting an uncontrolled flow of people and information, by introducing ideological pluralism, by trying to set the smaller members of the community against the Soviet superpower, and by attacking the validity of a universal model of socialism.

The regimes have reacted with particular sensitivity to anything they regard as constituting a real, or even a potential, challenge to the idea of the universal model, since rejection of this idea entails rejection of the specific status and exemplary role of the Soviet Union. In their defense of the central (Soviet) model, the ideologists have focused their counterattacks on the Chinese, the dispersed Czechoslovak reformers, the Garaudy school in France, and the West European social democrats, denouncing them as advocates of "national roads" to socialism, of "democratic socialism," or of "third ideologies." They have also denounced "bourgeois capitalists" for allegedly encouraging nationalist hostility to the universal model of socialism, and more recently they have quarreled with Christian social teachings as expressions of false humanism. Furthermore, the ideologists have kept under fire the "legend" of the "modernization of capitalism" as another, and not entirely unsuccessful, device for undermining the prestige of the socialist model.* On top of all this, the ideologists have also taken exception to the theory of convergence, because speculation about the blending of the capitalist and socialist systems eliminates socialism as the real answer to the problems of mankind, something no Marxist-Leninist can ever accept. The regimes do not believe in the convergence of the systems, but they see a convergence in the final aims of their opponents--bourgeois capitalists, opportunists, nationalists, revisionists of the Right and of the Left:

> In advocating national models of socialism, they
> try to distort and undermine true socialism in
> the socialist countries, to weaken the fraternal
> relations between those states, and to kindle na-
> tionalist feelings which have nothing to do with
> respect for integrity and national characteris-
> tics. They try to justify the theory of social-
> ist "pluralism," from which it would follow that
> each country or group of countries would have its
> own brand of socialism, distinct from the scien-
> tific socialism of Marx, Engels, and Lenin which
> has found its embodiment in the Soviet Union and
> other socialist countries. . . .

---

*"It is the constant obligation of our whole ideological front to minimize the obvious appeal of contemporary capitalism," wrote the prominent Polish ideologist Jerzy Lukaszewicz. ("Some Problems of the Party Ideological Front," Nowe Drogi, Warsaw, April 1973.)

Socialism, as a new social system, is basically one and the same thing for all countries.[13]

At this point, special mention should be made of Hungary. Frequently in the earlier stages of its economic reform, and sporadically even today, Hungary has been described, mainly by foreign observers, as experimenting with a new model of socialism. Such an attempt, even if limited in scope and chaperoned by declarations of loyalty to Moscow, would be a more serious affair in the eyes of the Soviet Union than Rumania's deviations in the field of foreign policy. As a consequence, the Hungarian regime has vehemently protested against "slanderous speculations" about the construction of a new model of socialism and has used every opportunity to rebut the charge that its reform program is deviationist in character. When Andras Hegedus and two of his sociologist colleagues were expelled from the party in June 1973, one of the charges against them was that of mapping a new model of socialism, inspired by ultraleftist Western ideas.[14]

At this stage, however, it appears that of all the enemies of socialist unity in both East and West, the Soviet bloc leaders are especially concerned about the Chinese. The attacks on Peking are becoming increasingly acrimonious. The Maoist leaders have been denounced not only for rejecting the Soviet concept of socialist unity but also for constantly interfering in the internal affairs of the Warsaw Pact states, of joining forces in Europe with elements hostile to European security and cooperation, and for developing their own, separate contacts with the Common Market, the NATO countries, and the imperialists in general. But the greatest sin the Maoists committed was to describe the Soviet Union as a social-imperialist superpower with hegemonistic ambitions, which deals with its capitalist counterpart at the expense of socialist interests and especially those of the small- and medium-sized countries. Indeed, the charge that it is a superpower entails denial of the Soviet Union's claim to be the chief unifying factor in the socialist world, the unselfish spokesman for socialist interests in the international arena, and the protagonist of European security and cooperation. What makes Peking's offense even worse is that the charge was forcefully spelled out at the very moment when Brezhnev was involving himself personally in East-West rapprochement. A certain "I. Alexandrov," allegedly a pseudonym for a high-ranking CPSU official, retorted:

. . . This false premise, which is taken up by
anti-Sovietists of all the various shades, tes-
tifies more strikingly than anything else to
Peking's complete renunciation of class principles in international politics, and to its complete departure from the common policy of the
socialist countries.

. . . All this demagoguery about "superpowers" serves as a cloak for Peking's unprin-
cipled compact with the bourgeois states, and
as a justification for the hegemonistic preten-
sions of the Chinese leaders to leadership of
the third world.[15]

As a response to the Chinese (and their potential allies in the West), the East European regimes have engaged
in a campaign within a campaign in support of the Leninist
foreign policy of the Soviet Union, the construction of
socialist unity, and Brezhnev's personal contribution to
all this. One of the high points of this subcampaign was
the Crimean meeting of the Soviet bloc leaders in July
1973, at which the need for further unity was stressed.
The CPSU Politburo has acknowledged with satisfaction the
"unshakable determination" expressed at this meeting to
strengthen the position of the socialist community, further
cooperation among socialist states, and coordinate more
closely their actions in the international arena.[16]

News media commentaries preceding and following the
Crimean summit outlined several important future tasks:
maintenance of military power (the combat readiness of the
armed forces should be "permanently increased"); intrabloc
political cooperation; closer coordination of foreign policies; acceleration of the process of economic integration
("particularly in the spheres of production, science, and
technology"); more cooperation in ideology and political-
educational work; and collective resolution of the "topical
theoretical and political problems" of contemporary socialism.

THE DEVELOPMENT OF THE "NEW MAN"

This brings us from consideration of the over-all construction of socialist unity to the day-to-day problems of
ideological work, to the practical tasks involved in consolidating the influence of Marxism-Leninism in public life.

Can they be carried out by relying on old tenets and interpretations, by repeating compromised vulgar slogans, by
adapting outworn teaching and proselytizing methods? Certainly, many aspects of the campaign consist of no more
than this. At the same time, however, one must not overlook
the many significant efforts to bring Marxist-Leninist doctrine closer to the modern realities--in a word, to give it
the appearance of the Weltanschauung of the technological
age and to broaden its social base with more refined methods. The existence of such trends cannot be dismissed even
if in many cases they become mired in declamatory statements,
or are diverted or distorted by the intervention of neocon-
servative forces.

A good case in point is the call for a new communist
morality, for the creation of a truly convincing model of
"socialist humanism" to help in the development of the "new
man" envisioned by Marx. This experiment can invoke the
authority of Brezhnev himself. In his report to the 24th
CPSU Congress, the Soviet leader inserted a short statement
about the role of man in a socialist society. The molding
of the "new man," the comprehensively developed individual,
he said, is just as important in the construction of communism as the creation of its material and technical base.[17]
This statement has been interpreted as conferring the highest official approval on the task of determining the nature
of this new man and the way in which he should develop his
capacities under socialism. In the course of these inquiries, some interesting "discoveries" have been made. For
instance, Soviet scholars now have publicly admitted that
their approach to man has been rather one-sided; he was
seen almost exclusively as a production force, not as a
personality in his own right.[18]

East European authors have made even more profound and
more concrete observations. They have warned, for example,
that it is not sufficient to prepare man exclusively for
his public role in society, to educate him to become a good
worker and a good citizen. There is also a private sector
in human life, the innermost core of the individual, which
contrasts with the realities of the external world and poses
questions of its own: What is the purpose of my existence?
Who am I? What is happiness and how can I attain it? Why
must I suffer and how can I surmount my difficulties? What
lies at the end of life and where does death acquire its
power?*

----

*Even Kurt Hager, SED CC secretary and Politburo mem-
ber, had admitted the existence of this "other side" of the

What is surprising here is that some of these "revela-
tions" show a striking resemblance to the criticism made by
many "revisionists," "neo-Marxists," and other "reformers"
against the one-sided, distorted, mechanistic Marxist-Leninist concept of the human being. The new, although still
very cautious, reflections about the existentialist aspects
of human life, and the listing of questions that sooner or
later bemuse every man, sound like passages from an early
Marxist contribution to the Christian-Marxist dialogue.

Needless to say, the regimes show no signs of reopen-
ing the dialogue or taking over anything worthwhile from
the ideological reformers. It is remarkable, however, that
they have recognized the existence of the more human side
of man as well as the inability of their present ideological tools to come to grips with this issue. But obviously
(and this must be a frustrating requisite for all sincere
explorers in the field) the new tools must be found within
Marxism-Leninism, not adapted from other doctrines, models,
or experiments--one of the "fatal mistakes" made by the
Czechoslovak reformers and by "dialoguers" of the Garaudy
type. The assumption, and most probably the highest party
order, is that the potentials of Marxist-Leninist ideology
are sufficient to provide answers to all the questions facing modern man. There is, however, no visible agreement
on how the work should proceed and what form it should take.

A more profound elaboration of the principles of socialist humanism, of its image of man and his role in society, is indispensable, it is felt, for two reasons.

The first is domestic. It should be demonstrated to
the masses that socialism is not fighting simply to create
a consumer society, or to achieve the highest possible
standard of living, with its purely material benefits (as
capitalism does, it is added) but also to make possible the
self-realization of man as a whole so that the humanistic
aspects of life may be enjoyed. Socialist humanism should
help to develop a new human personality and to eliminate
the influence of hostile ideologies that have offered help
to man in precisely those areas where the traditional
Marxist-Leninist propaganda methods have been inadequate.
One of these hostile ideologies is religion, and its continuing influence on man in socialist society should be
superseded by elaboration of the humanist aspects of socialism.

---

problem. Cf. his speech at the ninth CC plenum, Neues
Deutschland, East Berlin, May 30, 1973.

Another hostile force that should be combated as an obstacle to socialist humanism is the petit-bourgeois mentality. The socialist regimes have invested this with many "negative" attributes, such as extreme individualism, disregard of the interests of society, vulgar materialism, corruption, and repudiation of many of the higher values. From the point of view of ideological consolidation, however, the most grievous offenses are an alleged lack of "socialist awareness," a receptiveness to foreign propaganda, and the idealization of the Western system of production. The ideology of the petite bourgeoisie, the regime experts say, is fed from three main sources: survivals from the past, the general economic improvement, and the spirit of Western consumerism. If one is to believe the many long studies that have appeared, no segment of socialist society is immune from these "malign influences," but two groups are exceptionally vulnerable: the lower middle class (sometimes this term stands for the workers) and the younger generation (because of its lack of experience and greater exposure to hostile propaganda).

Inquiries into the deeper roots of this mentality have concluded that its elimination will be a long and difficult process. What complicates the task, the studies insist, is that, in principle as well as in practice, socialism has nothing against the good life: the attainment of material affluence is one of its central goals. The problem is how to define the good life and find the point at which an individual's way of life clashes with the interests of the community, necessitating some kind of intervention from above. A correct answer to this problem, one can assume, would be especially welcome in Hungary, where there is widespread dissatisfaction in the ranks of the workers with the affluent life led by certain categories of people and a growing demand for the "narrowing down of democratic rights." The regime's dilemma is how to oppose effectively any unpleasant manifestations of the petit-bourgeois mentality without imposing serious restrictions on the functioning of "socialist democracy."[19]

The second argument put forward by regime ideologues for more substantial elaboration of socialist humanism is international in nature. But here propaganda considerations visibly prevail over sincere, even if very cautious and restricted, reformist ambitions. If socialism, it is argued, wants to mount an ideological offensive against the West, it must present a clear alternative to capitalism and show that socialist democracy, being superior to bourgeois democracy, can create a new scale of values corresponding to

the true ambitions of modern man. Below is a quotation
from a belligerent article in a Czechoslovak paper that is
fairly representative of the rather aggressive and triumphal
current in the campaign:

> Today bourgeois ideologists are calling for a
> change in priorities in life in the capitalist
> countries, which is constantly devalued by the
> growing number of intercapitalist conflicts
> and the inability of capitalism to master the
> problems of the advancing scientific-technical
> revolution. We should therefore continue to
> demonstrate that capitalism is unable to create
> this new scale of values of life, but that it
> is created in the socialist world. Creating
> the conditions for a free and all-embracing de-
> velopment of man, creating a socialist way of
> life and a new position for man in society, are
> parts of this process. In the ideological con-
> frontation with capitalism it is still impor-
> tant, and will continue to be so in future, to
> point out the decreasing difference between the
> socialist and capitalist worlds so far as con-
> sumer goods are concerned and the fact that in
> some respects socialism is surpassing capital-
> ism.
>   Owing to man's new and different position
> in society under a socialist way of life, so-
> cialism has created yet another aspect through
> which to prove its superiority over capitalism,
> and this aspect will become increasingly attrac-
> tive to the working masses in the capitalist
> countries.[20]

LEARNING FROM ONE'S MISTAKES

Moving closer to the more practical organizational aspects of the campaign, it is symptomatic that the regimes
have shown a willingness to learn from their past mistakes.
In the first, Stalinist, phase it was generally assumed
that the political takeover of state power would automati-
cally resolve all ideological issues and create a deeply
rooted socialist awareness and that the party would have
nothing to do but to tell the masses how to build the new
world (or order them to do so). Today, however, even in a
country like Czechoslovakia, it is admitted that this as-

sumption was mistaken. The development of socialist awareness and the building of socialism constitute an extremely
complicated process that requires thorough discussion and
clarification of many sensitive subjects plus the skill to
adapt Marxism-Leninism to modern conditions without losing
any of its essence. Consequently, those engaged in this
work not only need a good basic knowledge of Marxism-Leninism and the ability and endurance necessary to conduct constructive dialogues with their opponents but also require
a good critical sense, which will enable them to distinguish
between what is true and what is false, ideologically speaking. They must be particularly well equipped to refute the
"imperialist arguments" that reach the socialist countries
through direct or indirect channels.

As indicated earlier, the East European regimes are
convinced that it is not always direct, overt Western ideological activity that constitutes the real danger, but that
which may reach the country, and enter the minds of the
people, through side channels, often sneaking in unnoticed
as harmless scientific material, particular methods of research, or a fashionable expression. Such apparent trifles
can become a source of serious ideological aberration, and
certain categories of intellectuals, such as journalists,
artists, social scientists, and students of the humanities,
can easily turn into unwitting carriers of the germ of
ideological infection.* They should therefore be made
aware of their sensitive position and play a more positive

---

*In Hungary, journalists and social scientists have been
attacked by the minister of culture for freely borrowing
from the professional vocabulary of Western sociological
schools and for displaying a neutral attitude toward Western research methods and organizational systems. (Gyorgy
Aczel, "Selected Cultural Problems of Ideological and Cultural Life," a report delivered at the national agitprop
conference in Budapest, 24-25 January 1973, published in
Bulletin der Botschaft der Ungarischen Volksrepublik in der
DDR, East Berlin, 6 April 1973.) At the time he wrote this
article Aczel was a secretary of the HSWP Central Committee; he has since been removed from that post and transferred to a government position. In Poland, a similar
charge was made against members of these two professions,
who were in this case joined by artists. It was said that
they failed to approach Western philosophical concepts with
the necessary critical attitude and that those who write
for the press do not "adequately reveal" the weaknesses of

and active role in sealing off the inlets through which subversive Western propaganda infiltrates, in defending socialist ideology, and in developing the "socialist man."

The regimes seem to be more or less resigned to the
fact that many of the older generation, including party
members, remain captives of their past, show a lack of
flexibility, and fall easy prey to hostile influences. In
the long run, it is stated, the offensive should orient itself toward the young, who have grown up entirely under socialism. Here, too, however, difficulties can arise: their
ideological education can, and in most cases does, suffer
from reactionary family ties; they have no personal experience of "capitalist oppression"; and they are becoming a
major target of Western overtures, thanks to the spread of
universalist youth cultures and subcultures. This, however,
merely strengthens the argument that ideological education
should be concentrated on the younger generation.

As a result, each socialist regime is making elaborate
preparations to improve and expand the ideological education of its young people in both the public and party school
systems. In at least one country, Poland, preparations
have been made to carry the ideological campaign into the
home, and thus reach those who seek to find refuge there
from regimentation.[21] Everywhere the long-term goal is to
develop the young people's "socialist personalities," to
immunize them against foreign influences, and to teach them
how to ensure the victory of socialism in its historic confrontation with "capitalism."[22]

Authoritative regime sources have repeatedly stressed
that the ideological struggle is being waged against anti-
socialism, not against individuals. Its chief instruments
are patient discussion and convincing argument; "administrative methods" should be avoided whenever possible. But
between these two extremes there is a wide range of techniques available to, and used by, the regimes. In the last
two years, for example, all of them have passed resolutions
calling for greater vigilance on the ideological-cultural
front. In most cases this implies a tightening of control
on editorial offices, publishing houses, research institutes,
enterprises, and individuals involved in East-West exchange.*

---

the Western system. "Schematism" and "excessive simplifi-
cation" often are used in presenting the capitalist world
(Lukaszewicz, op. cit.).

*One of the rare public complaints about the stiffening
bureaucratic control of Western study trips appeared in the

It also involves giving instruction on how to behave toward foreign tourists and, most important, applying greater selectivity in deciding which Western cultural products should be admitted.

From time to time, however, the regimes do not hesitate to use harsher methods ("administrative solutions") in dealing with those who tamper with ideological consolidation. Such cases have been regularly reported in Czechoslovakia and the Soviet Union, and the latter has distinguished itself by misusing psychiatry and staging a series of trials to remove ideological offenders from the public scene. But administrative intervention in the ideological-cultural field--albeit much milder--can occur under relatively more liberal regimes as well. A recent cause célèbre was the expulsion of sociologist Andras Hegedus and philosophers Janos Kis and Mihaly Vajda from the Hungarian party for "ideological and political views . . . opposed to Marxism-Leninism and to the policy of the HSWP."*

Sizing up the specific tasks of socialist propaganda, regime experts, especially in the smaller countries, have concluded that the creators of this propaganda, if it is to succeed, cannot afford to dissipate its impact by dealing separately with every detail of, and every subject raised by, the ideological confrontation. Nor should socialist propaganda be limited, it is suggested, exclusively to the refutation of "capitalist" or other hostile views, or allow itself to be maneuvered into handling topics of the West's choosing.

COUNTEROFFENSIVE, CONTROL, NONINTERFERENCE

It is usually at this point that the more militant elements among the regime ideologues and propagandists inject the subject of a counteroffensive, in the sense that the socialist community should not limit itself to conduct-

---

Polish press, in an article by Sz. A. Peniazek, "Trying to Get out into the World," Polityka, Warsaw, 14 July 1973.

*On this point, see also p. 34. Two months after the expulsions the party reiterated the validity of its middle-of-the-road policy in political, socioeconomic, and ideological affairs in two editorials in the party daily, in which the author expressed the hope that social conflicts could be resolved by public discussion rather than administrative methods. (Nepszabadsag, 18 and 22 August 1973.)

ing an ideological campaign at home but should use its resources to transfer the ideological conflict to the capitalist states, that is, to mount an ideological offensive in
the West and concentrate it on issues of its own choice.
In practical terms this would mean emphasizing two general
topics: the great potential of socialism to create a new
society and a more meaningful way of life (as opposed to
capitalism) and the inability of the West to resolve the
human problems emanating from the technological-scientific
revolution. The ultimate aim of such an offensive, it is
said, should be to speed up the liberation of the working
masses in the West "from the servitude of the bourgeoisie
and a petit-bourgeois ideology"--in short, to "create the
conditions needed for the political victory of the workers'
movement."[23]

The unfolding of an ideological campaign in the socialist countries and the possibility of extending it to the
West is considered fully compatible with the regimes' concept of East-West cooperation. As described earlier, such
cooperation should be based on the principle of peaceful
coexistence, but in East European eyes peaceful coexistence
does not imply ideological peace, but rather presupposes a
sharpening of the ideological struggle. Western advocacy
of a freer flow of people, ideas, and information, however,
is not accepted as a constructive contribution to this ideological struggle. The apparent inconsistency is "resolved"
by the Soviet bloc's thesis of "good" and "bad" propaganda,
of justified and unjustified ideological offensive. The
difference between the two is determined by the considerations of the class warfare:

a) The ideological offensive of the socialist regimes
   is characterized as an organic component of class
   warfare on an international scale. Hence the socialist regimes' endeavor to intensify the ideological struggle is a contribution to the promotion of the socialist revolution, to the fulfillment of the historical mission of the working
   class. Consequently it cannot be inconsistent
   with the spirit of peaceful coexistence. As to
   the West, under the pretext of engaging in cultural-ideological exchanges it wants to subvert
   the socialist community of states, the bastion
   of real peace and progress. Thus the idea of
   liberal East-West exchange is antisocialist in
   intent and runs counter to the principle of peaceful coexistence and the grain of history.

43

b) More concretely, the socialist regimes present
the practical difference between the two ideological offensives as follows: while the socialist
regimes are engaged in honest, objective propaga-
tion of the advantages of the socialist system
and of the true, oppressive nature of "capitalism,"
the West disseminates misinformation, slander,
national hatred, and dubious "works" of culture,
misusing the channels of East-West cooperation.
The latter has been dismissed by regime sources
as continuation of the cold war, as interference
in the internal affairs of the socialist countries
that clearly violates the principle of peaceful
coexistence.

Hence, the implication is, what the two
sides are doing is really not comparable. One is
pursuing its historical mission to promote progress; the other is doing all it can to arrest
progress. On this basis, the regime ideologues
feel justified not only in defending the socialist positions against Western "machinations" but
also in launching a counteroffensive against the
bourgeois-capitalist-imperialist ideology of the
West. The constant threat to socialism and progress must be destroyed in its own nest.[24]

Most of the arguments advanced by party ideologues
have been taken over and widely used by the East bloc delegations to the CSCE in the protracted debates on the "freer
flow" proposal. They have charged that the Western proposal
could result in a return to cold-war tactics by the capitalist countries, to a broadening of their "campaign of
misinformation," to the importing of antihuman, politically
and morally harmful cultural material into the socialist
camp, and to large-scale interference in the internal affairs of the socialist states. This has culminated in a
recommendation by the regimes that East-West exchanges in
the related fields be broadened, with the proviso, however,
that, directly or indirectly, the state remain in control
of the flow of exchange and that the ultimate agreement
contain a specific reference to noninterference in the internal affairs of the interested states. The vagueness of
the Soviet bloc concept of noninterference and its arbitrary interpretation of the principle of peaceful coexistence can only make East-West negotiations on the subject
more complicated.

Fear of Western ideas and an inclination to identify
Western culture with violence, chauvinism, and so forth
are among the few things Rumania shares with the rest of
the bloc in this connection. Control over cultural activities seems to be more rigorous in the RSR than in any other
bloc country except the Soviet Union and Czechoslovakia,
and since the freer flow issue was first raised the Rumanian
leaders have frequently stated that cultural cooperation
cannot disregard the normal rules of interstate relations
and cannot justify "intrusion into other people's internal
affairs."[25]

Beyond this, however, Rumania plays no active role in
the bloc's integration campaign. As mentioned earlier,
it is the only East European country that (so far) has not
signed any agreements on ideological cooperation. The
Ceausescu regime by no means recognizes the leading role of
the Soviet Union. It approaches the applying of universal
laws to the building of socialism with extreme caution,
and when it does do so the accent very soon shifts from the
general to the particular. Rumania has not demonstrated
any notable interest in disseminating the bloc concept of
peaceful coexistence and has avoided making sweeping accu-
sations of ideological subversion against the West. Nor
does the regime see any need for an individual or a collective counteroffensive against the West, and the Rumanian
propaganda machine has shown no great eagerness to deal
publicly with the freer flow controversy.

A SUMMING UP

In the last year or so the drive to achieve ideological disarmament, to consolidate Marxist-Leninist ideological influence in all sectors of public life, has become
integral to the political endeavors of the Soviet bloc.
This is partly a reaction to the rising spirit of consumerism, to the political uninterestedness of the population
in the bloc countries. But it was also inspired by the
regimes' suspicion--nay, fear--that the broadening of East-
West contacts, in the framework of European security and
cooperation, might encourage the trends mentioned above
and, ultimately, constitute a serious threat to the general
position of Marxist-Leninist ideology.

The campaign is not intended merely to preserve the
ideological status quo. It also encompasses a limited experiment to change the profile of Marxism-Leninism, to in-

crease its responsiveness to modern problems, and to make it more attractive to the masses both in the bloc and in the rest of the world. Some pledges to carry the ideological struggle into the "enemy camp," to eliminate the influence of the "decaying bourgeois ideology," were also heard.

All in all, however, the program to consolidate Marxist-Leninist ideology with the help of delimitation (<u>Abgrenzung</u>) and control indicates an unwillingness to face an open encounter with an ideologically and culturally pluralistic Europe. While the socialist regimes are almost enthusiastic about pan-European cooperation in economic-technological-scientific areas, they take a more than cautious attitude toward such cooperation in the cultural field or any other area that might affect their ideological monopoly. The Soviet bloc has tried to make the world understand that European unity cannot eliminate the existing social systems; rather it must maintain the strict separation between the two parts of Europe. But such stipulations have not prevented some East European ideologues and propagandists from fiddling about with plans for the annihilation of bourgeois-capitalist ideology, and precisely through the facilities provided by pan-European cooperation.

In considering the "reideologization" program in the Soviet bloc and its broader offensive projects, however, one should keep several significant points in mind. First of all, most of those who have so far come out in favor of a new ideological policy (for example, "hardening the line," "vigilance," <u>Abgrenzung</u>, "control," "counteroffensive") are members of the official party leaderships or officials in party ideological departments and institutes. Even if their basic determination to implement the central decision cannot be doubted (and at least the first East-West discussions about the "freer flow" proposal have confirmed this), a great deal of what they have to say on the subject sounds like routine, obligatory recitation of official directives, which will have no immediate practical consequences. Another point is that other forces in the communist parties, the so-called more liberal elements (not to speak of the general public) have had very little chance to contribute to the ideological "discussion." The pragmatic elements, the people involved in East-West economic cooperation, have found themselves in a similar situation: they have not been able to speak up and express their views on the general prospects for tightening the ideological reins. But despite their silence, the ultimate influence of these groups on the shaping of the Soviet bloc's policy of East-West cooperation must not be underrated.

As the history of East-West contacts has so far manifested, it is difficult--in fact, impossible--to maintain
artificial dividing lines between the many spheres of East-
West cooperation. It is to be hoped that no campaign on
the part of the Soviet bloc to achieve ideological consolidation will be able to rescind this "natural law" of East-
West normalization or to seriously damage the built-in
automatism of East-West cultural exchanges.

The Soviet dissidents, of course, constitute a special
case. They do not fit into any of the categories mentioned
here, and their protests against the restrictive intellectual policy of the Soviet government, including its attitude toward pan-European cooperation, have been ignored,
or even repudiated, by Moscow as illegal, partisan actions
by a small group of political troublemakers. But the regime's deep embarrassment at the protests is visible to all,
and they have compelled it at least to take a more cautious
stand on many of the ideological issues under discussion.
The long-term effects of the dissident movement cannot be
considered in the present context.

NOTES

1. Yu. Kashev in <u>Novoye Vremya</u>, Moscow, 4 May 1973.
2. This paragraph was based mainly on the following
sources: J. Sokol, "Peaceful Coexistence and Ideological
Subversion," <u>Wojsko Ludowe</u>, vol. 23 (Warsaw, May 1972); V.
Knyazinski, "<u>Détente</u> and the Problems of the Ideological
Struggle," <u>Mezhdunarodnaya Zhizn</u>, no. 3 (Moscow, 1973);
Miklos Ovari, "Several Practical Problems in Mass Political
Work After the November 1972 CC Resolution," <u>Bulletin der
Botschaft der Ungarischen Volksrepublik in der DDR</u>, East
Berlin, 26 April 1973; Y. Nikolayev, "Cooperation and Ideo-
logical Struggle," <u>International Affairs</u>, no. 4 (Moscow,
1973); J. Lukaszewicz, "Some Problems of the Party Ideolog-
ical Front," <u>Nowe Drogi</u>, Warsaw, April 1973; Tamas Palos,
"Ideological Struggle--Class Struggle," <u>Partelet</u>, vol. 18
(Budapest, April 1973); Lajos Racz, "More Sensitivity Is
Needed in Ideology as Well," <u>Csongrad Megyei Hirlap</u>, Szeged,
13 May 1973; <u>Rabotnichesko Delo</u>, Sofia, 31 May 1973; J.
Kucera, "Ideological Offensive," <u>Tribuna</u>, Prague, 20 June
1973; Moscow Domestic Service (Yuriy Zhukov's TV program),
7 July 1973; Radio Moscow in Czech, 18 July 1973.
3. The Soviet bloc source material on peaceful coexistence is particularly voluminous. For the present
sketchy roundup the following articles were taken into con-

sideration: A. Sovetov, "Peaceful Coexistence, A Real Factor in International Relations," Mezhdunarodnaya Zhizn,
no. 8 (1972); R. Garai, "New Conditions and Phenomena in
the Policy of Peaceful Coexistence," Partelet, vol. 17
(September 1972); "The Characterization of Present International Power Relations (A Discussion)," Nemzetkozi Szemle,
vol. 17, no. 1 (Budapest, 1973); Nikolayev, op. cit.; Kucera,
op. cit.

    4. Professor Y. Bogush, "Leninist Foreign Policy,"
International Affairs, no. 5 (1973).

    5. K. Katushev, "The World Socialist System: Main
Trends and Developments," Kommunist, no. 5 (Moscow, 1972).

    6. Paul Markowski, "The Common Foreign Policy of the
Socialist Community of States and Peaceful Coexistence,"
Deutsche Aussenpolitik, vol. 13, no. 4 (East Berlin, 1973).

    7. Radio Moscow, 15 August 1973.

    8. Rude Pravo, Prague, 25 August 1972, as reported
by Ceteka on the same day.

    9. See also Guenther Steltner, "Cooperation in the
Socialist Community of States on a New Scale," Einheit,
vol. 28, no. 5 (East Berlin, 1973).

    10. Radio Moscow's Hungarian service, 4 August 1973.

    11. For example, by Jerzy Lukaszewicz, a Polish CC
secretary, in Pravda, Moscow, 28 August 1973. A detailed
roundup of the East European agreements will be found in
"Bilateral Ideological Agreements Multiply in Eastern Europe," East European Background Report/11, Radio Free Europe
Research, East European Research and Analysis (henceforth
EERA), 17 July 1973.

    12. Nepszabadsag, Budapest, 24 July 1973.

    13. Radio Moscow, 20 September 1972.

    14. See William F. Robinson, "Hegedus, Two Other
Scholars Expelled from Hungarian Communist Party," Hungarian BR/9, RFER (EERA), 25 June 1973.

    15. "In the Interests of Peace and Socialism," Pravda,
7 August 1973.

    16. TASS, 3 August 1973.

    17. As quoted in Pravda, 5 January 1972, by Academician
F. Konstantinov, president of the Philosophical Society in
the USSR.

    18. Ibid.

    19. See, for example, J. Farago, "Power and Democracy,"
Nepszabadsag, 18 August 1973.

    20. Kucera, op. cit.

    21. See Polish SR/29, RFER (EERA), 24 August 1973,
Item 1.

22.   Karel Horak, "The Ideological Indoctrination of Youth Must Be Improved," Zivot Strany, Prague, March 1973; Gerhard Neuner, "Theoretical Problems of the Development and Education of Socialist Personalities in Connection with Establishing the Content of Secondary School Education," Pedagogik, East Berlin, April 1973; "The Sejm Resolution on the Upbringing of Youth," Monitor Polski, Warsaw, 17 April 1973; Lukaszewicz, "Some Problems."

23.   Kucera, op. cit.; Lukaszewicz, "Some Problems"; Harold Neubert, "Peaceful Coexistence Aids World Revolutionary Struggle," Einheit, vol. 28, no. 5 (1973).

24.   Cf., for example, Nikolayev, op. cit.; Gerhard Dengler, "Socialist Information for Other Countries and Imperialist Propaganda," German Foreign Policy, no. 6 (East Berlin, 1972); Palos, op. cit.; Voice of the GDR (domestic service), 30 June 1973.

25.   Scinteia, Bucharest, 16 May 1973.

3

ECONOMIC IMPULSES
TOWARD DÉTENTE
Henry Schaefer

In the early postwar years the imposition of the Soviet systemic and development models on Eastern Europe and the deteriorating political situation severely limited the scope of East-West economic relations. In fact the USSR rejected economic cooperation with the West, refusing to participate in the preparations for an International Trade Organization and to become involved, or let the East Europeans become involved, with the General Agreement on Tariffs and Trade (GATT) and the Marshall Plan. (Czechoslovakia, a founding member of GATT, became inactive after the communist take-over in 1948.) The Soviets objected to efforts to liberal-ize trade, including the most-favored-nation principle, and opposed efforts to reestablish multilateralism.[1] There was no possibility that labor or capital would flow between East and West and, in large part because of Western restric-tions, relatively little likelihood that technology would do so. Communist earnings from services, including tourism, were minimal, and economic relations were confined essen-tially to a modest amount of trade conducted within the framework of bilateral barter agreements.

ECONOMIC PRESSURES IN EASTERN EUROPE

In Eastern Europe, however, by the late 1950s the re-serves of manpower and raw materials that had allowed rapid extensive development were becoming exhausted, and a number of states began to feel the need to turn to more intensive development policies and to acquire the more advanced tech-nology and capital equipment that such policies necessitate. Initially, in Eastern Europe as well as in the USSR there was considerable reluctance to form continuing ties with the West, and an attempt was made to meet these growing economic needs by invigorating Comecon and by purchasing licenses and turnkey plants from the West. These efforts have not, however, enabled the East European states to effect a change in the commodity structure of their exports to the West as they have industrialized.

By the mid-1960s foreign trade problems had become a major reason for the increasing attention devoted to the question of broader economic reforms in Eastern Europe, particularly in the more industrialized and trade-dependent countries—notably Czechoslovakia, East Germany, and Hungary.[2] Efforts were made to increase the role and financial interest of producing enterprises in foreign trade and to develop closer ties between these enterprises and foreign trade enterprises. Even optimistic observers, however, noted that the scope for reform in the foreign trade sector was "narrow in comparison with the domestic sector," and that because of a number of inhibiting factors, "changes in the methods of plan control in foreign trade [had] been intermittent and relatively slow-paced."[3] Moreover, a negative feature of a number of these reform efforts was their tendency to blur authority and responsibility in the foreign trade sphere. At the same time the liberalization of trade restrictions and payment arrangements had done little to overcome the "latent force[s]" promoting bilateralism and "hamper[ing] real multilateralization of trade and payments" between East and West.[4] Whatever the hopes for the future, there was little sign that the broader reforms getting under way yet offered much prospect of overcoming the structural impasse in exports to the West, or that they would significantly facilitate the acquisition of Western technology, equipment, and know-how increasingly necessary to promote intensive economic development.

Recognition of their continuing inability to penetrate Western industrial markets and of the limited potential of their various efforts at trade reform helped to lead the East European states to consider closer, long-term economic ties with the West. The development of economic cooperation as a framework for such links has thus been both a logical extension of the purchase of licenses and turnkey plants that emerged in the late 1950s and a reaction to the failure of these technological and capital equipment acquisitions to solve the problems of achieving up-to-date technological levels and of selling industrial products in the West.

The beginning of East-West economic cooperation is often dated from about 1964, when Western firms began sup-

plementing their production capacity by contracting with
communist firms for supplies of finished or semifinished
goods manufactured with the aid of documentation and know-
how, and sometimes machinery and equipment, provided by
the Western firm.[5] Since then economic cooperation arrangements have taken on more diverse and complex forms, some
of which involve both partners in management and give them
a share in the risks and rewards of the venture. When located in the West, cooperative arrangements have usually
taken the form of corporate joint ventures typical of the
economic and legal institutions of market economies. Because both institutions and precedent have been absent in
the planned economies, arrangements operating (in part at
least) in the East have required greater negotiation and
more detailed agreement on each aspect of their operations.
The gathering of the factors of production as well as such
questions as investment returns and management prerogatives
have all had to be negotiated and spelled out in any agreement. In an operational sense, if not in an ownership
sense, however, the more complicated arrangements operating
in Eastern Europe have anticipated the sort of long and
close collaboration that is associated with joint ventures
in the West. Reflecting East European interests and capabilities, the primary forms that economic cooperation with
the West has taken have been:

1. the supplying by the Western partner of technology,
   managerial know-how, or engineering services,
   frequently in conjunction with licensing
2. subcontracting by the Eastern partner
3. coproduction involving the sharing of processing
   or component production
4. joint marketing
5. cooperation on third markets in supplying plant
   or equipment, often in conjunction with one or
   more of the above forms

THE EARLY SOVIET APPROACH

Postwar economic relations between the Soviet Union
and the West developed more according to political than to
economic dictates. Although the Soviets proposed an all-
European cooperation agreement in the mid-1950s in an effort to forestall the establishment of the European Economic Community, it was not until after the tensions of the
1958-61 period that the USSR really began to try to develop

a new policy toward Western Europe that could incorporate
economic relations into the broader framework of "peaceful
coexistence." The potential and durability of the EEC were
increasingly acknowledged, and Khrushchev went so far as
to suggest economic cooperation between Eastern and Western
economic groupings and to propose a world-wide trade organization in which the communist states would participate.[6]
In part these Soviet ploys undoubtedly reflected a greater
recognition of the economic needs of Eastern Europe and of
the legitimacy of their fears of the EEC's commercial policies, but they appear to have been primarily an attempt to
forestall both the consolidation of the emerging Franco-
German axis into the "backbone" of EEC integration and the
feared emergence of a West European economic "power center"
comparable to that of the United States.[7] In any case,
Khrushchev did not have time to follow up these bold but
ill-considered ideas, and after his ouster they were not
pursued by his successors.

Within a short time after their assumption of power,
however, Brezhnev and Kosygin indicated that they were prepared to engage in more extensive economic ties with the
West on a bilateral basis. The first step toward the giant
Togliatti automotive complex was taken when a protocol on
scientific and technological cooperation with Fiat was
signed in mid-1965, and the Soviet Union's efforts to sell
patents and licenses in the West, which had begun in earnest
in 1962 with the setting up of the specialized agency
Licensintorg, were stepped up after its accession to the international agreement for patent protection in July 1965.
The next year, on Soviet initiative, talks on deliveries
of natural gas in exchange for pipe got under way with Austria, Italy, and France, and after French President de
Gaulle's visit to Moscow and the signing of the Soviet
Union's first intergovernmental agreement on scientific,
technological, and economic cooperation with a Western country, Franco-Soviet cooperation began to develop under the
guidance of a new high-level commission. This agreement,
and subsequent ones with other West European countries,
also provided for a number of working groups, which on the
Soviet side have been subject to tight central control
through the State Committee on Science and Technology.

A number of cooperative arrangements with Western
enterprises were also undertaken during this period. However, cooperation in research and development rather than
in production or marketing was preferred, and in the relatively few arrangements involving industrial production the
Soviets, unlike the Eastern Europeans, were normally the

principal partner.[8] The Soviets apparently desired to maintain close control over their economic cooperation with the West and to limit the number of such arrangements, yet through the very magnitude of some of their proposals, particularly the gas-for-pipe deal, it was clear that they expected to enlist a maximum of Western governmental support and involvement. In view of the Western countries chosen, this large-scale economic courting appears to have been an integral part of the USSR's new, more differentiated approach to the West, which involved a hardening attitude toward the United States coupled with a stepped-up policy of détente toward Western Europe, with the notable (temporary) exception of West Germany--a policy reflected at the 23rd CPSU conference in March 1966.[9] But, while a purely bilateral approach to economic cooperation with the West served certain immediate Soviet economic and technological needs, and perhaps to a limited extent furthered the goal of isolating West Germany and fragmenting Western Europe, it had two fundamental weaknesses: it neglected the economic needs of Eastern Europe and it failed really to confront the evolving forces of integration in Western Europe.

TOWARD A GROUP APPROACH

Nevertheless, the Soviet leadership was still unwilling to revive Khrushchev's proposals and chose to proceed cautiously in bringing Eastern Europe into a group approach. The first signs of a renewed search for a broader framework for pan-European economic cooperation emerged in mid-1966. East-West economic cooperation had not been part of the security conference idea when it was reactivated in early 1965 to head off Western moves toward a multilateral nuclear force,[10] and the conference project itself had faded by late 1965 as NATO support for such a force waned. The conference proposal, however, appeared in quite different guise at the Bucharest meeting of the Warsaw Pact in July 1966, having been transformed into part of the broader détente strategy aimed at Western Europe.[11]

The Bucharest Declaration made all-European economic cooperation an integral, if still vague, part of the security conference campaign. It called for a "broadening of economic relations between European states, and the elimination of the discrimination and obstacles existing in this area . . . the strengthening of economic and trade ties, and the multiplication of contacts and forms of cooperation

in the fields of science, technology, culture, and art, as
well as in other fields." It suggested that an all-European
conference discuss these questions, and that the accord
reached at the conference be expressed in terms of an "all-
European declaration."[12]

As it turned out, the Soviet Union was not immediately
able to exploit effectively these rather tentative programmatic ideas about institutionalizing East-West economic cooperation in developing its strategy for Europe. Hints
were soon forthcoming that the West Germans would be welcome in the development of all-European cooperation if they
would only "recognize the groundlessness of their entire
postwar political thinking."[13] But six months after the
Bucharest declaration the new Kiesinger-Brandt government
scored a major breakthrough by establishing diplomatic relations with Rumania, thereby dealing a severe blow to Soviet hopes that the Warsaw Pact states would present a
united political and economic front vis-à-vis the West.
Although, at first, the USSR was relatively open-minded
toward the new West German government's policy statements,
Ulbricht's urgings and the disruptive impact of the precipitous recognition of Rumania served to stiffen the Soviet position during early 1967 and, as at Karlovy Vary in
April, pan-European cooperation came to be advocated rather
perfunctorily and less for the sake of "security" than to
help Western Europe to "get rid of the dictation of the
dollar."[14]

Preoccupied with consolidating the bloc, the Soviet
Union did not pursue the security conference project or the
idea of East-West economic cooperation with any real enthusiasm during 1967 and instead turned increasingly to a campaign against American and West German bridge-building policies, which allegedly were coordinated and subversive in
their intent. Although they were well aware of the need
to develop a more viable, long-term policy in the face of
Western developments, the Soviets' policy in Europe not
only "inadequately bridged the divergent interests of the
Warsaw Pact allies [but also] inadequately responded to the
new opportunities and challenges in Western Europe. . . .
Moscow seemed unable to define its own position in such a
manner as to seize the initiative in European affairs."[15]

During early 1968 Soviet information media continued
to push for pan-European cooperation in strongly anti-
American terms, putting it forward as the way in which
Europeans could become "masters of their own house" and as
"a good material basis" for European security.[16] Yet the
principles of such cooperation remained vague, and concrete

proposals were not forthcoming. Moreover, West German imperialism was found to be "clamoring louder and louder for
political as well as economic domination in Western Europe"
and to have made a "political and military deal [with] aggressive circles in Washington."[17] The illusory quality
of the Soviets' hope of disrupting West European, as well
as Atlantic, unity with pan-European cooperation schemes
ensured that the vast majority in the West would remain
wary and uninterested.

At this time, moreover, Soviet fears of the possible
impact of East-West cooperation on Eastern Europe were
rapidly increasing. Expanded relations with the West were
a basic feature of the program to revitalize the Czechoslovak economy during the Prague Spring, and the mounting Soviet attacks on Czechoslovak plans and on alleged imperialist (particularly West German) machinations prior to the
invasion of the CSSR in August 1968 reflected concern over
the economic weakness of Eastern Europe and over its receptivity to cooperation offers by the West. As the USSR's
attention turned increasingly to developments in Czechoslovakia, the lack of Western response to halfhearted Soviet
overtures on pan-European economic cooperation was undoubtedly welcome.

NEW DEPARTURES

After the invasion of Czechoslovakia, the Soviet Union
quickly reaffirmed its commitment to the idea of a conference and to the program for European security adopted at
Bucharest in 1966. Expanded East-West economic cooperation
was still to be a part of all this, but a much strengthened
Soviet desire for a shift to a more collective Eastern
bloc approach soon became evident, one of the first, and
more unusual, indications of this coming in the handling
of a UN speech by Gromyko less than two months after the
invasion (on 3 October 1968). The foreign minister endorsed the conference idea, the Bucharest program, and the
Brezhnev Doctrine, and talked of extended bilateral contacts
between East and West European states. The latter reference
did not, however, appear in _Pravda_, which claimed to repro-
duce the full text.[18] The fact that the Soviets were eager
to pursue their own bilateral economic relations with the
West was also soon made clear, and despite some initial reluctance in the West to expand economic ties with the invaders, by the turn of the year the Soviets were already
laying new plans for economic cooperation with Austria and

France, as well as initiating contacts with the EEC and West Germany.

In an apparently authoritative outline of the Soviet view in early March 1969, Mikhail Lesechko, the Soviet representative to Comecon, called on the members of that organization to expand their cooperation with the West while arguing that the situation required closer coordination of the East's world market activities, noting that "much remains to be done in this [latter] respect."[19] Shortly thereafter the Warsaw Pact countries met and issued the "Budapest Appeal," renewing the call for a European conference. While conciliatory toward the West, this declaration contained little of substance. Reflecting the drive to strengthen bloc cohesion, including the Warsaw Pact, it did not criticize NATO or call for the dissolution of military blocs, but the time was evidently not yet ripe for new initiatives on economic cooperation as a substitute focal point for the bloc campaign for a conference and for the strengthening of European "security." While reiterating the call for "all-round cooperation on an all-European basis" made in the Bucharest declaration, in proposing more specific spheres for cooperation it omitted the earlier declaration's references to scientific-technological cooperation and focused on "great projects" in such areas as power, transportation, and health.[20]

In part this calculated vagueness merely illustrated anew that while the "West gains more from the reality of détente . . . the East gains more from the mere appearance of it."[21] But in the immediate postinvasion situation it also reflected the great reluctance on the part of the Soviets to let things move too rapidly when a new drive to strengthen Comecon was just being launched and certain of its members still appeared eager to press on unilaterally with the development of economic ties with the West. The phrasing of the Budapest Appeal was designed to signal the East's continued interest in East-West economic cooperation and to help remove Western doubts raised by the invasion and by the subsequent neoisolationist voices in the East, but it was not supposed to provide overeager Eastern Europeans with an opening for the accelerated pursuit of such cooperation on their own.

A month later, however, the Soviets upped the ante significantly in their avid courting of West Germany by offering to supply it with large quantities of gas and oil. (The offer was reportedly first made by Soviet Foreign Trade Minister Nikolki S. Patolichev to German Economic Minister Karl Schiller at the Hannover Trade Fair in April 1969.)

As talks quickly got under way, Brezhnev affirmed that "observance of the principle of peaceful coexistence opens up broader opportunities for the development of relations between [socialist and capitalist] states," and that "we make no exception for any capitalist state."[22]

By the end of October 1969, after Willy Brandt's election as chancellor of the FRG, the time was ripe for a major new Eastern initiative on the European conference question. The Comecon summit in April had helped to consolidate the bloc by giving the drive for closer economic cohesion new momentum, while the EEC's evolution and prospects for expansion were increasingly seen as motivation for, as well as providing a barrier to, the East's plans for pan-European economic cooperation. Accordingly, in the Prague Declaration of October 1969, East-West "commercial, economic, technological, and scientific relations" were boosted to the position of one of the two main questions to be taken up at a European conference,[23] which now came to be generally referred to in the Eastern news media as the "conference on security and cooperation."

The Soviet Union now became an even greater advocate of pan-European cooperation, which by 1970 superseded the faded proposals for dissolving military pacts and for disarmament and came to be seen as the most tangible possible contribution to détente, at least in its initial stages. Proposals were made for cooperation in such fields as pollution control, nuclear research, and medicine and scientific-technological cooperation was increasingly offered as a counter to Western Europe's alleged overdependence on the United States. With the emphasis shifting from the military to the economic and with the courting of West Germany stepped up, the EEC and Western "discrimination" loomed ever larger as the arch-villain on the European scene, to a considerable extent displacing West German "revanchists" and even NATO. At the same time Soviet-West German talks on the gas-for-pipe proposal progressed rapidly, and in February 1970 an agreement to send gas through Czechoslovakia to Bavaria was signed.

By the spring of 1970 the conference idea itself began to reflect these shifts in the concept of détente. The concentration on a single conference was replaced by proposals for a series of conferences and for the establishment of a "permanent regional organization for security and cooperation in Europe."[24] It was subsequently suggested that this regional organ could adopt some of the practices of existing regional organizations.[25] The concept of pan-European economic cooperation was beginning to take on institutional form; yet, while making some concessions to Western positions and finding the conference to be urgent, the pact memorandum issued in Budapest in June 1970 added little of substance to the economic cooperation idea, merely formalizing the proposal for a permanent regional organization.

At the same time more explicit, if unimaginative, guidelines were now presented[26] for the framework and forms of East-West economic cooperation to be permitted socialist countries. The stress was on organizational rather than institutional innovation, there being foreseen "a common pattern of . . . cooperation . . . jointly worked out long-term programs . . . organized, as a rule, through a system of joint branch working groups, whose activity is coordinated and directed by appropriate intergovernmental agencies." Cooperation was to be "built . . . on a firm legal-contractual basis and . . . regulated by intergovernmental agreement [which] creates definite possibilities for planning the development of such cooperation, [for] the governments of the capitalist countries cannot disregard the international commitments they have assumed." All this would permit "foreign economic ties . . . [to be] reflected in national economic plans and programs." It would also permit the development of (well-supervised) direct contacts in order to carry out the approved forms of cooperation, which were to include Western investment in the development of "certain kinds of natural resources" in the socialist countries, perhaps on a multilateral basis; licensing and equipment deliveries leading to the "more-or-less long-term exchange of goods"; "cooperation and specialization in machine building through reciprocal deliveries" often involving a parallel marketing arrangement; "joint scientific research and cooperation in applying the results in industry"; cooperation in "supplying complete sets of equipment to developing states"; and "production and trade cooperation through the activity of joint commercial companies . . . set up in capitalist countries." It was found that strict limits must be maintained on this development of East-West economic cooperation, because, among other things, "primary consideration" had to be given to the "possible social and political consequences of specific contacts with capitalist countries," and the socialist countries "cannot permit relaxation of control over their own economy."

This last point received increasing attention. It was claimed that the problems that arise in developing economic cooperation are almost entirely the fault of Western governments and that any attempt to alter the existing socialist system or to weaken the coordination of their economic policy is unacceptable. Building on the old Leninist arguments for cooperating with the capitalists--that is, the emerging need for an international division of labor, growing capitalist contradictions, and new socialist economic successes--it was found that not only did the growth of the socialist states' economic potential create the material basis for expanded economic relations with the West but it served as a guarantee of their economic and political independence. Moreover, observers were reminded that while mutually beneficial economically, "production and commercial cooperation between countries which belong to opposed socio-economic systems [remains] one of the forms of the world-wide historical struggle between socialism and capitalism."[27]

PEAKING OUT

Thus by 1971 the acceptable organizational forms, institutional limitations, political reservations, and ideological rationale for expanding economic cooperation with the West had been spelled out pretty clearly. With the acceptance of the Comecon integration program in July all that organization's members, including Rumania, were pledged to coordinate their foreign economic policies more closely and were committed to developing closer cooperation with fellow Comecon members in a long, comprehensive list of economic spheres. With the program out of the way, the Soviets quickly moved to develop the image of Comecon as a promoter of bloc cohesion and as a weapon to be used against the imperialists, viewing the coordination of its members' activities in the world market as an objective demand of the planned socialist economy, particularly during integration. At the same time, the program's respect for sovereignty and national interests, its strictly voluntary nature, and its open character were contrasted to closed Western integration groupings such as the EEC, and it even appeared to be suggested that Comecon might serve as the prototype for the permanent regional organization sought under the aegis of a security conference.[28]

Yet, despite Western pressures and increasingly concrete references in the East to the possibility of "some forms of business relations" between the EEC and Comecon,*

---

*This phrase was used by Brezhnev in his speech marking the 50th anniversary of the Soviet State (Radio Moscow, 21

there was no apparent attempt to devise a counterpart to the EEC Commission for Comecon and to give it analogous powers as a commercial spokesman and community negotiator. In the past it had been the Warsaw Pact, via its Political Consultative Committee, that had presented the Eastern position on security and cooperation, including economic matters. As the likelihood of a European conference increased and the date was firmed up, it became the practice to give such overt, bloc-type pronouncements a decreasing role, rather than shift authority in the economic field to Comecon.

There almost appeared to be less stress on economic relations as one of the pillars of European security. A less rigid and restrictive attitude toward the agenda of the security conference began to emerge in 1971, but no new ideas on economic cooperation were offered in the declaration issued at the January 1972 summit meeting in Prague, in which such cooperation was described only as one of the seven very general "basic principles of European security and relations among European states."[29] Up to the start of the conference, in fact, there were no further substantive Eastern bloc contributions to the discussion of East-West economic relations, and there was a tendency to give cooperation a secondary role so far as the conference itself was concerned. Such downgrading of expanded East-West ties in part reflected the growth of concern about their potential political-ideological impact and the mounting resistance to Western calls for a freer flow of people and ideas.

It also evidently reflected problems with Soviet economic capabilities and performance. While nominally receiving priority for the past five years, economic relations with France had not developed well, and, with the "grandiose projects" anticipated after de Gaulle's visit in 1966 having "dwindled away in their execution,"[30] the dissatisfaction on both sides came to be openly acknowledged. But by now disenchantment with Soviet economic performance was not confined to France. It was increasingly acknowledged that Fiat's project in Togliatti had not been financially profitable; in Britain, even before the massive ouster of Soviet espionage agents (in September 1971) soured relations, there were sighs of unhappiness about Soviet cooperation arrangements; and in Austria there was growing concern as the Soviets gradually backed off from earlier promises of expanded gas deliveries.

December 1972) and was subsequently repeated by various Soviet commentators.

The shifting Soviet approach could also be attributed in part to the problem of timing and to an emerging preoccupation with the USSR's own pressing economic needs. The accelerated campaign for expanded East-West economic cooperation during 1969-70 had been part of the drive for an early convening of a European conference. By the time it became clear that the inauguration of such a conference would take longer than had been hoped, most of the economic cards had been played, and it was in fact becoming necessary to counter overly enthusiastic Western (including neutral) responses, which went too far, particularly on questions of institutional change. At the same time mounting economic difficulties within the Soviet Union appeared to have focused attention on bilateral cooperation projects with new partners, notably West Germany and the United States, which promised more immediate benefits than the ambitious, but still vague and long-range, multilateral proposals that had been pushed in conjunction with the conference campaign.

The seriousness of the Soviets' intent can be seen in their stepped-up activities in a broad range of economic spheres. They have made increasing efforts to enter Western services and technology markets, for instance, through sales of patents and licenses, insurance underwriting, and even the setting up of a Western computer operation; they have attempted to expand relations with multinational West European groups, including Euratom and the new European Trade Union Confederation founded in early 1973; and they have stepped up their banking and financial activities in the West and are joining the universal copyright convention (which may have more positive implications for technical literature than for other types). Membership has been achieved in such organizations as the new International Institute for Applied Systems Analysis in Vienna, and increasing interest has been shown in international monetary affairs, including the International Monetary Fund.

With the preparatory talks under way and the holding of a European conference seemingly assured, parallel with this active pursuit of their own economic interests the Soviets showed enhanced concern about the framework within which expanded East-West economic relations would take place. It was reaffirmed at top Soviet levels that economics, as well as politics and ideology, would remain a sphere of class struggle.[31] "Imperialist circles," according to one writer, have attempted to use trade "for purposes hostile to socialism, or to launch unfounded attacks on the foreign trade monopoly, [because] they clearly realize the great role it has to play in the economic competition between the two opposing social and economic systems," and he ended by saying that it is "of course absolutely unrealistic to make the development of economic cooperation between the USSR and the capitalist world dependent on change in the economic and foreign trade mechanism in our country."[32]

In support of this line and in spite of the shift of Soviet attention to other Western economic partners, Franco-Soviet relations continued to be held up as the model for bilateral East-West economic links: systematic, long-term intergovernmental agreements with their attendant commissions, working groups, and political puffery were seen as the ideal way to conduct economic relations between states. The 10-year cooperation program being worked out under the 1971 agreement with France was highly touted, and it was found particularly significant that this agreement stipulates that both sides will endeavor "to encourage the participation of each country's organizations, enterprises, and companies in realizing the existing five-year and other forthcoming plans of both countries."[33] In fact, it was claimed that at the European conference the "Soviet Union and France will have something to say and something to show, for what they have already done and what they are doing is surely worth imitating."[34]

The Soviets indeed tried hard to imitate the Franco-Soviet pattern of cooperative arrangements in their economic relations with other Western states. A 10-year cooperation agreement with Germany was among the documents signed during Brezhnev's visit to Bonn in May of 1973, at which time similar agreements were being urged on Italy, Belgium, and Britain. This effort suggested that the Soviets were greatly interested in establishing a precedential pattern prior to the European conference, particularly with members of the EEC. Besides inducing Western states to begin to adopt Eastern concepts and forms of cooperation, this was designed to emphasize the nonbloc nature of the conference and to minimize the role of the EEC Commission in it.

MOVING AHEAD IN EASTERN EUROPE

Encouraged by the Soviet turn to economic cooperation with the West and by the favorable atmosphere provided by the movement toward détente, the East European states, with the exception of East Germany, continued to move ahead with new plans for economic cooperation with Western countries on a bilateral basis. While their enthusiasm for such ties

and their willingness to innovate to achieve them varied
considerably, their motivations were much the same, and
still more purely economic than those of the Soviet Union
or East Germany. In broad terms, the interest shown in
economic cooperation with the West has appeared to vary with
the level of development of the country, the state of economic reform, and the foreign policy of the regime, but
the significance of these factors has varied considerably.
At the one extreme has been Bulgaria, which, being among
the less developed and less reform-minded and yet the most
Soviet-oriented, has been the least active in its pursuit
of Western economic ties, not seeking any form of Western
investment and limiting production cooperation arrangements.
The situation in the other countries, however, has been
more complex.

    In Czechoslovakia economic reform, and especially room
for maneuvering in foreign policy, have been highly restricted since the invasion. Yet the retrenchment in economic cooperation with the West after 1968 was much more
limited than one might have anticipated. The forms of this
cooperation have been restricted, central control has been
reinforced, and the idea of Western investment has not been
raised, but cooperation itself has been actively and increasingly pursued. Aside from the general respectability
accorded such relations since 1969, this policy would appear to be explained largely by Czechoslovakia's advanced
level of development and pressing economic and technological needs and hence, ironically, by the partial acceptance
on the part of the regime and the Soviet Union of the arguments for expanding economic relations with the West advanced during the spring of 1968.

    In Poland, which in East European terms is at an inter-
mediate stage of development and has taken the most erratic
approach to economic reform over the years, economic policy
toward the West has been closely linked to over-all foreign
policy. This relationship is especially evident in the
change of attitude under Gierek, who abandoned the balanced-
trade obsession of Gomulka and made Western economic ties
an integral part of Poland's development and modernization
plans. Poland has welcomed new forms of economic cooperation and on the eve of the conference was debating how to
introduce, or to effectively simulate, some form of Western
investment.

    Although at a relatively low level of development and
eschewing any real economic reform, Rumania has been very
active for many years in seeking to expand economic relations with the West. This activity, however, was largely

confined to the trade sphere until the latter part of the 1960s, when economic cooperation began to be encouraged. Rumania then quickly moved to the forefront of those in Eastern Europe who encourage Western cooperation and investment, notably through the passage of a law providing for foreign participation in joint ventures located in Rumania in early 1971 and of the associated implementing decrees in late 1972. Throughout, economic ties with the West have been for Rumania essentially an extension of its over-all foreign policy.

It has been Hungary, however, that has been most successful in developing economic cooperation with the West. This can in large part be attributed to the letter and the spirit of the economic reform introduced in 1968, which has provided much the best institutional framework, outside that of Yugoslavia, for the formation of such links at the enterprise level. This success has been achieved even though Hungary is not one of the most developed countries, has not strayed appreciably from close foreign policy coordination with the Soviet Union, and has only cautiously offered the possibility of joint investment.

These variations in approach to the expansion of economic ties with the West have affected the individual positions of these countries on the economic aspects of détente and a European conference in rather predictable ways--for example, Czechoslovakia dwells on ideological dangers, Rumania on international principles, and Hungary on direct contacts. But the over-all impression has been one of great caution, especially as the conference approached. Whereas such safe and immediate concerns as Western "discrimination" through quotas, lack of MFN treatment, and the EEC's agricultural policy have remained constant and common themes for all (including the Soviet Union), little or nothing has been suggested as a possible quid pro quo for the removal of such barriers, the idea of institutional change, in particular any implication that the East's trading practices might alter to any significant degree in order to promote economic relations with the West, being virtually taboo. Possibilities that were rather freely discussed five to ten years ago--such as the introduction of operational tariffs, multilateralism, and convertibility, or further modifications of the foreign trade monopoly-- came to be alluded to only as distant prospects to be considered once Comecon's own integration program provisions for institutional modifications are completed. The word appears to have been sent and received that these are subjects concerning which the positions of Western and neutral negotiators at Helsinki, the ECE, and elsewhere were to be given no support from the East. There have remained, moreover, strong advocates of delimiting change.

Outside the Soviet Union itself, the protagonist of keeping accommodation within bounds has been East Germany, whose approach to East-West economic relations has been unique in Eastern Europe. For many years, the GDR rejected cooperation for itself and strongly resisted involvement in it by the rest of Eastern Europe. In large part this position was based on political-ideological considerations and the concern for a cohesive bloc approach to the West with a view to establishing East Germany's legitimacy and transforming its interests into socialist international interests. It also had a strong economic basis. East Germany's special economic relationships with West Germany and the privileged access to the EEC that this has provided have served to reinforce East Germany's position as the leading technological power in Eastern Europe. The expansion of East-West economic and scientific-technological co-operation can only serve to undermine this position, as Soviet and East European dependency on East German expertise and advanced products is reduced.

Accordingly, as economic cooperation developed, the East Germans fought a rear-guard action. They argued for a limited, carefully controlled, common policy on East-West cooperation, even at one point maintaining that, as the most advanced countries, East Germany and the Soviet Union were best suited to absorb advanced Western processes and to lead the bloc in the economic-technological struggle with imperialism. They stressed the need for strong resistance to bridge building, to convergence theories, to Western integration practices, and to any encroachment on the socialist foreign trade monopoly.

Yet by 1970, with the increasing momentum toward détente, the Eastern bloc's growing stress on all-European economic ties, and their own renewed drive for recognition, there were signs that the East Germans were relenting somewhat. Contingent upon Comecon's progress toward integration, which East Germany had come to espouse much more sincerely, expanded economic cooperation with the West began to be seen as a logical counterpart to improved East-West political relations. Particularly after the spring of 1971, during which the Soviets launched their peace offensive (at the 24th party congress) and Erich Honecker assumed the leadership of the SED from the inflexible Walter Ulbricht, East German information media began to echo Soviet views on the virtues of economic relations with

the West. The Soviets' approach and their long-term agreement with France--with which East Germany also signed a
cooperation agreement in 1972--rather than the more innovative cooperation arrangements favored in most of Eastern
Europe, were held up as models, but there appeared to be
less of a tendency to try to instruct the rest of Eastern
Europe on how to proceed.

As preparatory talks for the European security conference got under way, the question of East-West economic
relations received closer attention. While a greater willingness to participate was voiced, the stress was on the
framework and the preconditions for such new links. Although a highly selective attitude toward East-West economic relations reflected their general approach to détente,
it would appear that the East Germans were now stepping up
their preparations for the future, for the not-too-distant
day when they would be generally recognized and have gained
membership in the UN, when the European conferees, including the Soviet Union, would have placed their stamp of approval on the acceptable forms of East-West economic links,
and when the rest of Eastern Europe would have normalized
relations with West Germany and perhaps with the EEC.
While attempting to influence the Eastern bloc's stance on
the economic cooperation issue, the Honecker regime appeared
resigned to the fact that in the economic sphere, as elsewhere, its intrabloc power to dictate had waned with its
claim to special status, and that when the day of full
legitimacy arrived East Germany would have to compete not
only with, but for, economic cooperation with the West.

LOOKING AHEAD

In gradually moving back toward some of Khrushchev's
embryonic ideas about economic engagement with the West,
his successors have been very careful to try to select only
what is "good," as the East Germans and Lenin had advised.
They have also taken the precaution of ensuring that for
Eastern Europe integration under Comecon comes first.
Nevertheless, the largely fortuitous coincidence of the
rising Western need for fuel and raw materials and the rising Eastern need for technology and capital has served to
force the pace of détente on both sides. It propelled
economic cooperation into a more significant role in the
Soviet peace offensive, in Eastern Europe's relations with
the West, and in the bloc's drive for a European conference
and helped to expand the Soviet concept of selective engage-

ment with the West into one of total engagement. At the
same time, it reinforced the USSR's determination to use
the conference, and particularly the more extensive foreign
policy coordination it is seen to necessitate, to control
and shape Eastern Europe's economic relations with the
West and to resist institutional innovations in the economic
sphere, as elsewhere, which might undermine their political-
ideological hegemony in the course of the greater exposure
to the West resulting from peaceful coexistence.

As with the economic reform movement and the Comecon
integration program, perhaps the clearest message of the
Eastern bloc approach to expanded East-West economic relations is that the still-prevailing orthodoxy wants no real
part of the underlying economic institutional realities of
the West. This probably helps to explain the lack of innovation in the Soviet and bloc positions on East-West economic
relations after 1970 and the evident groping for ways to
sustain some semblance of progress in this area as the
European conference was delayed longer than originally
hoped. While the reluctance to talk of new institutional
approaches may in part have reflected a desire to have something left to negotiate at the European conference itself,
the campaign against "concessions" in the economic sphere
suggested that the resistance to change would remain very
strong. Moreover, the parallel campaign for ideological
strengthening and for equating, even more firmly, the
existing economic system with socialism indicated that whatever compromises were reached in the negotiations over the
freer movement of people and ideas, every effort would be
made to isolate economic institutions from the impact of
these same people and ideas.

Yet in the East these restrictions, whether political,
ideological, or institutional, are viewed not as inhibitions
to expanded East-West economic relations but as the manda-
tory framework within which such relations can safely be
conducted. Soviet commentators have in fact argued that
the forms of industrial cooperation developing between East
and West European countries are already diverse and that
with experience new forms are "bound to arise," and they
have viewed the "presence of many parallel, duplicatory,
and relatively small-scale production lines and enterprises"
in Europe not as an "inevitable historical pattern, but
rather as the consequences of protracted political tension,"
maintaining that

over the long run, the European economy could have
a significantly more comprehensive character based

upon a complementary structure among the economies of its individual states. The socialist
and capitalist nations could develop individual
sectors and types of production designed to sat-
isfy one another's requirements for a long period
of time.[35]

This vision of the future is of particular significance
for the more advanced states of Eastern Europe. East-West
economic ties are no longer a phenomenon to be tolerated
on the margin, to be treated as an aberration when too actively pursued by a Ceausescu or a Sik, but an integral
part of peaceful coexistence. While the form and scope of
such relations remain questions to be thrashed out essentially in private East bloc councils and not subjects for
serious negotiation with the West, the basic decision to
expand East-West economic relations and to integrate them
into the emerging broader détente policy was quickly made
in the aftermath of the Czechoslovak invasion and does not
appear to have been seriously compromised by the array of
strictures and reservations voiced since.
  This policy was made possible by the achievement of
military parity, has been reinforced by the growing need
for outside economic and technological help, and has facilitated the achievement of the goals of containing the
EEC and filling the void left by the decline of American
preeminence. But to sustain their strength and strategy
vis-à-vis the West and to maintain the political and ideological credibility of peaceful coexistence, greater economic success, both within the Soviet Union and for Comecon
as a whole, is essential. This will not come easily.
Welcome as the go-ahead on East-West economic relations
may be for themselves, there has been growing concern among
East Europeans over the economic impact of the Soviet surge
into Western markets. It is feared that the Soviets not
only will bid up prices and utilize their political muscle
to skim off the technological cream, but also will have
less fuel and raw material available for delivery to Eastern Europe because of new Western commitments. While increasingly "integrated" within Comecon, the East European
states may find themselves much less integrated into Europe
as a whole than is necessary for their successful future
economic development.
  It remains a moot question whether the new consumerism
at home, integration under Comecon, and expanded Western
ties will provide the substitute for institutional reforms
for which they were designed or will only serve to demon-

strate more clearly the need for fundamental change. Aside from their obvious political opportunism the voices in the East that have begun exploring the ideas of Eastern engagement in the troubled international monetary system suggest that, however confident for the short run, there are some at least who may anticipate the eventual need for some institutional accommodation in the interest of substantially expanding East-West economic ties.

NOTES

1. For a summary of Soviet attitudes at this time see Alvin Rubinstein, The Soviets in International Organizations (Princeton, N.J.: Princeton University Press, 1964), pp. 10-13.

2. For a more detailed discussion of the reforms introduced and contemplated as of mid-1968, see the UN ECE Economic Bulletin for Europe, vol. 20, no. 1 (1968).

3. Ibid., pp. 44-45.

4. Ibid., p. 52.

5. See, for example, the useful study prepared by the UNCTAD Secretariat for the Trade and Development Board, entitled Industrial Cooperation in Trade Between Socialist Countries of Eastern Europe and Developed Market Economy Countries (Geneva: TD/B/247, 19 June 1969).

6. See the "Theses on the European Community" by the Moscow Institute of World Economy and International Relations, published in Pravda, Moscow, 26 August 1962; Khrushchev's article in Kommunist, no. 12 (Moscow, August 1962); and Zbigniew Brzezinski in Foreign Affairs, vol. 42, no. 3 (New York, April 1964).

7. Moscow Institute of World Economy and International Relations, op. cit.

8. UNCTAD Secretariat, op. cit.

9. See K. E. Birnbaum, Peace in Europe (London: Oxford University Press, 1970), pp. 48, 56-57.

10. Communiqué of the Political Consultative Committee of the Warsaw Pact, 20 January 1965, published in Pravda, 22 January 1965.

11. See A. Ross Johnson, "The Warsaw Pact's Campaign for 'European Security,'" Rand Report R/565/PR, November 1970; and Birnbaum, op. cit.

12. "Declaration on Strengthening Peace and Security in Europe," Pravda and Izvestia, Moscow, 9 July 1966.

13. Naumov in Pravda, 21 September 1966, as cited in Birnbaum, op. cit., pp. 56-57.

14. See Brezhnev's speech at Karlovy Vary, April 1967, as cited in Birnbaum, op. cit., p. 72.

15. Fritz Ermarth, "Internationalism, Security and Legitimacy: The Challenge to Soviet Interests in Eastern Europe, 1964-1968," Rand Memorandum RM/5909/PR, March 1969.

16. Y. Zhukov in Pravda, 12 March 1968; and E. Novo-seltsev and N. Khomutov in International Affairs, Moscow, March 1968.

17. V. Cheprakov in International Affairs, April 1968.

18. See Birnbaum, op. cit., p. 95.

19. Ekonomicheskaya Gazeta, no. 10 (Moscow, March 1969).

20. Magyar Tauirati Troda (hereafter MTI), 18 March 1969.

21. T. Stanley and D. Whitt, Détente Diplomacy: United States and European Security in the 1970s (New York: Dunel-len, 1970), p. 96.

22. Speech to the International Conference of Commu-nist and Workers' Parties, 7 June 1969, as reported in Pravda and Izvestia, 8 June 1969.

23. MTI text, 31 October 1969.

24. V. Shatrov and N. Yuryev in International Affairs, April 1970.

25. "New Stage in Preparation for All-European Confer-ence," International Affairs, September 1970.

26. By A. Vetrov in International Affairs, September 1970.

27. L. Khodov, Voprosy Ekonomiki, Moscow, December 1970.

28. See Henry Schaefer, Comecon and the Politics of Integration (New York: Praeger Publishers, 1972), pp. 187-190.

29. "Declaration on Peace, Security, and Co-operation in Europe," Trybuna Ludu, Warsaw, 27 January 1972; and Charles Andras, "The Seven Pillars of Europe," East-West Background Report/2, RFER (EERA), 16 March 1972.

30. Stanley and Whitt, op. cit., p. 29.

31. Brezhnev's speech on 21 December 1972; and the editorial entitled "On Behalf of Peace and Friendship Among Peoples" in Kommunist, no. 7 (May 1973).

32. I. Kovan in Foreign Trade, no. 4 (Moscow, 1973).

33. Cited by V. Kazakevich in International Affairs, August 1972.

34. Y. Zhukov in Pravda, 7 June 1972. For more de-tails on Franco-Soviet cooperation see A. Krasikov in Ekonomicheskaya Gazeta, no. 3 (January 1973).

35. L. Pronyakova and V. Yevmakov in International Affairs, December 1972; and N. Shmelev in Mirovaya Eko-nomika i Mezhdunarodnive Otnoshenia, Moscow, January 1973.

4

**THE MILITARY
DIMENSION**
Lawrence L. Whetten

The Soviet Union has a long, well-documented record
of interest in European security matters, dating at least
from Foreign Minister Molotov's call, in 1954, for a multilateral conference on the issue. In recent years Moscow's
interest in international security matters has been expanded
to include strategic arms limitations talks (SALT) with
the United States, the CSCE, and the MFR negotiations.*
The Soviets have consistently placed a high priority on
participation in and the results of the SALT deliberations,
but they have been equally consistent in their reservations
about the purpose and utility of MFR. Their reluctant
agreement to participate in the Vienna talks was a consequence of determined Western diplomacy. The scale of East-
West differences on these three levels of security issues
indicates the interrelationship of all three with the national security interests of each member of both military
alliances and the divisions that have historically separated the two pacts on matters relating to normalization
of relations.
    For years the West has maintained that progress toward
military disengagement or military détente was a prerequisite for any movement toward political reconciliation. For

---

*MFR (Mutual Force Reductions) is the abbreviation used
here for what was formerly known as Mutual and Balanced
Force Reductions (MBFR). In October 1973, as East-West
negotiations on the problem opened in Vienna, it was decided that the conference would deal with Mutual Reduction
of Forces and Armaments and Associated Measures in Central
Europe.

its part, the East has insisted that the relaxation of political tensions was the precondition for reduction of the military confrontation. The West felt that it had habitually dealt with the Warsaw Pact countries with restraint and in good faith but could no longer rely on either predictions or proclamations of Soviet intentions and that military capabilities were more reliable indicators of possible political options. But the Warsaw Pact nations held that regional tensions were a result of NATO's refusal to accept the consequences of World War II and the present political-territorial realities in Eastern Europe; these political attitudes, they said, would have to be altered before the threat to the Warsaw Pact nations would subside. These contradictory positions created a deadlock that barred significant advance toward either political or military détente.

The socialist interpretation of the flow of events was confirmed by the head of the Polish delegation to the Vienna Preparatory Consultations for MFR, Minister Plenipotentiary Tadeusz Strulak, when he said at a May 1973 press conference that the progress made over the last two years in fostering détente and normalizing relations among European states was a result "above all, of the signing of the treaties between the Soviet Union and Poland and the FRG, the four-power agreement on West Berlin, the treaty between the two German states, and the recognition of the German Democratic Republic by the majority of states of the world." Strulak stressed that the Polish government considered all these basic conditions for further relaxation of tension, normalization, and joint construction of a system of European security, including progress toward military détente.[1]

To some extent East-West differences over concepts of security, which have delayed efforts to bring about the security conference, are a result of differing perceptions. Historically, Russia has been sensitive about territorial imperatives and acutely aware of its vulnerability along both its 2,000-mile European and its 4,000-mile Far Eastern frontiers. Although its eastern border is longer and the communications links more vulnerable, the western frontier has traditionally been of greater concern because there are few natural barriers and distances to vital industrial and political centers are much shorter. One of the basic aims that motivated Soviet policy during World War II was the concern to secure decisive influence over any potentially destabilizing factors in contiguous regions considered vital to the USSR's security.

Since 1945 the Soviet Union has claimed the Elbe River as its strategic frontier, and it is now seeking final and universal recognition for this, which would give it a 400-to-600-mile buffer on its western flank. This zone may appear relatively small and insignificant in the nuclear age (it can be crossed by a missile in five minutes' flight time), but the Soviets are keenly aware that Russia proper cannot be invaded by any contemporary power unless these western approaches are first occupied and secured, by either diplomacy or force.

Soviet security policy since World War II has been directed primarily toward ensuring physical control over this western glacis and exerting a decisive influence over factors in Central and Eastern Europe that threaten these traditional approaches to the Russian heartland. Thus, from a security point of view, Moscow has felt compelled to ensure friendly governments in Eastern Europe and an influential role in developments related to the German problem. Either a strong united Germany or the development of Titoist national communist governments in Central Europe would compromise the Soviet security zone. Thus the Soviet Union has gained acceptance of the division of Germany and legitimized it through the normalization treaty with the FRG and the four-power Berlin agreement, which provide international ratification of its terms for a de facto peace settlement of World War II, including its own continued military presence in Central Europe. The maintenance of 31 divisions in this area gives the Soviet Union extensive influence over the internal and external policies of the states of Eastern Europe. The presence of Soviet troops thus performs both a political and military function in guaranteeing the reliability and viability of the present governments in Central Europe and in ensuring physical defense of the approaches to the Soviet Union.

Certain difficulties, however, attend the achievement of security and the legitimization of Soviet hegemony in Eastern Europe, despite the presence of large numbers of its forces. Even after nearly a quarter of a century, socialist rule in Eastern Europe has not fully gained public acceptance and endorsement--a fact, paradoxically, due more to success than failure. The ruling elites have succeeded in most cases in uprooting traditional agrarian social structures and imposing industrialization and modernization from above. But the process is incomplete, and these societies remain in a highly transitional stage in which instability and unrest are endemic. Communist political autocracy and frustrations stemming from unfulfilled egalitarian ideological expectations inject uncertainties in addition to those of societies in similar stages of industrial development. Thus the internal dynamics of these societies as they progress from mobilization to modernization, as they shift from utopian aspirations to development targets, will probably continue to generate social unrest and political instability, which loom as omnipresent threats to vital Soviet interests. Further, as has been demonstrated several times in recent years, the close interdependence of the Warsaw Pact countries nurtures the process of mutual infection by the virus of social protest, compounding Moscow's security problems.

From the Soviet viewpoint, the security aspect of the CSCE is tortuous. Industrial modernization, and the corresponding degree of greater stability which it may promise, can best be accelerated through trade with and technological inputs from the West. The accompanying relaxation of tensions will result in the social conflicts in Eastern Europe becoming more an issue in the broader context of international affairs, which, in turn, may foment continued unrest and instability to the detriment of Soviet security interests and European détente. The Soviets' way out of this imbroglio is to attempt to isolate and insulate from the broader context of European détente Eastern Europe's difficulties and their own proclaimed right to act on behalf of socialism to suppress unrest by force. Thus, during the preparatory conference and the first round of the CSCE, the Soviets attempted to focus attention on issues that would resolve their security dilemma: preservation of the political status quo and of the territorial status quo, recognition of East Germany, national sovereignty, noninterference in national affairs, the renunciation of force, and expansion of trade and technological exchanges.

Some observers have argued that Moscow has acted cynically in advancing these issues and is seeking objectives in the West denied it during the cold war because of tension and Western opposition. Others hold that the USSR has come to recognize severe economic impediments to economic growth, which have compelled expanded collaboration with the West--for example, the very real possibility of accepting the United States as a permanent supplier of grain. But however important these secondary goals may be, Moscow's overriding objective in the CSCE is strategic: ensuring physical security, achieving political legitimization, and perpetuating the dependence of Eastern Europe in a manner that will exclude the use of force whenever possible but not preclude it altogether if necessary.

At the July 1973 Helsinki meeting of foreign ministers Gromyko surprised many delegates by stressing these points unmistakably. He played down the principle that sovereignty and noninterference should be accorded to "all states ir- respective of their political, economic and social systems" so laboriously hammered out in earlier sessions. He re- ferred to the concepts of peaceful coexistence and coopera- tion among states with different social systems and called upon Western delegates to recognize that peaceful coexis- tence should be "fully applied in Europe, crossed as it is from north to south by a visible boundary between the two social worlds." He called for unrestricted commercial re- lations, provided such contacts are subject to "strict ob- servance of the laws, customs, and traditions" of the states concerned. Under questioning by the press, neither he nor official spokesmen would accept the possibility that fron- tiers could be changed peacefully by mutual consent. The return to these hard-line features of Soviet policy indi- cated that while Moscow was prepared to negotiate about the nature of détente, its precise characteristics remain vague. While Western states have gradually come to acknowl- edge the qualified role they are to play in the moderniza- tion of Eastern Europe, Andrei Gromyko's declaration reaf- firmed earlier assumptions that security matters east of the Elbe are to remain the exclusive prerogative of the Soviets. The reassertion of a tough Soviet position resur- rects the fundamental reservations of the skeptical school of analysts of Soviet foreign policy about the relationship that Moscow envisions between the political and the mili- tary aspects of European détente. Will the USSR be able to convert the mainly political CSCE into a peace confer- ence codifying the results of World War II largely on So- viet terms, while minimizing Western demands for military disengagement as the price for normality by delay and tac- tical maneuvering? Moscow's performances at the MFR talks and SALT II are still inconclusive on this cardinal point.

MUTUAL FORCE REDUCTIONS

The concepts of Warsaw Pact solidarity and Soviet lead- ership of the military alliance remain firmly entrenched and million-men armies still face each other across the European Divide. Pressure to reduce these forces or to institute a military disengagement has come largely from the West.

The Soviet Union, as noted above, maintains 31 divisions in Eastern Europe: 20 divisions in the GDR (10 tank); 2 tank divisions in Poland; 5 divisions in Czechoslovakia (2 tank); and 4 in Hungary (2 tank). This force includes some 7,850 medium T-62 tanks, with about 1,500 T-54/55s stored in forward depots. Soviet tactical air forces comprise some 1,250 aircraft deployed in these four countries.

Eastern Europe's national armed forces vary remarkably in size, quality of equipment, level of training, and defense expenditures. Bulgaria has an army of 120,000 with 8 motorized rifle divisions and 5 tank brigades, equipped with 2,000 T-34, T-54, and T-55 tanks. Rumania has a larger standing army of 141,000 with 7 motorized divisions, 2 tank divisions and 1,700 tanks, and assorted brigades with equipment similar to Bulgaria's. The Hungarian Army is 90,000 with 4 motorized rifle divisions and 1 tank division and an aggregate of 1,500 tanks. Czechoslovakia has an army of 150,000 consisting of 5 motorized rifle and 5 tank divisions with a total of 3,500 medium tanks, including some modern T-62s. The GDR has a small but well-equipped army of 90,000 in 4 motorized rifle divisions and 2 tank divisions, with a total of 2,000 tanks, many in the T-62 category. Poland has the largest army, 200,000, with 5 tank, 8 motorized rifle, 1 airborne, and 1 amphibious assault division, and with a total of 3,400 tanks, including some T-62s. When other types of equipment are compared, the military effectiveness of the national forces declines progressively from north to south.

Ratios of defense expenditures to national economic wealth also reveal marked discrepancies. While there has been a steady growth in GNP in both alliances (the USSR's GNP remains half that of the United States), there has also been a general decline in the percentage of GNP allocated for defense in the NATO countries and a rise among the Pact states. The U.S. defense budget rose from $78,700 million in 1971 to $83,400 million in 1972. But as a percentage of GNP, defense expenditure fell from 9.3 in 1968 to 7.3 in 1971. During the same period, the USSR percentage remained constant. The budgets of other Pact countries rose one or two percentage points to a high of 5.9 for East Germany and 5.8 for Czechoslovakia In NATO countries percentages fell by two to three points--for instance, Canada from 2.7 to 1.8; France, 4.8 to 3.1; FRG, 3.6 to 2.8; Greece, 4.9 to 3.3; and Turkey, 4.5 to 3.3. Percentages for Eastern Europe for 1971 were substantially lower than those of most Middle East states--for instance, Egypt, 21.7;

Iran, 8.5; Iraq, 6.5; Israel, 23.9; Jordan, 11.3; Saudi Arabia, 8.9; Sudan, 7.4; and Syria, 9.8.

When defense expenditures per capita are compared, national variations are even sharper. Figures for Bulgaria, Hungary, and Rumania are less than half those for Czechoslovakia and East Germany. They are roughly equivalent to those for Greece and Portugal, but two or three times higher than those for Turkey. They are also about the same as those of representative nonaligned nations.[2]

Several generalizations can be drawn from these and related figures. The military resources and expenditures in terms of real assets or economic capabilities are sharply divided in both alliances along lines of national preferences. Length of service, size of armed forces, and the percentage of men of military age in service also seem to reflect nonmilitary considerations to the point where no standard criteria exist on either side. Military manpower levels among the southern Pact members are the same or lower than those of most nonaligned nations, and defense expenditures for all East European states are four to six times less than those of Egypt or Israel; yet all these states started at approximately equal training and equipment levels in the mid-1950s.

From these observations it appears that national peculiarities and historical, geostrategic, and economic imperatives have precluded the establishment of alliance-wide consensuses on the nature of the threat or the importance of global security commitments. In other words, the temperatures of the cold war have fluctuated rather sharply in the two groups of allies, forcing both great powers reluctantly to assume greater defense burdens. Both have complained for years to the other members of their groups about this imbalance in burden-sharing.[3]

The first formal Soviet acknowledgment of the proposal to reduce forces was made by Brezhnev in his May 1971 speech in Tbilisi; this was followed by the June Budapest Appeal, but the issue was ignored in other speeches on the subject of European security. Moscow later refused to receive retiring NATO Secretary-General Manlio Brosio, who had been commissioned in May 1971 to explore personally the Warsaw Pact's position on MFR. Not until their January 1972 summit conference did the socialist countries again proclaim MFR a matter of priority. Finally, on his return from Moscow on 7 September 1972, Henry Kissinger reported to newsmen that the USSR had offered a compromise on the linkage between the political and military factors. Moscow proposed opening talks on force reductions in 1973,

after the preparatory conference for the CSCE was under
way--a timing that was acceptable to the United States.

The lukewarm-to-cool Soviet attitude toward MFR can
be attributed to a number of factors. First, MFR was not
a high priority issue; Moscow regarded the CSCE as of far
greater importance, and therefore the Warsaw Pact had probably not studied the issue and its implications in sufficient detail to warrant early discussions. Second, when
it became apparent that West European capitals were becoming
increasingly responsive to the idea of a security conference but that the United States was still demanding progress on MFR before the conference, some concession had to
be made. Yet at no time had the Soviets formally stated
what they expected from MFR, the course they wanted the
talks to take, or the impact they anticipated they would
have on the higher-priority CSCE--indicating, among other
things, possibly tardy homework. Third, MFR is infinitely
more complex than SALT. The Western Allies had been studying the question since 1969 but had only attained the
first level of understanding of the scope of the problem
and had reached no consensus on either objectives or criteria for measuring military asymmetries. It appeared
that the Soviets were much further behind in their preparatory analyses, especially since they had to incorporate
the uncertainties of the political mission of their forces
in Eastern Europe into their over-all estimates of preferred
force strengths. Fourth, the timing of Brezhnev's Tbilisi
speech, one week before a U.S. Senate vote on Senator Mike
Mansfield's proposed unilateral American troop cut, suggests that Moscow saw greater advantages in mutual reductions than in unilateral Western action. Brezhnev clearly
demonstrated serious Soviet interest in checking any possibility of enhanced cohesion within NATO that might result
from precipitous U.S. action. And fifth, it would have been
in the Soviet interest to gain time and ensure deliberation
in troop reductions in Europe and transfers to the Far East,
in calculating and registering the usefulness of MFR as
political leverage, and in studying the all-important questions of new weapons systems and strategies for both a
"SALT-ed" and an "MFR-ed" Europe.

A further point: Any Western move that would have
forced the Soviet hand at that time or presented Moscow
with a fait accompli would have been widely regarded as
detrimental. Pressure for Moscow to follow a unilateral
U.S. cut would probably have had a destabilizing impact on
Eastern Europe, especially on East Germany where the number
of Soviet troops is regarded as a measure of Soviet polit-

ical support. Likewise, a sharp Soviet reduction would
have eroded the present tenuous relations with Peking,
which could be expected to denounce the action as anti-
Chinese. Until there had been at least some discussion
with the West, unilateral moves would have been regarded
by some friends and adversaries alike as ill-conceived,
sporadic decisions that would complicate matters and expose
Eastern Europe to increased Western influence without ensuring greater Soviet diplomatic flexibility. Thus Moscow
moved cautiously until it had assessed the effect force reduction talks were likely to have on the fabric and cohesion of the Warsaw Pact.

Several additional observations should be made about
the Soviet approach to the problem. First, there is no
easy formula for regulating the number of foreign troops
stationed in both Eastern and Western Europe and there is
no precise ratio between them and indigenous forces. Most
important, there is no clear understanding about the relationship of physical force to political influence; it is
exceedingly difficult to predict how many and what kind of
troops are necessary to protect a nation's and an alliance's
interests against political, not military, challenges. Thus
the most valid argument for preserving the present Soviet
troop strength is that it is these existing force levels
that have deterred expansion of Western political influence.
A lower posture might encourage Western assertiveness.

Yet there is evidence that military reductions can
take place without adverse results for either side. In
the 1950s the Soviets withdrew one corps from the Group of
Soviet Forces, and Germany made an estimated reduction of
50,000 troops. At the same time the United States began
thinning its forces. Both sides were then participating
in commandant exchanges between the East-West zones and
encouraging the interchange of military observers of field
maneuvers (Soviet officers actually attended several British tank exercises at Pembroke before these exchanges were
discontinued). Again, the United States reduced 20 percent
of its forces in Germany between 1965 and 1968 to a "dual-
based" status (that is, stationed in the United States and
training annually in Europe) without creating an enhanced
threat from the USSR or a precipitous failure of confidence
among West Europeans.

In this light, did the intervention in Czechoslovakia
increase the threat against NATO or improve regional stability? However one argues the point and the justification
for permanently locating five additional Soviet divisions
in Eastern Europe, the intervention unquestionably estab-

lished Moscow's vital interest in preserving stability
within its strategic perimeters and its allegedly legal
right to do so. With 1956 and 1968 as clear indications
of the Soviets' intention to use force if necessary to protect their interests in Eastern Europe, the size of their
physical presence there becomes less critical. They can
move as quickly and decisively with two divisions near
Prague as with five.

Second, the nature of the European confrontation has
changed. Formerly it was set primarily within the context
of ideological challenge and military threat, but this context has now been superseded by competition for influence
and political rivalry. There is still a real need for military security, but it is now primarily a means of providing
reassurance and stability rather than deterrence.

Unilateral troop cuts were one-sided moves and were
subject to reversal or acceleration without undue reference
to an adversary's reactions. Therefore, at least theoretically, unilateral actions may be less durable and subject
to more vagaries than multilateral or negotiated decisions.
The mere process of negotiation will increase the interest
and influence of each side in the defensive affairs of the
other and accordingly enhance their stakes in responsible
actions and long-term undertakings. This aspect of the
multilateral approach will be an important contribution to
the Soviet insistence on "equal security," a concept that
presupposes the continuation of the two security systems
in something like the present constellation of power.

SYMMETRICAL OR ASYMMETRICAL FORCE REDUCTIONS

There seem, then, to be intrinsic military reasons
within the context of the present European configuration
that justify Moscow's accepting the risks of multilateral
talks about reduced force postures, besides the budgetary,
economic, and internal political arguments customarily offered. Yet the main parties concerned remain widely divided about the envisioned objectives of the exercise: to
promote political détente, accelerate change in the East
or fragmentation in the West, consolidate the respective
spheres, or merely engineer military disengagement. Moreover the parties are also undecided about an appropriate
agenda.

For example, assuming that military disengagement is
the goal, there are two basic schools of thought among
Western analysts about the preferred means of achieving

troop reductions: percentage reductions and cuts that reflect existing asymmetries. The percentage-cut school argues that whether or not one questions the criteria for
force strengths, they have acquired an aura of historical
validity. Clearly neither side has consulted the other in
establishing its standards, and each has attempted to exploit its own comparative advantages to the detriment of
its adversaries whenever possible. Asymmetries exist in
intentions, interests, and capabilities, and each side has
institutionalized definitions of these terms that would
economize resources while maximizing deterrence. Three
fundamental asymmetries have emerged and been incorporated
into the deterrence posture of both sides: geographic--
the USSR is a European power by virtue of geography, while
the United States is present on the continent only for reasons of policy; strategic--Moscow has demonstrated that it
considers the Elbe River its strategic border, while the
U.S. commitment remains in fact uncertain and untested;
political--as a means of legitimizing the Soviet model for
communist development, political stability reinforced by
Soviet troops is essential in Eastern Europe, whereas the
United States has only a very limited desire to exercise
political hegemony over NATO.

The percentage-reduction school maintains that no cuts
are conceivable until the West accepts the implications of
the Soviet attitude to these asymmetries, especially the
political mission of Soviet garrisons in Eastern Europe.
The only way, therefore, to meet Soviet security and stability requirements is to reduce troop strengths on each
side by fixed percentages--first by 10 percent as a sign
of good faith, then by 20 percent to reflect mutually attractive budgetary economies, and finally by 30 percent to
ensure mutual security.[4] Theoretically, it is argued, percentage cuts down to a specific level would reduce the size
of the respective force structures without adversely affecting existing asymmetries.

The asymmetrical reduction school argues that the advantages and disadvantages inherent in the postures of both
sides are so marked that percentage cuts risk a dispropor-
tionate loss of advantages and accordingly contribute to
insecurity and instability. The following asymmetries are
cited most often:

1. The Warsaw Pact has important reservoirs of manpower and material in Eastern Europe and can resupply from
the USSR in days by land routes, up to an estimated 70,000
men, with equipment, per day, while the vast bulk of NATO's
reserves are located in North America and must be shipped

over vulnerable sea lanes, involving weeks and months of delay.

2. Equipment characteristics differ, with the Warsaw Pact stressing shock, standardization, and mobility, and NATO emphasizing a greater defensive capability and national weapons production: the Pact has more operational tanks in Europe than NATO has, but NATO has a far greater anti-tank capability[5] and maintains a much wider variety of munitions and delivery systems, giving the West greater flexibility and efficiency in weapons employment.[6]

3. Defense spending by the Warsaw Pact nations has gradually increased over the past 10 years, while it has steadily declined among the Western nations.

4. Wide discrepancies will persist for the remainder of the decade in training levels, with the Soviets only simulating combat exposure and the West digesting the experience of Southeast Asia (a large percentage of U.S. troops are combat veterans while there are few in the Soviet ranks).

5. The reliability of allies remains difficult to measure: the Rumanians are unlikely to declare war merely to protect East Germany's security, and Norway and Iceland are unlikely to support Greece against Bulgaria in a localized fracas.

If the single factor of weapons and equipment inventories is considered, using only each side's respective assessment of effectiveness, reliability, and possibilities of servicing, one can easily grasp the complexity of establishing agreed standards for evaluating asymmetrical advantages and assessing appropriate cuts. And when all inputs are taken into account, the exercise becomes infinitely more complicated than SALT. The difficulty of defining a precise, mutually acceptable formula for reduction is the strongest argument for seeking alternative methods.

The Soviet reaction to these two approaches is instructive. In the first comment on MFR in any Soviet periodical, the authoritative Academy of Sciences published a detailed rejection of asymmetric reductions. The article argued that the 1:3, 1:4, or 1:6 variants in troop cuts were based on erroneous Western assumptions about the impact of geography. First, the reduced units should be disbanded, not merely withdrawn from forward positions. In emergencies, Western Europe would be able to mobilize and deploy reserves at least as easily as the USSR, which would have to call up men from, say, Central Asia. Second, geography would be as big a stumbling block to the USSR as to the United States in an emergency. The USSR has extensive borders to defend, and reinforcing Eastern Europe is not merely a matter of dispatching troops from western military districts in the Soviet Union but of moving units over 6,000 miles from the far eastern districts. (The USSR presently has 31 divisions deployed in Eastern Europe, 60 in the European USSR, 8 between the Volga and Baikal, 21 in the Caucasus, and 44 along the Chinese border--49 if those near Baikal are included.)[7] Third, since any outbreak of hostilities would probably escalate rapidly to a full-scale conflict, the over-all global balance between NATO and Warsaw Pact forces must be taken into account. When total forces are included, NATO has a substantial advantage. (In fairness it should be noted that American units from Panama, Okinawa, and Alaska and the 300,000-man Italian Army can hardly be regarded as either readily available or as effective reserves until fully acclimatized and in combat positions.) Finally, both nuclear and conventional forces must be included in any reductions. The article concludes:

> In our opinion, if we approach the question of reducing armed forces and arms in Central Europe from a realistic position, the only possible principle is that of equal reduction. And this approach would accord with the main condition laid down at the time of the Oreanda meeting between Secretary-General of the CPSU CC L.I. Brezhnev and Chancellor of the FRG W. Brandt-- that no harm should be done to the countries taking part in such a reduction [the principle of equal security].[8]

These are strong reservations, and if the experience of SALT is a valid precedent the Soviets can be expected to insist on a rejection of asymmetric reductions. And from the West's viewpoint, the percentage cut formula is too simplisitic and would enhance the Warsaw Pact's existing advantages. Cutting both sides by equal slices would weaken the West more than the East because of the offensive capabilities, centralized geographic dispositions, and reserve mobilization advantages the Warsaw Pact enjoys. Therefore, equal percentage cuts would inflict unequal reductions in the West's real strength.

In his Foreign Policy Report to the U.S. Congress on 3 May 1973, President Nixon pointed out the difficulty of defining the types of troops to be cut:

Reductions provide an inherent advantage for
the side that has postured its forces along offensive lines. Offensive forces would retain
the initiative to concentrate and attack, while
the defense must continue to defend the same
geographical front with fewer forces. Major
deployments of equipment, especially those with
offensive capabilities, are therefore an important element in the reduction process. How can
equivalence be established between different
categories of equipment? What ratios would be
equitable? . . . Mixed, asymmetrical reductions?
This means reductions would be made by different amounts in various categories of weapons or
man-power. It could prove extremely complex to
define equivalence between different weapon
systems.[9]

Clearly, a solution is hard to find.
    One possible starting point is the asymmetry in the
sense of threat and insecurity felt on both sides of the
Elbe. Historically, each has seen the other as a threat.
However graphic these conflicting perceptions may be,*[10]
it is safe to assume that the Soviet view of NATO's strength
is that it is greater in many categories than that of the
Warsaw Pact. The latter is superior in conventional arms,
but the East European forces are generally not as well
equipped as their NATO counterparts. From the Soviet viewpoint, Warsaw Pact forces are largely defense-oriented,
as its strength in fighter aircraft shows. While the West
has concentrated on self-propelled guns, the East has re-
lied on the less mobile towed artillery. Tank forces in
the forward area have an offensive capability, but not the
indigenous logistic support for sustained operations.
Finally, in tactical nuclear weapons the Warsaw Pact has

---

    *Rude Pravo, Prague, 1 June 1973, charged that a far
greater concentration of combat-ready troops existed in the
FRG than in any comparable East European territory and that
Bonn had the advantage of quicker mobilization, including
the transfer of units to attack positions. On the other
side, see West German Defense Minister Georg Leber's assertion that he feels "secure" despite the recent modernization of Warsaw Pact forces (Die Zeit, Hamburg, 23 June
1973); and the assertion by SACEUR General Andrew J. Goodpaster that the Warsaw Pact is a greater threat than ever.

access to fewer (but larger-yield) warheads stored only in the USSR; the FRG has over 900 artillery pieces that have a nuclear capability, with warheads available within helicopter flight range.

FORCE REDUCTION TALKS: PARTICIPANTS AND PARAMETERS

It can be assumed that each side sees the threat posed by the other through very different eyes and that this cleavage was a main factor behind the tough position adopted by the Soviets at the preparatory consultations for MFR in Vienna. These talks began on 22 November 1972 but were quickly adjourned until 31 January 1973. Protracted informal consultations delayed the convening of a plenary session for over 14 weeks, until May 14. The first and perhaps easiest problem was to decide whose troops should be included in the initial cuts: the two great powers, or all who station forces in Europe (such as Britain, Belgium, and France), or indigenous national forces. The delegates finally agreed that only the two great powers should be involved in the first cut for several reasons: U.S. Congressional pressures; the symbolic effect this would have on the commitment of the great powers to the process of détente; the centrality of such forces to each side's offensive capability.

The second obstacle was the question of who should take part in the talks. The West sought to restrict participation at the working level so that the vigor of the deliberations would be focused on the most dangerous area, Central Europe, instead of being dissipated over national issues from other regions. Membership was to be confined to seven Western nations--the United States, Britain, Canada, the FRG, Holland, Belgium, and Luxembourg--and five from the East--the Soviet Union, Poland, East Germany, Czechoslovakia, and Hungary (that is, the states that could directly threaten or support operations against the Federal Republic of Germany). The Warsaw Pact was caught off guard because of Rumania's known demand for an open conference in which any participant could raise any issue of national importance. To ensure that such latitude did not impede progress, a compromise was worked out for the final communiqué, which provided for two categories of members: full participants with decision-making powers and states with special status that gave them the right to raise any topic relevant to the subject under discussion.

This formula was agreed upon after the Soviets changed
tactics sometime in March: they abandoned the neutrals
(whom they had earlier sponsored), sacrificed Rumania without much ado, and insisted that Italy be given full status
to balance Hungary. The Soviets argued that the inclusion
of 165,000 Hungarian and 40,000 Soviet troops in Hungary
would create a structural imbalance in the talks unless the
300,000 Italian and 10,000 American troops in Italy were
also brought into the reckoning. More to the point, they
reasoned that the inclusion of their forces stationed in
Hungary would mean that all Soviet troops stationed abroad
would be included in the conference's sums, but only a portion of the U.S. forces overseas, thus distorting the picture during the next round of cuts. Finally, a Soviet official hit the nail on the head when he commented infor-
mally that the reasons for not including the four Soviet
divisions in Hungary were the "political-geographical" mission they still performed and the need to defend the southern tier of the Warsaw Pact.

From the Soviet military viewpoint there are both
tactical and strategic advantages to be derived from excluding their forces in Hungary from any reduction:

● Relative to any potential enemy in the area, they
comprise powerful armor and tactical air units that can be
employed offensively as well as to protect vital communications and the headquarters of the Southern Forces Front;

● They serve the political function of guaranteeing
the reliability of the Hungarian regime;

● They are strategically well placed, along with the
Soviet Navy, to exert pressure during any crisis that might
arise when the political succession is at stake in Yugoslavia, Albania, or Rumania;

● Should military action ever be required in the Balkans, undiminished Soviet strength could secure communications with the Ukraine, serve as a spearhead for combined
Hungarian, Bulgarian, and Soviet operations against Yugoslavia, or lend military weight to a Warsaw Pact encircle-
ment of Rumania.

The United States accepted the Soviet position, but
its allies objected strongly. Hungary, they said, provides
a conduit through the Danube Valley to Bavaria along which
there would be virtually no resistance; if it were excluded
from the reckoning, it would act as a reservoir from which
men and materiel could be shifted north or south; and there
was no assurance that Soviet troops withdrawn from the
northern tier would not be transferred to Hungary. Under
strong combined U.S.-USSR pressure, however, the NATO allies

accepted a compromise whereby Hungary would be classified
as a special-status nation and the West would reserve the
right to question its status or other issues relevant to
Hungary at a later date--a clear concession to the Soviets.*

The Hungarian question introduced the whole question
of verification. The SALT negotiations made progress in
part because of the effectiveness of satellite surveillance;
verification of the strength of bodies of troops in a given
area is far more difficult. In World War II, in the occupation of Czechoslovakia, and in the Suez Canal build-up
the Soviets demonstrated a high degree of expertise in making clandestine troop movements. Their skill in this type
of operation, superior to that of the West, is precisely
the reason for their refusal to accept any form of on-site
inspection.

The verification problem in MFR affects not only troop
withdrawals but also the final disposition of forces and
equipment. West German Defense Minister Leber claims that
1,500 new T-62 Soviet tanks have been brought into East
Germany alone since 1966 and that the replaced T-55s and
T-54s have not been scrapped but stored in forward depots
where they can be brought back into service at short notice
and issued to reinforcement units. Further, in the annual
Warsaw Pact exercise, Shield 72, the Soviets introduced a
massive airlift, similar to the U.S. Reforger and Crested
Cap exercises in which dual-based units are transported by
air from the United States to Germany. But the Soviets
made a significant innovation: they mobilized a major segment of their civilian airline fleet for this purpose.
This is the first evidence that the USSR has considered
and experimented with the possibility of using the technique of dual-basing to compensate for a withdrawal of combat units.[11] But the numbers, types, and locations of such
units, if they exist, must be verified before they can be
accepted by the West. This single example illustrates the
complexity of the verification problem, which was left unresolved during the preparatory consultations.

The question of the types of weapons and equipment to
be cut was also raised. It was the Soviet side that intro-

---

*While the right to raise relevant issues was explicitly
stated in the June communiqué, the West directed its spokesman, the head of the Dutch delegation, Ambassador Bryan
Quarles, to publicly restate this reservation on the Hungarian question. In particular, it was feared that verification of troops in Hungary could be circumvented by its
absence.

duced the additional words "and arms" into the full title of the MFR conference. It was generally assumed that the Warsaw Pact would use this rubric to raise its traditional demand that tactical nuclear weapons be included along with manpower cuts. Nuclear weapons are always a delicate question, and especially in this context. As Nixon asked in his 3 May 1973 report: "How do we reconcile reductions in roughly balanced conventional forces with the fact that the strategic balance is no longer clearly favorable to the Alliance?"[12] Historically the NATO allies have maintained their conventional forces at a low level and have thus accepted the likelihood of rapid escalation to the nuclear phase. Since selected categories of theater nuclear weapons were being discussed under the aegis of SALT II, the Soviets apparently decided not to tamper with this delicate balance and agreed to limit MFR to conventional weapons, even though their numerical superiority could bring with it bargaining disadvantages.

To judge from press reports, the size of the initial cut in great-power conventional forces stationed in Central Europe was also discussed. The Soviets reportedly rejected out of hand any asymmetrical compromise, pointing to their concessions on tactical nuclear weapons and the confinement of the reductions to Central Europe. According to the latest figures, there are 350,000 Soviet troops in Eastern Europe and 310,000 U.S. troops in Europe as a whole, but only 190,000 of them in West Germany. Total ground forces in Europe are 1,410,000 for NATO versus 1,350,000 for the Warsaw Pact. These figures indicate that a percentage cut, if it were confined to the two major powers, would work to the Soviets' disadvantage: a 10 percent reduction would cost them 35,000 troops against 19,000 for the United States. These figures enable the Soviets to counter the popular Western argument that percentage cuts in Central Europe down to a fixed point would preserve the existing asymmetries intact without impairing either side's security.

The Soviets devoted the bulk of their efforts during the consultations to rejecting the term "balanced reductions" and refuting the principle behind it, and to gaining acceptance of the need for "mutual reductions." This was the most divisive issue that arose during the preliminary consultations, first between East and West and then, when the United States sided with the Soviet Union, within NATO. (In the long term, however, it had the virtues of forcing NATO to decide finally upon a common objective for MFR and of creating a unified Western stand on the issue of reduction.) It was not until Brezhnev's visits to the FRG in May and to the United States in June that the term "balanced" was dropped from the title of the conference and the substitute wording agreed upon for the final June 19 communiqué:

> [The participants] agreed that, in the negotia-
> tions, an understanding should be reached to con-
> duct them in such a way as to ensure the most ef-
> fective and thorough approach to the consideration
> of the subject matter, with due regard to its
> complexity. They also agreed that specific ar-
> rangements will have to be carefully worked out
> in scope and timing in such a way that they will
> in all respects and at every point conform to
> the principle of undiminished security for each
> party.*

NATO spokesmen argued that the inclusion of the Western term "undiminished security" amounted to acceptance of
the underlying principle of the West's interpretation of
balanced reductions; the trick was to find a formula that
all could agree would not impair their security. But this
explanation brought the argument full circle: there was
no perceptible difference between the Western understanding
of "undiminished security" and the Soviets' original term
"equal security." (As the Polish Army daily pointed out,
this concept was much closer to the oft-stated French posi-

---

*As a trade-off Brezhnev agreed that the formal talks
would commence on 31 October 1973; the Soviets had been insisting that the MFR talks be postponed until after the com-
pletion of the CSCE. He gained, however, a seemingly important Western concession on the format and content of the
agenda. NATO had insisted upon a detailed, itemized listing of issues that would both prescribe the dimensions of
the conference and allow a systematic point-by-point assessment. This mechanism would provide built-in brakes against
unwanted public euphoria and leverage against obstruction-
ism; if agreement was not reached on any point, progress to
the next could be impeded. Moscow sought and gained acceptance on the format used successfully in SALT: a statement
of guidelines and principles, allowing work to proceed on
an ad hoc basis. U.S. concurrence ultimately compelled
allied endorsement, but the lack of rigidity may work in
the West's favor by reducing built-in obstacles and permitting the "good intentions" of all parties greater scope in
influencing the negotiations.

tion that "mutual force reductions" could produce a shared benefit in undiminished individual security and predicted the ultimate participation by France when the premises of the conference would accordingly be changed.[13]

THE NEXT PHASE OF NEGOTIATIONS

After the largely informal, unrecorded preparatory consultations, what can be expected from the equally informal working groups that began deliberations in October 1973? What alternatives are there to those already presented and what format are accords likely to take? Nixon apparently postulated the minimum and maximum U.S. expectations in his May report to Congress. He rejected percentage cuts because they gave advantages to the Soviets and preferred "mixed, asymmetrical" cuts, meaning reductions of varying amounts in various categories of weapons or manpower, if equivalence can be tabulated between different kinds of weapons. Ideally he would presumably want reductions to equal levels, with the imposition of common ceilings on both sides.[14] Both approaches are unrealistic --the first because of difficulties in equating, for example, tanks and artillery, and the second because it does not take account of the political mission of the Soviet garrisons, which adds an extra quantitative dimension.

On the other side Rumania, in its maverick role, has frequently demanded more comprehensive security measures, including a ban on the production of all weapons, especially nuclear ones, and their gradual liquidation; nuclear-free zones in various parts of the world; elimination of military bases and the withdrawal of troops from foreign soil; reduction of national troop levels; and the creation of conditions for the abolition of military blocs.[15] Desirable as these aims may be, they look somewhat utopian under present circumstances and have little relevance to contemporary negotiations, except to remind us of the awesome scale of the ultimate goals.

Others have presented the case for reductions of military budgets through example or individual initiative.[16] While there may be some historical evidence of a correlation in the budgetary restraints exercised by the great powers at various periods, these individual reductions may have been as much the product of other economic and political imperatives as the result of a general desire for disarmament. Moreover, because of differing inflationary rates, pay scales, procurement costs, and so on, military

91

budgets provide no easy answer to the comparability problem. At any rate, to attack the source, as the advocates of this method propose, rather than the more tangible end products such as troops or arms, is likely to create even greater confusion and ambiguity in the minds of a public anxious to see immediate and concrete results.

To repeat the question: What can be expected from the working groups by the end of 1975? Two alternatives may be acceptable to both sides. The first of these is that, to compensate for the asymmetries involved, a formula should be devised for fixed ceilings only on offensive capabilities on the central front. These fixed ceilings should roughly equate the offensive capacities of the two sides and should include conventional armor and tactical nuclear weapons and interdiction aircraft. (It is assumed that medium-range delivery vehicles will be covered at the SALT II negotiations.) They should be equated to a minimal threat posture for each of a series of incremental reductions. By incorporating only the most destabilizing factor in the over-all equation--offensive capabilities--the other asymmetries can be avoided with little risk, and greater unanimity can be expected on the most dangerous single aspect of the confrontation. With an agreed ceiling on offensive capabilities, the formula can then more readily accommodate relatively large percentage cuts in manpower. This alternative would allow both sides unrestrained freedom of action in devising appropriate defenses for theater-level (that is, all-European) hostilities. Thus percentage reductions in in-being forces (both stationed and indigenous) and fixed cuts in offensive weapons should be the most effective check on the hostile intentions of an opponent. Finally, this formula reduces a country's power to launch a surprise attack without impairing either its mobilization and defensive capabilities, or its ability to absorb unexpected attacks.

The second alternative is a function of the normalization process. If the problems of agreed reduction prove too complex, it may be prudent to place the main emphasis on the political factors of the confrontation and to reconsider the mutual interests involved. In other words, it may become imperative to stress ends rather than means and to concentrate on defining the concept of normalization and building up mutual confidence in what it should achieve. Once this has been done, it would be possible and indeed preferable for each side to take unilateral action that will complement the normalization process between East and West and conduce to agreement on ultimate force levels. In the interim the multilateral discussions could focus on functional aspects of disengagement, as several NATO delegations have already advocated.

The wider horizons of the second alternative make it possible to look beyond mere troop reductions to a fuller evaluation of functional factors and disengagement techniques. A wide selection of methods of reducing military tension could be submitted for consideration by the participants in the MFR talks, such as exchange of observers for military maneuvers; removal of travel restrictions on accredited military attachés; prior notification of large-scale maneuvers; construction of "hot-line" communications at the tactical level to cope with inadvertent border penetrations; emplacement of unmanned electronic sensors along frontiers and probable penetration routes; and creation of a joint standing committee to establish criteria for provocative and precautionary activities. Such methods would encourage military disengagement and prompt a de facto understanding of the nature of political normalization. Further, they would lessen the necessity for verification or would rely on unilateral surveillance procedures and thereby improve the political acceptability of a functional approach. The second alternative, then, is the use of interim solutions, making the military status quo cheaper and the political status quo more viable without substantially altering either, as preconditions for advancing normalization. At this early juncture, it seems possible that both alternatives will eventually be considered multilaterally, perhaps simultaneously; the CSCE could then concentrate on the political definition of normalization while force reductions were handled by the MFR talks.

There are several general negotiating techniques that can be used in such cases. First, Correlated Systems Trade-Offs is a variation on the zero-sum bargaining principle where a loss for one side is regarded as a gain for the other--for example, an equal number of F-4s and TU-16s, F-111s and Tu-22s could be cut. The difficulty with the correlation technique, as noted in the Nixon report, is that it gives too little weight to weapons' characteristics and cannot be used to tackle the chief source of the threat to both sides: their differing offensive capabilities in tanks and aircraft. While the weapons' roles may be similar, their characteristics are so dissimilar that policing a reduction would be very difficult.

Second, there is the technique of Noncorrelated Systems Trade-Offs--for example, one wing of F-4s is withdrawn from a theater in exchange for withdrawal of one tank divi-

sion. The problem here is that theater forces cannot be
satisfactorily correlated on a military basis alone. For
example, antitank defenses are likely to improve in the
near future to a degree that will sharply curtail the effectiveness of the tank, reducing its value as a bargaining
counter vis-à-vis the flexible F-4 aircraft. Thus reductions of noncorrelated weapons would be political rather
than military decisions.

Finally, the method of Unilateral Concessions, or Reductions by Mutual Example can be used where military trading is not feasible and the payoff is largely political
The difficulty with unilateral action of this kind is not
merely the problem of determining its military impact, but
also that of ascertaining the political risks involved and
the incentives to reciprocity it provides. Political implication and the uncertainty associated with it increase
as one moves down the scale from the first to the third of
these techniques, and at the outset of the working group
talks in Vienna it seems unlikely that the last of them
will receive much attention. But if the technical problems
connected with establishing agreed criteria for correlations
lead to frustration and stalemate, the political stakes for
reaching agreement may gradually increase, and unilateral
reductions may become more attractive--provided the mutual
interest in achieving accord remains undiminished.

As the talks got under way in October 1973, the Soviet
Union introduced several new proposals that altered the
course of the negotiations. In general the new recommenda-
tions broadened the scope of the reductions and tackled
subjects formerly taboo, such as tactical nuclear weapons.
In a major policy statement to the Moscow World Congress
of Peace-Loving Forces on October 26, Leonid Brezhnev stated:

> We consider it necessary to agree on the reduction
> in a defined area of Central Europe of both foreign
> and national land and air forces of the countries
> participating in the negotiations. . . . It would
> seem that one must recognize that the cuts should
> also apply to units armed with nuclear weapons.
> . . . Whether the reductions are to be by equal
> percentages or by equal numbers will have to be
> discussed by the participants. . . . From our
> point of view it is important that any future
> cuts do not disturb the existing balance of power
> in Central Europe and in the European continent
> in general. If this principle is upset, the whole
> question will become a bone of contention and an

object of unending disputes. . . . The Soviet
Union will be ready for realistic action in this
area as early as 1975.[17]

Two weeks later the head of the Soviet delegation in
Vienna, Oleg Khlestov, presented a formal position paper
that detailed Brezhnev's suggestions. Troop cuts were to
be made in three phases. In the first, 20,000 NATO and
Warsaw Pact forces would be cut by 1975. Thereafter percentages would be used: in phase two there would be a 5
percent cut by all countries with troops in Central Europe
in 1976, and phase three would include a 10 percent reduction in 1977 by all members of both alliances. (According
to press reports, the Soviets favored a 15 percent drop,
but the East Europeans held out for something less drastic.)
In each phase there were to be matching reductions in weapons and equipment, including air forces and nuclear delivery systems.

The U.S. delegation in general welcomed these changes
in the Soviet position. Moscow had in effect canceled the
laborious negotiations conducted during the spring, but had
moved closer to the core of the problem, possibly with some
benefit to the speed of the over-all negotiating process.
The compromise between numbers and percentages would, of
course, preserve the USSR's existing military preponderance
in Eastern Europe if it included national forces as well
as those of the great powers, and a reduction of its allies' strength in all three phases would ensure the Soviets
continuing asymmetrical advantages. If the Soviets hold
to their demand for allied cuts in phase one or accept a
formula whereby each side can establish its own reduction
mix, the NATO response will be complicated. There is still
strong Congressional pressure for an immediate reduction
in American forces abroad that cannot be ignored, yet the
FRG was the strongest NATO advocate of allied reductions
during phase one and can be expected to reiterate its demand. The USSR, however, might be induced to limit the
initial cuts to Soviet and American troops if the West
agrees to simultaneous reductions in nuclear weapons launchers.

The Soviets cannot include nuclear warheads in the
proposed reductions because none of the Warsaw Pact's warheads are stored in Central Europe. Only launchers and
delivery vehicles can therefore be considered. This is a
complicated problem since most systems, especially those
in NATO, are capable of firing both nuclear and conventional missiles. NATO has approximately 7,000 warheads

for between 2,000 and 2,500 delivery vehicles, while the
Warsaw Pact has about half that number in each category.
Yet the FRG alone has 900 artillery pieces that are "dual
capable." Aircraft are even more difficult to differen-
tiate. All the U.S. combat air units in Europe are equipped
with F-4s, which are dual capable, and no verifiable dis-
tinction can be made between F-4s assigned to ground support missions and those designated for nuclear strikes.
The United States has already agreed not to provide aircraft with a nuclear capability as replacements for Allied
forces equipped with the F-104 strike aircraft. It is not
clear what the Soviets can offer as a trade-off. The USSR
has placed greater emphasis on single mission aircraft,
and an attempt to reduce, say, equal numbers of Su-7s and
F-4s would work to the Soviets' advantage (the F-4 can
carry four times the payload of the Su-7). Nuclear missile
systems are therefore more likely candidates for reduction;
both sides have surface-to-surface missiles designed primarily for nuclear warheads, and the SCUD-B and Pershing
missiles could be eliminated without impairing the conventional capability of either grouping. Despite the complexity of finding an equitable formula for cutting general
purpose forces and nuclear weapons systems, the Soviet proposal for the first time raises the prospect that the Warsaw Pact countries are prepared to deal seriously on troop
reductions.

THE IMPLICATIONS OF MUTUAL FORCE
REDUCTIONS FOR EASTERN EUROPE

Although both the Soviet Union and the United States
consult with the members of their respective military alliances and make an effort to consider the views of the
smaller states, in the final analysis the mutual force reduction talks are primarily a bilateral great-power issue.
The bulk of the striking power of both alliances is in Soviet and American hands. Despite the fact that their direct involvement is limited, the East European states will
nevertheless be considerably affected by the results of
any decisions on force reductions. At present the potential
impact is difficult to gauge, but some indications exist.
Some East European states have not unequivocally accepted the Soviet Union's interpretation of the nature and
extent of the physical threat to their own security. Be-
neath a diplomatic panoply of jointly reached and enunciated
defense policies, diverse perceptions can and do exist,

though they are rarely subject to public scrutiny. Perhaps
the best known and clearest example of this occurred in
January 1967, when Rumania in effect rejected the Warsaw
Pact countries' position that West German revanchism was
the main source of European tension by establishing full
diplomatic relations with the FRG. This fundamental policy
shift precipitated a serious crisis over precisely what
the security requirements of Eastern Europe really were,
and the initial reaction, led by East Germany, portrayed
the potential threat as having been exacerbated by the
Bonn-Bucharest flirtation. The Rumanian aberration resulted
in a series of bilateral mutual defense treaties between
East Germany and other East European states designed to
reinforce the commitments incorporated in the Warsaw Pact
and to preclude other individual approaches to West Germany.
Rumania has declined to participate fully in Warsaw Pact
exercises, and the 1972 defense law has shifted Rumanian
military doctrine away from Soviet defense concepts and
toward Yugoslav or even Chinese concepts of all-national
defense against any aggressor threatening the country's
sovereignty or territorial integrity.

Depending on the character of the indigenous leadership (which has been subject to fairly significant variations over the past 10 years), the internal political role
of the Soviet military presence has obviously been the subject of differing interpretations. For example, East Germany, Czechoslovakia, and Poland have in the past tended
to view their strategic position with greater apprehension
than either their southern allies or the Soviet Union, as
well as from the different perspectives of specific national
interests. Until the present network of treaties with Bonn
became a reality, they considered themselves more exposed
to West German pressure; and, because the pivot of the bilateral relationship of each of them with Bonn was a matter
of fundamental policy, they looked upon the Soviet military
alliance as an essential guarantor of the national position.
Collective security formed a useful barrier to a gradual
increase of West German influence, as well as a visible
guarantee against an erosion of the Soviet commitment to
their own positions.

Because of these varying national estimates and definitions of the threat to national security, the size of
the Soviet military presence is--in the GDR at least--re-
garded as a measure of the political relationship to the
Soviet Union in terms of the latter's vital interests.
East Berlin, for example, tends to see the 20 Soviet divisions on its soil as evidence that the GDR is the Warsaw

Pact country most vulnerable to Western pressures, and accordingly the most important link in the Soviet strategic chain. Thus, unilateral Soviet reductions in troop strength may be expected to encounter the resistance of the East German leadership.

By the same token, Soviet forces in Poland are not necessarily a measure of the Soviet commitment to Polish political objectives vis-à-vis West Germany, but they serve as a visible reminder of the identity of Soviet and Polish interest in the permanence of the Oder-Neisse boundary. The December 1970 treaty has reduced their diplomatic and political significance in this context, but from a strategic point of view it is clear that no increase in indigenous forces could compensate for the value of the Soviet divisions. Few would doubt, however, that the primary reason for stationing two Soviet divisions on Polish territory since 1945 is to strengthen Moscow's hand in dealing with domestic political upheavals; in December 1970, for example, Soviet troops stood poised to intervene should the leaders of Poland fail to resolve the crisis.

In Czechoslovakia discontent with the country's allocated role in Warsaw Pact security policy surfaced during the short-lived reform in 1968. At a celebrated press conference in July of that year General Vaclav Prchlik complained about Prague's inability to influence the formation of military policy because Moscow had arrogated this responsibility to itself. Prchlik called for a reorganization of the Warsaw Pact command structure that would allow its members a genuine voice in the making of policy. One infers from this that Prchlik was reflecting the opinions of at least part of the officer corps that Czechoslovakia might find military responsibilities assigned to it that were not completely in accord with its national interests as seen from Prague. The example of joint defense of Soviet interests given by the May 1970 Mutual Defense Pact illustrates these reservations. Since the August 1968 invasion, the Soviet military presence has served the primary purpose of ensuring domestic stability by guaranteeing the reliability of the political leadership. The Husak regime would probably welcome a symbolic withdrawal of a portion of the Soviet forces as a means of enhancing in the public eye its credibility as a leadership, but there is every reason to believe that any wholesale withdrawal would be viewed with misgivings in both capitals.

On the other hand, from the point of view of expenditures, it is unlikely that the East European states in which Soviet troops are stationed would favor unilateral reductions of these forces. Since the Warsaw Pact countries have adopted a burden-sharing plan by which the host countries pay for garrisoning costs, there is little financial incentive for them to seek a cut in stationed as opposed to indigenous forces; it is cheaper to pay for stationed Soviet troops than for their own national forces. Sizable increases in the latter would raise personnel and equipment costs and expand defense budgets. Moreover, some countries, such as East Germany, are reluctant to accept reductions of Soviet troops on military grounds. A sharp unilateral Soviet cut would require an increase in East Germany's armed forces, and a stronger <u>Volksarmee</u> would be worrying to all countries with interests in Central Europe. Thus, there are important military, political, and economic reasons why the countries of Central Europe should prefer a strong Soviet presence and a gradual reduction in their own national forces.

From the East European point of view, the timing of the cuts is in a sense as important as their size. Because of the weighty political significance of the Soviet military presence, the East Europeans have shown themselves anxious to devise political buttresses to offset any reductions that may occur, and the CSCE is viewed as an important vehicle for providing international ratification of the existing situation in Eastern Europe on Warsaw Pact terms. This is regarded as an indispensable precondition for developing the political parameters of détente in Europe, after which limited military disengagement can be more safely pursued.

A second method used in the attempt to strengthen the political position within the Warsaw Pact is the renewal of the ideological campaign. The initiative in developing an integrated ideological campaign to counter the (assumed) increased political challenge from the West appears to have come primarily from Eastern Europe. It is important to note that the East Europeans to some extent feel that they have a different historical and cultural background from that of the USSR and that they are more susceptible to influences from the West. Accordingly, a series of bilateral treaties dealing with ideological cooperation has been negotiated between East Germany, Poland, Czechoslovakia, Hungary, and Bulgaria. This integrated ideological campaign will have to show positive results before the governments concerned feel sufficiently secure to accept significant military reductions. The stress on ideology has been reflected in the military sphere as well; in Czechoslovakia, for example, the importance of ideological training has received a new and vigorous emphasis.

In the ongoing MFR talks the Soviets can be expected
to seek reductions in selected Western weapons systems that
they regard as detrimental to the security of Eastern Europe, without pressing for package or "basket" settlements
that might lead to structural adjustments and instability
in the fabric of either alliance. In general, the USSR is
likely to draw the line at the point where military disengagement impinges on concepts, reductions, or policies that
hold any risk of altering the present structure and stability of the Soviet alliance and security system, including
its political ramifications. This line of reasoning empha-
sizes the political undertones of the MFR talks and high-
lights the gravity of such undertakings when so little
consensus exists about their political utility. Nonetheless, the momentum of the drive toward arms limitation is
provided by political factors; unless their primacy is maintained that momentum could be lost. While both sides have
had difficulty in assessing accurately the potential impact
of military disengagement on their alliance structures, it
has been even more difficult for them to weigh the consequences of failure. The dangers of disenchantment in Western Europe and resignation in Eastern Europe may be far
more crippling to the normalization process than the risks
of miscalculation about specific security measures. Fear
of failure alone is likely to produce some positive results,
and it seems safe to assume that the Soviets are sufficiently
committed to the process of détente that they will make a
more generous contribution to both CSCE and MFR than would
have been the case if they had been engaged in purely defensive maneuvering to weaken the Western alliance.

NOTES

1. Polska Agencja Prasova (hereafter PAP), 16 May
1973.
2. The Military Balance, 1972-1973 (London: International Institute of Strategic Studies (hereafter IISS),
1973), p. 72.
3. Lawrence L. Whetten, "Legal Basis for the Soviet
Military Presence in Czechoslovakia," Revue du droit international 47, no. 4 (Geneva, November-December 1969): 287-
299.
4. Christoph Bertram, "Mutual Force Reduction in Europe: The Political Aspects," Adelphi Papers No. 84, IISS,
January 1972; and Timothy W. Stanley and Barnell M. Whitt,
Détente Diplomacy: United States and European Diplomacy
in the 1970s (New York: Dunellen, 1970).

5. The Military Balance, 1971-1972 (IISS, 1971), p. 78.

6. For an example of the difficulties in technical asymmetries see Neville Brown, "The Tactical Air Balance in Europe," The World Today 28, no. 9 (London, September 1971): 385-393.

7. The Military Balance, 1972-1973, p. 7.

8. Mirovaya Ekonomika i Mezhdunarodniye Otnoshenia, Moscow, June 1972, pp. 87-89. See also r.r.g., "Soviet Commentary Rejects Asymmetric Approach to MBFR," CAA Research Report No. 1453, Radio Free Europe Research, 19 June 1972.

9. President Nixon's Foreign Policy Report to the U.S. Congress (Washington, D.C.: U.S. Government Printing Office, 3 May 1973).

10. See the general "Threat Estimate" carried in Neues Deutschland, East Berlin, 30 May 1973.

11. John Erickson, "Soviet Shield '72," Royal United Service Institution, London, December 1972.

12. President Nixon's Foreign Policy Report.

13. Zolnierz Wolnosci, Warsaw, 5 June 1973.

14. President Nixon's Foreign Policy Report.

15. See, for example, the statement by Rumanian Deputy Foreign Minister Nicolae Ecobescu, Radio Bucharest, Domestic Service, 10 June 1973. See also Chapter 9, below.

16. For example, Andrew J. Pierre, "Limiting Soviet and American Conventional Forces," Survival 15, no. 2 (London, March-April 1973): 59-64; and Charles L. Schutze, et al., Setting National Priorities--The 1973 Budget (Washington, D.C.: Brookings Institute, 1972).

17. Radio Moscow, 26 October 1973.

5

EAST GERMANY:
THE SPECIAL CASE
John Dornberg

Whatever motivations may have been behind the various
Soviet calls for a European security conference--and these
have changed with the times and exigencies of the world
situation since Vyacheslav Molotov first proposed the idea
in 1954--East Germany has been guided by a single, basic
thought. For the GDR such a conference had always appeared
as the logical and most convenient venue for attaining at
least de facto, and possibly de jure, recognition of its
sovereignty and independence.

GDR Foreign Minister Otto Winzer himself underscored
this aim in the autumn of 1969, following the October 30-
31 Warsaw Pact conference in Prague at which the appeal for
early convening of an all-European meeting on security and
the renunciation of force was revived. In a signed editorial in Neues Deutschland on 4 November 1969, Winzer
pleaded the urgency of convening such a conference, and
then wrote:

> The preparation and holding of a security confer-
> ence creates new possibilities for general and
> equal inclusion of the GDR and also of the West
> German Federal Republic in pan-European relations.
> Participation, with equal rights, in a European
> renunciation-of-force agreement would best serve
> to ensure peace in Europe under the present inter-
> national circumstances, and in addition would be
> a contribution to détente between the two German
> states.

Indeed, although the GDR paid proper lip service to
the professed twofold purpose of the conference--that is,

renunciation of force and expansion of trade, economic, scientific, and technological relations--it was the potential role of the conference as a vehicle for obtaining recognition that most interested East Berlin.

Moreover, East Germany was adamant that the conference should serve as the only vehicle for a renunciation-of-force agreement on a multilateral basis. It was strenuously opposed to any and all bilateral agreements, for it feared, justifiably, that such pacts, possibly between Bonn and Moscow and Bonn and Warsaw, might tend to isolate the GDR and reduce its chance of realizing its maximum demand of de facto recognition.

In his Neues Deutschland article Winzer left no doubt as to the GDR's position on this:

> The Bonn government has declared that it considers the successful conclusion of a bilateral renunciation-of-force [treaty] as an "important step on the road toward a European security conference." This interpretation raises some doubts. Although a pan-European agreement on the renunciation of force does not, in fact, preclude bilateral agreements, it would be wrong to consider bilateral agreements a necessary antecedent step on the road toward a security conference and preparation for a future all-European [treaty network].

In a subsequent interview that he gave to the editors of the East German weekly Horizont (published in no. 46, 1969), Winzer presented the GDR's views and the reasons for them even more clearly. Describing as an "untenable precondition" a Bonn foreign ministry official's statement that bilateral renunciation-of-force agreements should remain a West German "policy instrument" to be followed, later perhaps, by a multilateral network of such agreements, Winzer said: "Bonn's intention is to force the GDR to enter into so-called 'intra-German' negotiations by which [West Germany] aims to deny [the GDR] sovereign statehood and international independence."

The whole question of bilateral agreements had, of course, been raised by the advent of the Social Democratic-Free Democratic coalition government of Willy Brandt and Walter Scheel in October 1969, just before the Prague Warsaw Pact meeting and Winzer's Neues Deutschland editorial. It was apparent at the time that Moscow was far more interested in testing the intentions of the new Bonn government than was East Berlin and that the Soviet and East German

103

positions were drifting apart rather significantly. In
fact, it was this divergence and East Germany's staunch
opposition to bilateral negotiations and agreements that
led to a communist-bloc crisis in the latter half of November and prompted the holding of the summit conference of
"leading figures of the fraternal socialist countries" in
Moscow in December 1969.

The first signs of serious disagreement, besides the
Winzer article and interview, were the very divergent editorial interpretations that the Soviet and East German party
and government news media were giving to the significance
of the governmental change that had taken place in Bonn.
By mid-November the Soviet position could best be described
as a pronounced willingness to enter into both exploratory
and substantive talks with Bonn, whereas East Berlin,
afraid of isolation and apprehensive lest its policy aims
be overtaken by uncontrollable developments, was pleading
with Moscow to go slow.

The East German view, however, found only limited sympathetic resonance in the Soviet capital. One prominent
Soviet publicist with high-level government and party connections told this author in a private conversation during
those weeks: "We should give [the East Germans] a little
time. After all, we cannot really expect them to jettison
a 20-year-old policy within 20 days." But views that sympathetic to the East German position were hard to find in
Moscow.

The interests of the GDR were in many ways contrary
to the national and economic interests of the USSR and
other East European countries. They could argue for better,
possibly bilateral, relations with the Federal Republic
while pointing out that the GDR itself continued to profit
from its special status and from the "interzonal" or intra-
German trade agreement, which gave East Germany a special
relationship with the Common Market. Indeed, East Germany's
position could be challenged. On the one hand, East Berlin
was insisting on a course of action by which it hoped to
gain full diplomatic recognition from the West, especially
West Germany. On the other hand, it wanted very much to
preserve the economic advantages devolving from the "interzonal" trade agreement.

By the time the twice-postponed Moscow summit meeting
opened on December 3, the mood of the East German leadership was described as "tense and gloomy." As one East Berlin party official put it in a conversation with correspondent David Binder, "the atmosphere is electrically charged
and the thunderbolts are already striking from the clouds."[1]

How stormy the Moscow summit really was may never be fully known in the West. Suffice it to say that the communiqué, though it talked about an "atmosphere of comradely cooperation," did concede that the participants in the talks had "exchanged their points of view," which in communist communiqué parlance can generally be regarded as indicating disagreement.[2]

The extent of the disagreement was underscored by East German party leader Walter Ulbricht in an interview he gave to Neues Deutschland on 6 December 1969 after his return to East Berlin. Although Ulbricht claimed that he was "very satisfied" with the outcome of the meeting, he pointedly ignored the favorable assessment of the new Bonn government that had been expressed in the communiqué. Instead, he devoted most of his remarks to the question of a European security conference, stressing that this had been the main issue under discussion and represented the main thrust of the communiqué, which was decidedly not the case.

Three days after the Ulbricht interview was published the Soviet Foreign Affairs Ministry's V. M. Falin, now the USSR's ambassador in Bonn, called Helmut Allardt, then the West German ambassador in Moscow, to tell him that Foreign Minister Andrei Gromyko was ready to begin discussing a renunciation-of-force agreement that very afternoon. What transpired over the next three years is more or less recorded history: the Bonn treaties with Moscow and Warsaw, the four-power agreement on Berlin, the basic treaty between the two Germanies (which is tantamount to de jure recognition of the GDR by the FRG in all but name).

Throughout this period differences of opinion and policy continued to burden the relationship between Moscow and East Berlin, and Ulbricht made no secret of his opposition or his intention to drag his heels. Although he had abandoned his demands for diplomatic recognition by West Germany soon after the historic meetings between FRG Chancellor Willy Brandt and East German Premier Willi Stoph in Erfurt and Kassel on 19 March and 21 May 1970, Ulbricht continued to employ delaying tactics over the Berlin question and to emphasize his independent stance in a number of ways. For example, he received the new Chinese ambassador in East Berlin with ostentatious courtesy. He made conciliatory moves toward Rumania. And he made a special point of trying to improve relations with the Italian communists. In fact, Ulbricht proved so obstructive that he was replaced as party leader in May 1971 by his "crown prince," Erich Honecker.

In retrospect, Ulbricht's tactics seem like grossly miscalculated and futile gestures that merely sealed his own political fate. For by the time the foreign ministers met in Helsinki to open the European security conference that Ulbricht had once envisioned as the principal venue for East Germany's full acceptance as a sovereign state the GDR had already been formally recognized by more than 80 countries and was on the threshold of membership in the United Nations. An apparently acceptable modus vivendi short of formal diplomatic recognition by Bonn had been found in the agreement to exchange "permanent representatives." In fact, the only world power that had not yet formally recognized the GDR was the United States. But even that was only a matter of time, for preliminary, low-level talks on establishing diplomatic relations between Washington and East Berlin were already scheduled.

Considering that the vast majority, if not all, of its objectives had been achieved in advance of the conference itself, one could justifiably ask what interests, if any, the German Democratic Republic still had, or has, in pursuing the goal of agreement on security and cooperation in Europe. That question is not easily answered.

Obviously there are some general goals in which East German interests coincide with those of the Soviet Union and the other East European states. Thus, one might note that although the GDR has obtained de jure and/or de facto recognition from all the participants in the conference, it has yet to obtain formal recognition of the European status quo--specifically, of its own boundaries. Like the Soviet Union, it no doubt has a certain interest in reducing the American presence in Europe and feels that this can be accomplished through a series of renunciation-of-force agreements that would obviate the need for continuing U.S. military commitment. No doubt, too, the GDR has an interest in the establishment of some type of permanent European control organization in which it could continue to play an active diplomatic role, the result of which would be an enhancement of the GDR's prestige.

EAST–WEST ECONOMIC AND TECHNOLOGICAL COOPERATION

But the conference basket that most strongly motivates the USSR and the East European countries to participate in the Geneva talks--trade and economic, scientific, and technological cooperation--can be only of secondary, if not peripheral, interest to the GDR, in view of that country's unique position within Comecon and its special status vis-à-vis the Common Market. One should consider, first of all, that the GDR is already a major economic power in its own right, and falls into an entirely different category from that of its European socialist partners. As an industrial power and trading nation the GDR ranks sixth in all of Europe, behind the USSR, West Germany, Great Britain, France, and Italy. Within Comecon itself it not only takes the second spot, behind the Soviet Union, in industrial output but actually far outpaces the USSR in the quality, sophistication, and technological advancement of some of its products and industrial installations. Although it comprises only 0.4 percent of Comecon's territorial area and has less than 4.6 percent of its population, East Germany annually accounts for more than 15 percent of the organization's total exports. With 3.7 billion rubles out of 26 billion, it accounted for more than 14 percent of the Soviet Union's total 1972 trade turnover and is the USSR's largest single trading partner, delivering many of the advanced and sophisticated products--optical goods and precision instruments, machine tools, textiles, chemicals, and plastics--which the USSR would otherwise have to purchase for hard currency in the West.

Bar none, the GDR is the most viable economic power in the socialist bloc and as such has entered the European security and cooperation talks with aims and objectives quite different from those of its Comecon partners and on a basis completely different from theirs. This is not to say that East Germany is not also in need of and in the market for some of the technologically advanced products and processes or the cooperative undertakings that a successful conclusion of the CSCE may produce. But more than any of its allies and partners the GDR plays the role of "giver" rather than "taker."

Beyond that, however, there is the special status resulting from what used to be called interzonal trade but is now, in deference to East German sensibilities, politely referred to as "intra-German" trade. The East Germans, in fact, prefer to label it "inter-German" or simply foreign trade. Regardless of what it is called, in 1972 it reached the prodigious value of more than DM 5.3 billion or approximately $2.2 billion, in two-way volume. Since it is treated as domestic German trade, it is free of tariffs or quotas and affords the GDR indirect access to the Common Market.

Inter-German trade is, of course, an anachronism carried over from the period when the Federal Republic insisted there was but one German state and cared little what it might cost to maintain that fiction. It has always given rise to resentment and disgruntlement in both Comecon and the Common Market, and there are members of both who would like to see it abolished. Some Common Market members do not like it that East Germany has special access to the EEC or are envious of West Germany's access to the East German market.

Inter-German trade was always an anomaly and no one made it seem more anomalous than Walter Ulbricht himself, who observed in 1969: "In the bitter struggle between socialism and imperialism there is a growing need for the community of socialist countries to resolve all scientific, technological, and economic problems with their own resources and means."[3] And while interzonal trade continued to flourish, Ulbricht warned the other socialist countries, notably Rumania and Hungary, that "those who aspire to become travelers between two worlds . . . will sooner or later become dependent on the world of monopolies and banks." But in Comecon it was hard to find anyone who was doing quite as much traveling between two worlds, and becoming quite as dependent on the world of monopolies and banks, as Walter Ulbricht.

Ulbricht is gone now and his successor, Erich Honecker, contends that instead of convergence "an objective process of delimitation characterizes the relationship between the socialist GDR and the imperialist FRG." But Honecker, it seems, is doing even more traveling than Ulbricht between the two worlds of socialism and imperialism, for inter-German trade is flourishing. Last year's value of 5.3 billion marks represented more than double that of 1965, and by 1975 the total is expected to reach a two-way volume of DM 8 billion.

Every month some 5,000 East German trucks roll westward loaded with sugar and underwear, cameras and hosiery, pork and typewriters, men's suits and refrigerators, toys, television sets, and teddy bears. Able to produce at a lower cost for labor, the GDR supplies West German discount and mail order houses with anonymously labeled goods that can be sold as "German" without consumers' knowing which Germany they came from. Anonymous labeling, in fact, has even enabled the GDR to supply West German supermarkets with bargain-price sparkling wine, which it imports in bulk from such Comecon countries as Hungary, Bulgaria, and Rumania. Many of these "German" goods are subsequently re-exported by the Federal Republic, to the Common Market as well as to third-world countries. Their undisputed quality and the obvious satisfaction of the customers is further indication of the GDR's economic prowess, not to mention its political pragmatism.

When the trucks roll eastward again they are loaded with machine tools, computers, nonferrous metals, rolled steel, and, since the Eighth Congress of the Socialist Unity Party (SED) at which Honecker promised GDR citizens a "marked improvement in the material and cultural conditions of life," shoes, grocery products, textiles, and even beer from Dortmund (which may not be better than, but is at least different from, that brewed in Radeburg).

True, the trucks going east tend to carry more than those going west, but Bonn, eager to maintain the trade as a symbol of the "special relationship" between the two Germanies, has agreed to underwrite the East German trade deficit with an annual credit of up to DM 585 million, interest free. And while the GDR staunchly denies that there is a "special relationship," it cannot deny that West Germany is one of its principal trading partners, and a very special one at that.

CONCERN FOR FREEDOM OF MOVEMENT
AND INFORMATION

While it is difficult under these circumstances to say what really persuasive interests the GDR may still have in seeing the conclusion of a European security and cooperation agreement, it is relatively easy to pinpoint East Germany's concerns and the potential impact of the CSCE on the German Democratic Republic. They are all to be found in "basket three"--that is, in the area of freedom of movement and a free flow of ideas and information.

In this respect East Germany's is indeed a special case, for no East European country, with the exception of the Soviet Union itself, has such tightly sealed borders and such restrictive exit and emigration policies as the GDR. On the other hand, no other East European country is as exposed to what it would consider pernicious influences from the West.

The reasons for this, of course, are historical and are to be found in the postwar division of Germany. There was, first of all, the postwar exodus, which by 1961, when the Berlin Wall was built, had resulted in the departure of an estimated 3.5 million people. The wall and the tightening of the zonal borders were designed to halt this emigration, and for all practical purposes they did. The flow, though it has increased lately as a consequence of the agreements between the two Germanies and relaxed surveillance on the transit roads between West Germany and West Berlin, has been reduced to a trickle. Until the end of 1972 the annual average number of escapees and refugees was approximately 5,000. The wall did more, of course, than merely halt the refugee flow. It consolidated the East German state and contributed immeasurably to making it the economic power it is today. And as living conditions in the GDR improved, East Germany's citizens became less anxious to escape.

True, there are many who, like one acquaintance of mine, entertained no thoughts of leaving or escaping until the wall was built and the border sealed. Only then did they want to leave because, as he told me, "You do not know what it means to be fenced in, to be denied the right to travel." He would walk to the West barefoot, he said on one occasion. But what if the wall were to come down? "Oh then, he replied, "I would prefer to remain here. I make an excellent living and I think I am better off than I would be in the Federal Republic. My only complaint is this arbitrary restricting of my movements, which makes me feel as if I were in prison, as if my government did not trust me." But the vast majority of East Germans are more or less content and no longer entertain thoughts of leaving, and their number increases with each year that conditions improve and the generational balance in the population shifts.

It would seem that the regime ought to be able to afford to open its borders and abolish its restrictive exit policies by the middle of this decade. The likelihood that it will do so, however, is slight, for the memory of the mass exodus of the 1950s is too vivid in the minds of the present leadership. Even after 25 years in power the regime does not appear to trust the people or to have necessary confidence in its own accomplishments. Its fears are strengthened by the increase in escapes and defections since the relaxation of travel regulations (especially between the Federal Republic and West Berlin) that have been in effect since the signing of the FRG-GDR treaties and the four-power agreement on Berlin. Thus the wall remains. And as long as the wall is there, East Germany will remain particularly susceptible to the sort of pressures and demands for freer movement that are contained in "basket three" of the European security talks.

But the wall is merely one side of the coin, for despite the fact that the GDR is physically the most sealed-off country in Eastern Europe, it also enjoys more contacts with the West and more exposure to Western influences than any other. One need merely consider the family ties between East and West Germans to appreciate this. Statistics for East Germany, unfortunately, are not available; according to West German government sources, however, nearly 20 percent of West Germans and West Berliners, or approximately 12 million persons, still have blood relations in the GDR. They not only write to each other--and, more recently, telephone each other--but since the treaty package they again visit each other.

The movement is primarily west to east, but it is considerable. Between the signing of the basic treaty in December 1972 and 30 August 1973, a period of eight months, more than 7 million West Germans and West Berliners paid visits to East Germany. Many are one-day affairs made possible by the addition of 15 road and 7 rail crossing points on the border and the new regulations that allow residents of counties close and adjacent to the border to enter the other Germany for 24-hour periods for up to a total of 30 days a year. Theoretically, this new regulation applies to both West and East Germans, though in practice it is primarily West Germans who have been permitted to make use of it and to visit relatives on the other side. A similar agreement now exists in Berlin. However, there has been a pronounced increase in West German tourism in the GDR since the basic treaty was signed. In one direction, at any rate, the East German border and the Berlin Wall have become more permeable than ever before.

But there is yet another factor to consider: the impact of West German broadcasting, especially television, on the GDR. West Germany's First Program, telecast from transmitters near the border and from West Berlin, can be viewed by 80 percent of the East German population. The signal is received clearly in all but the southeastern corner of the GDR.

As the novelist Stefan Heym,* a former U.S. Army officer and American citizen now living in the GDR, put it in a recent article in The Guardian (7 July 1973):

---

*Heym is a Marxist by conviction. In trouble in the United States during the McCarthy era and disgusted by the direction U.S. policy was taking, he opted for life in his native (East) Germany, which he had fled when Hitler came

Much has been written about the difficulty of
crossing the Wall; but any electron jumps it
with ease. . . . Today the brand names and ad-
vertising slogans of certain West German products
have become household words in the East as well;
films shown by Western television are matters of
public discussion on East German trains and
streetcars; and Neues Deutschland has been known
to print polemics on subjects it never bothered
to report: the editors subconsciously assumed
that their readers would be familiar with the
story.

Heym attempted, somewhat sarcastically, to describe
the potential impact of the new freedom of movement in his
Guardian article. There are observations in it that apply
not only to East Germany but to Eastern Europe as a whole,
which deserve repetition here.

. . . With every new embassy bringing in its crew
of attachés, with every new group of Western visitors poking their noses through Checkpoint Char-
lie, with every new batch of West German second
cousins overwhelming their East German relatives
with their loving presence, this quiet, pleasant,
well-protected preserve named the German Democratic Republic is rapidly changing into a meeting
place of East and West.

Heym sees the "new opening" as the price the GDR must
pay for international recognition. Ideologists discomfited
by the influx of new ideas have attempted to counteract
the dangers with a policy of Abgrenzung (delimitation),
which is designed to "safeguard the republic from corrupt-
ing influences and subversion." Delimitation, he says, is
the consequence of the basic treaty between the two German

---

to power. After a brief period of glory in the early 1950s,
he soon found the official East German mind closed to his
provocative and independent ideas. Except for a brief
collection of his short stories, he found himself essentially unpublished in his own chosen country, though he had
no difficulty getting into print in the West with his icon-
oclastic views. He was severely censured by Honecker at a
Central Committee plenum in 1965, but recently an East German edition of his King David Report appeared.

states, which has propelled East Germany out of its isolation from the Western world. Previously it had been treated
as a pariah.

> In the media, in conferences, lectures, [and] semi-
> nars, people are being prepared for the arguments
> they will get to hear and the temptations they
> will have to resist; some categories of citizens
> are entirely forbidden to have contact with West-
> erners; others are warned to report to their near-
> est superior the gist of their talks with foreign-
> ers and any suspicious questions.

Heym contends that there are men and forces at work in the
GDR who "realize that a creative, modern approach to the
new problems is needed if the [GDR] is successfully to face
the new challenge. These men, while staying in close liaison with their opposite numbers in the Soviet Union, have
started ever so gently to turn the wheel." He maintains
that they have made changes in the economic as well as the
cultural field.
     "Mainly," he says, "these men seem to want to take a
more courageous stance in place of the sterile defensive
posture that was habitual with the anxiety-ridden political
sclerotics." He sees the "new opening" as potentially advantageous to socialism, as a means of showing the world
what the GDR has accomplished under it. "Have we nothing
to show the world for the years of devoted effort?" he asks.
"Have we no suggestions to offer on the marketplace newly
thrown open to us?" It may be difficult for "anxiety-ridden political sclerotics" who are unaccustomed to dealing
with any new thought except "by censor and police" to
grasp the idea that an opening works both ways.
     But, says Heym, "it would appear that time and circum-
stances were never more favorable to that kind of initiative. Interest in Marxist theory has revived in many places
and there is a great curiosity about socialist practice,
of which the GDR's is an important variant." According to
Heym, those men in the GDR who are trying to cure it of
its introversion are aware of the new opportunities. And,
he contends, "they also know the requirements for a successful breakthrough: subordination of the bureaucracy to the
needs of the citizen, and making the citizen's life more
rewarding morally and more stimulating intellectually."
Should they succeed, he says, they would give the GDR
"an image with a sparkle to it--the image of an enlightened
socialism."

"The people are there with whom to do the job," says Heym, "in spite of a not inconsiderable behind-the-scenes opposition of diehards with a vested interest in 'business-as-usual.' . . . If the challenge is met, the GDR may well come to take a leading part in European affairs and may influence, by its socialist example, developments in West Germany and elsewhere."

One would like to believe that Stefan Heym is right, but I cannot share his optimism, for everything indicates that the "diehards with a vested interest in 'business-as-usual'" are the ones who are turning the wheel, and not very gently at that.

Abgrenzung is a policy of ideological hatch-tightening that the East German regime has been practicing vigorously since relations between Bonn and East Berlin first came into flux. It takes a variety of forms. For example, to counter Willy Brandt's concept of "two German states within one German nation" and the West German concept that a "special relationship" will keep alive at least the idea of German unity, the GDR has embarked on a systematic policy of "de-Germanization." East German government and party officials consistently refer to their country only as "the republic," and painstakingly avoid calling it Germany or the German Democratic Republic. In fact, the terms "German" or "Germany" have been dropped wherever possible. The GDR's principal network, Radio Germany, has been renamed Voice of the GDR, and the Association of German Journalists is now known as the "Association of Journalists of the GDR." Postwar 10-pfennig pieces have been recalled and declared no longer legal tender because they have the word "Deutschland" on them. The old pan-German nationality sign on motor vehicles, a "D" in an oval, has been dropped by East Germany to be replaced by the letters "DDR." The idea seems to be that by simply using the initials GDR references to German and Germany can be avoided. One widely told joke had it that Honecker would, if he could, also have dropped the "G" from GDR and enrolled in the United Nations as simply the "Democratic Republic." Even the national anthem is no longer being sung, merely played or hummed, because there is a passage in it that refers to "Germany, our united fatherland." Indeed, the question being asked in East Berlin in the fall of 1973 was when the name of the official party newspaper, Neues Deutschland, would be changed.

For the ideologists of East Germany the "German question has been solved" and a "German nation" unifying the peoples of both postwar German states does not exist. As

Hermann Axen, a GDR Politburo member and Central Committee secretary, phrased it:

> In the arsenal of imperialism, nationalism in a
> somewhat refined form is occupying an ever greater
> place. Its newest variation is the claim launched
> by certain circles that "the German question has
> been left open" by the basic treaty between the
> GDR and the FRG. This is, of course, an attempt
> to mislead public opinion. The so-called German
> question has been solved once and for all accord-
> ing to the principles of international law. Every-
> thing that needed to be settled has been settled
> unequivocally and definitively by many interna-
> tional treaties, including the Basic Treaty. As
> a result, there is no "German question." Rather,
> there exist two sovereign, socially diametrically
> opposed, mutually independent German states and
> nations.[4]

Kurt Hager, also a Politburo member and Central Committee secretary and the SED's chief ideologist, insists
that the East German nation is "a new type of nation, a
socialist nation. [It] stands in unbridgeable contradiction to the old capitalist nation which continues to exist
in the FRG."[5]

There are other signs that, far from wanting to loosen
the reins, the East German leaders are pulling tighter.
They have mounted a massive campaign against "social democ-
ratism," which they equate with "bourgeois ideologies."
In fact, the SED's ideologists contend that "social democracy's unqualified 'yes' concerning the chances of imperialism's survival conforms to social democracy's 'no' to
socialism." There is a certain logic to the GDR's massive
ideological campaign against social democracy, of course.
That part of Germany that is now the GDR was traditionally
social democratic; in fact, it was one of the main power
bases of German social democracy. The East German social
democrats, as a party, ceased to exist when they melded
with the communists in 1946 to form the Socialist Unity
Party. But there are enough old social democratic war
horses around, two of them, it must be stressed, in the
SED Politburo, and enough young SED members who are dis-
gruntled with the party's ossification and inflexibility
and to whom social democracy or a "third road" to socialism
seems very alluring. The allure is personified by West
European social democratic leaders like Willy Brandt, Austria's Bruno Kreisky, and Sweden's Olaf Palme.

Underscoring the SED's official attitude toward such heretical currents Herbert Haeber, an East German social scientist, wrote in Neues Deutschland on 10 November 1972:

> As far as we are concerned, we are aware that socialism and imperialism, socialist and bourgeois ideology, are irreconcilable. In struggling to achieve peaceful coexistence we are always guided by the realization that we are establishing normal relations on the basis of international law between states of opposite social orders.

The SED's difficult ideological position in the light of the détente between East and West Germany and, in a larger sense, between East and West in general, became embarrassingly apparent to the rest of the world in November 1972, when the SED Politburo passed a 15-point resolution[6] on the tasks and duties of party agitation and propaganda. The primary task of agitation, according to the resolution, was "to develop people into socialist personalities," and, according to the resolution's preamble, the basic aim of propaganda and agitation is to instill "the revolutionary ideas of Marxism-Leninism, to demonstrate to the working people and the working class the fact that our ideas are being accepted in the world, to educate them in the spirit of communist ideals, to mobilize them for the implementation of party decisions, and to enable them to struggle even better against the policy and ideology of imperialism."

Having stressed that there can be no "ideological coexistence" and that socialist and bourgeois ideologies are "irreconcilable," the resolution went on to state:

> In view of the advance the policy of peaceful coexistence has made among states of different social orders and in view of the concomitant intensification of ideological confrontation, in view of the mass contacts of human beings of opposite ideologies and ways of living, the greatest degree of class awareness and activity are mandatory.

To make sure that these "mass contacts of human beings" are kept to a minimum the SED then issued a decree formally barring at least two million of its adult citizens --all those judged to be "holders of secrets or enjoying great trust"--from having any sort of contact with Western visitors. The category includes government officials at the ministerial level, party workers, trade union officials, and members of the armed forces and of the police.

Stefan Heym insists that there is a school of thought in the GDR "which would prefer to have a less narrow understanding of the concept of delimitation." These men, he says, feel that the country is in for a "protracted period of coexistence with the other German state and with the rest of the Western world," and that this requires a reappraisal of worn-out, traditional attitudes. "They see delimitation," says Heym, "not as a series of 'Off Limits' signs and police ordinances . . . but as a policy of maintaining safe and sane, no-nonsense Marxist guidelines while keeping an open mind."[7]

To judge from developments thus far, however, they appear to be an ineffectual minority. And as the GDR, flexing the muscles of its newly recognized sovereignty and prestige, moves into the protracted negotiations over European security and cooperation, the voices of these men seem to become increasingly inaudible.

NOTES

1. The New York Times, 2 December 1969.
2. Neues Deutschland, East Berlin, 5 December 1969.
3. Wirtschaft, East Berlin, 27 February 1969.
4. Horizont, no. 12 (East Berlin, 1973).
5. Neues Deutschland, 16 March 1973.
6. Published in Neues Deutschland, 11 November 1972.
7. The Guardian, London, 7 July 1973.

6

FOREIGN POLICY PERSPECTIVES AND EUROPEAN SECURITY: POLAND AND CZECHOSLOVAKIA

Robert W. Dean

This chapter examines the foreign policies of Poland and Czechoslovakia as they have evolved in response to broader international changes associated with East-West détente and domestic circumstances. As a result of their former enemy status vis-à-vis Germany both countries occupied forward positions in any advance toward European détente. The magnitude and legacy of their wartime catastrophes notwithstanding, a resolution of fundamental disputes with the Federal Republic of Germany was an integral part of any reordering of international relations in Europe, and the sine qua non of enhanced security for both. The problematic status of the Polish western territories and the politico-legal ambiguity of the 1938 Munich Agreement were indisputable sources of tension and uncertainty in Central Europe, which, although with time they had acquired a more academic character, remained the touchstone of relations with West Germany and stymied broader efforts toward normalization. Poland and Czechoslovakia, by their bilateral treaties that clarified these disputes on the basis of the existing status quo, have taken a decisive step away from the tension-ridden past and toward a future that envisages normalization with the FRG and makes possible the growth of bilateral ties with other Western states.

In both cases this initial phase of reconciliation has demonstrated the difficulties that are likely to accompany efforts toward further normalization and the expansion of ties. The incubus of the past has been removed, but this success, welcome as it ultimately was to all sides, released a host of secondary political, economic, and cultural issues, which in the end will comprise the fabric of détente. If the new period of diplomatic interest is governed by the same spirit of reconciliation that made the initial treaties possible, then forward movement is likely to remain a palpable feature of European détente.

That secondary bilateral issues have come to the fore in this way means that national foreign policy has ipso facto taken on a new significance. It would be mistaken to exaggerate the importance of this for the Warsaw Pact states, but it is nevertheless true that progress in détente includes not only multilateral understanding in MFR or CSCE negotiations but also the sum total of bilateral East-West accords. To some extent both Poland and Czechoslovakia, as members of the Warsaw Pact, must now go their separate ways together, to put it paradoxically.

Both countries have faced national upheavals within recent memory, albeit of a different nature. And it is the response to domestic trauma that has conditioned the development of their foreign policies. In Czechoslovakia until recently the hallmarks of foreign policy have been an exaggerated sense of caution, amounting almost to paralysis, in undertaking major initiatives in international relations. In Poland, the dust had hardly settled after the 1970 crisis and change of leadership when an active, outward-looking foreign policy was established. The contrast between the two countries thus far serves to underline the diversity of interest and approach to the general question of European security.

POLAND

Edward Gierek rose to power in December 1970 on a wave of violent popular upheaval. The workers' rebellion in the Baltic port cities was the ultimate product of years of an austere and makeshift economic policy, which promised a more abundant but increasingly distant future in exchange for what had come to be seen as an unending period of material sacrifice and deprivation. The new first secretary of the Polish United Workers' Party, long recognized for his pragmatic emphasis on efficiency and economic growth, has set in motion a series of measures that have generated a new material well-being for broad strata of the population. If Gierek's domestic policies have made important departures from those of his predecessor, Wladislaw Gomulka, the significant changes in foreign policy under his tenure have kept pace, and policy toward the West in particular has assumed a new sense of movement. This is the result of three interrelated factors.

119

First, the December 1970 Warsaw treaty with West Germany and the other agreements that have marked the process of East-West détente have provided Poland with a new maneuverability in foreign affairs. The country is less locked into position vis-à-vis the West, inasmuch as the earlier threats to its basic political-territorial claims, and the consequent need for strong reliance on the USSR for their protection, have largely disappeared. Article 1 of the bilateral treaty with the FRG states that the Oder-Neisse line forms Poland's western border and affirms its inviolability, pledges mutual respect for territorial integrity, and states that neither side maintains territorial claims against the other.

Second, foreign policy has been partially reconstructed to serve the needs of an ambitious program of domestic economic development. The financial and technological means of achieving economic modernization are to be found largely in the West, a fact that has necessitated revised foreign policy formulations that foresee a broad expansion of economic and political ties with Western states. Foreign policy has become the art of expanding the possible.

Third, foreign policy has acquired a national, "independent" dimension that postulates a more vigorous and meaningful role for the Polish state not only in East-West relations but within the Soviet community as well. This is in fact the counterpart of Gierek's domestic vision of "another Poland" wherein economic progress is to effect a metamorphosis of the entire profile of the nation. In foreign affairs it has meant expanding the country's purview to address issues of particular interest. Poland's leading role in formulating a Baltic Convention that limits the multilateral use of resources and provides for the environmental protection of that sea is an example. Here and elsewhere new directions in foreign policy seem fully consonant with the interests and policies of its dominant Soviet ally. And avoiding antagonisms in this regard remains the cardinal guideline for Warsaw.

The salient points on Poland's expanded horizons in the West have included Gierek's journeys to France in the fall of 1972 and to Belgium one year later, Premier Piotr Jaroszewicz's trip to Sweden in October 1972, and the numerous visits of Foreign Minister Stefan Olszowski to Western Europe. This invigorated diplomacy followed an initial period of consolidation after Gierek's assumption of power, in which an understandable emphasis was placed on Poland's relations with its Warsaw Pact allies. If its mainsprings are to be found in the accelerated pace of East-West con-

tacts in general, the scale of Polish activity exceeds
that of its socialist allies and sets it apart from them,
with the two exceptions of Rumania and the USSR.

Much of Polish diplomacy has centered on encouraging
support in the West for the projected Conference on Security
and Cooperation in Europe. Through the CSCE Warsaw hopes
to achieve the multilateral ratification and guarantee of
its political-territorial integrity as contained in the
bilateral treaty with the FRG. The new credence given the
European status quo as a result of this and other East-West
agreements suggests that Poland's view of its own security
has moved from the narrower focus of obtaining recognition
and defense of the Oder-Neisse line to broader, more comprehensive considerations of security. As suggested earlier, it has provided Warsaw with an expanding license for
the elaboration of economic relations with Western states
that are vital to plans for the nation's rapid economic
modernization.

Any discussion of the general problem of Polish security must stress Warsaw's conformity to the standard formulations and approach of the common bloc position vis-à-
vis European security, a pattern evident as actual negotiations got under way in Helsinki in the summer of 1973.
This essay suggests, however, that conformity shows only
one side of Polish political reality and that the motive
forces behind the Polish approach to and interest in European security are powered by more specifically national factors.

Domestic Discussion: A New Role
for Poland, East and West?

In the summer of 1970 a highly unusual exchange of
opinions appeared in the Warsaw daily Zycie Warszawy and
other important periodicals, whose leading pundits addressed
the question of the nation's role within the communist system and within Europe as a whole. This burst of introspec-
tion revealed a fundamental concern in an important segment
of the country's opinion-making intellectual elite over
the lack of national direction and sense of purpose, a national identity crisis that surely had broader social roots.
In focusing critically on the importance of national leadership, the discussion unknowingly anticipated Gomulka's
downfall. What is more relevant from the present point of
view, however, is that its stimulus was in large part recognition of the change that was taking place in interna-

tional relations in Europe and between the two superpowers. The rules of the game that had defined and limited Poland's international behavior for some 25 years were being transformed. The new era of détente would bring with it, as one scholar put it, "a shifting of forces within the blocs."[1] Within this more dynamic international setting, the Polish definition of national interest and the problem of national self-assertion on its behalf would gain a new importance. Indeed, it was candidly acknowledged that the lessening of tension would have a differentiating effect on all the states of the Warsaw Pact. General acceptance of the European political-territorial status quo had caused the overriding identity of interests to recede: "Differences are emerging among our states, arising from the different levels from which they began to build socialism, different traditions, and different historical experiences. Political and economic interests are not completely identical."[2] The discussion suggested that a process of national adaptation had begun in a changed international environment in which Polish aspirations to assume a more assertive international role, one proportional to its size and development potential, would be determined by the country's internal economic strength and political stability.

This attention to differences in national interests was not seen as foreshadowing antagonistic trends. It was clear that most participants in the discussion recognized a community of interests within the Soviet sphere that, with the political-territorial status quo ratified, would continue to generate cohesive pressures. Nevertheless, the opinion came through strongly that in the more differentiated milieu the onus of securing and extending national interests would fall on Polish shoulders, and here it was the country's internal performance that would have the determining effect in limiting or enhancing its international role in both East and West. A picture of the Warsaw Pact emerged in which Poland would not find its interests satisfactorily assured as a matter of course by the Soviet Union; the alliance had matured into one of mutual but more competitive interests.

> The future of every state depends on its contribution to some international community, on the role it plays in a group of states, on its economic and military strength, its technical and scientific creativity, its political, intellectual, and artistic activity. . . . [Amidst] rapidly changing international circumstances . . .

the mere fact that we exist guarantees nothing.
Our guarantee lies in the function we perform in
the international system of the political and
economic powers.[3]

It was generally acknowledged that the linkage between
internal factors and external capabilities was nowhere more
important than in economic performance. Here the problem,
in part social, of a sluggish and backward economy had to
be solved. The effectiveness of international economic cooperation as a path to domestic development, above all
within Comecon, would also be determined by Poland's ability to adopt a more assertive international stance. To
align regional economic cooperation more closely with Polish interests and to fend off negative effects of Comecon
and the international division of labor, it was "particularly important," one spokesman noted, "to have a strong
politico-economic position in the socialist bloc."*
Other articles in the series called attention to the
indispensable role of economic cooperation with the West
in modernizing the Polish economy and making it competitive. Said one observer, "Poland's membership in the community of socialist countries does not in itself guarantee
participation in the scientific-technological revolution."[4]
These prophetic contradictions of the official dogma
of optimism preceded the signing of the West German treaty
and the change of leadership in December 1970. Both events
appeared to confirm the prognosis of a changed setting in
the international environment and to encourage such aspirations among a sector of the Polish elite. West Germany's
ratification of the Polish treaty caused one commentator
to speak of "a new historical reality":

Today . . . the independent Polish state lies beyond the reach of direct outside danger. Its per-

---

*"The general line of our foreign policy calls not only
for the maintenance and consolidation of our potential and
our position in the socialist camp, but also for constant
vigilance and flexibility in our policy as the most effective defense of our national interests." (Andrzej Wielow-
ieyski, "Will the Polish Republic Bank on Youth?" Zycie
Warszawy, 25 June 1970. Cf. also Jerzy Bukowski, "For the
Proper Form of Social Discipline," ibid., 19-20 June 1970,
and Mieczyslaw Rakowski, "That Which Will Happen Tomorrow,"
Polityka, no. 14 (Warsaw, April 1970).

sonality, its historical legality, and its territorial and political shape are not only guaranteed by the alliance with the Soviet Union and
other socialist states, but have now finally been
approved by potential adversaries who, only a
short time ago, were far from eager to proffer
such binding declarations. And an independent
Polish state offers a truly unique possibility
for the survival of everything that constitutes
a nation: language, tradition, customs, a culture of its own. . . . We have reached the point
of maximum strategic advantage.[5]

The new guarantees of its national existence represented
by the treaty and the prospect of an emerging equilibrium
in Europe were therefore perceived as a turning point that,
while holding to the pivot of the Soviet alliance, provided
new opportunities for an independent momentum in Polish
foreign policy. "We can pause," to use one metaphor, "wipe
the sweat from our brows, and look around--throughout Eur-
ope--with the feelings of a man who has finished laying the
foundations and can now build the house."[6]

Other voices raised later in the domestic debate
stressed that the turning point of the treaties and the
status quo settlement would oblige Poland to revise its
role in European affairs. One author argued that the break
with the past signaled by the treaty must be accompanied
by a recasting of Poland's stereotyped role in Europe:

One such stereotype would be a conviction that the
present and future position of Poland in Europe
will continue to be determined by the same factors as in 1945. . . . With the coming into force
of the Eastern treaties, we have reached the
practical maximum of political advantage resulting from our [wartime] victory. . . .
    From now on, the position of Poland in Eur-
ope will be determined by the same factors as in
the case of other countries, because our rather
exceptional position during World War II will no
longer find reflection in postwar reality. . . .
    Other necessary factors here are our presence
and active participation in world-wide political
and nonpolitical enterprises. Finally, there are
our general level of cultural development, the
state of our infrastructure and productivity, our
consumption level, our social order, our openness

toward the outside world, our lack of phobias and
obsessions--[we must] reach in all these spheres
the level already attained in the highly developed
European countries.[7]

Thus, he claimed, the significance of European détente is
the new-found possibility that "we can work out for our-
selves a strong position in the world."
    The altered parameters of Polish foreign policy extend
as an equalizing factor to the Soviet bloc as well.

> . . . The alignment of forces in our camp is not
> a perpetuum mobile which was set in motion im-
> mediately after World War II. It requires con-
> stant recharging of energy. There is the need
> to maintain a constant community of interests,
> in which the interests of our partners must also
> be taken into account. The better the position
> we work out for ourselves, the stronger and more
> tenacious will be our alliance with the Soviet
> Union and with the other socialist countries and
> the proportionately greater will be the benefits
> we derive from this cooperation. . . . Current
> political events surely offer a very opportune
> moment for reflecting on these matters. . . .
> [But the treaty with the FRG and the internal
> changes of December 1970] by themselves . . .
> offer no guarantee but merely provide us with
> the chance of occupying a proper place in Europe
> under new conditions.[8]

This seems a clear recognition that the treaties have done
much to mitigate Poland's political debtor status within
the Warsaw Pact and above all vis-à-vis the USSR. Preconditions exist, therefore, for the exertion of greater Polish
influence within the communist community. Far from being
a disequilibrating factor, a more assertive Polish position, presumably in defense of the country's own interests,
will tend to have a congealing effect on the alliance inso-
far as it achieves the greater satisfaction of Polish needs.
Strains will be reduced and intra-alliance ties will become
more genuinely volitional. The argument is carefully framed
on the basis of loyalty to the alliance, but the thrust of
Polish aspirations comes through clearly.
    Another series of articles and commentaries that ap-
peared in 1972 focused on the domestic aspect of Poland's
accomplishments. In their attempts to fathom the public

psyche and explain the national character, they revealed similar frustrations over the nation's failure to achieve a status more commensurate with its size and potential, often focusing on the theme of national self-assertion and its relation to individual and collective self-esteem.[9]

These remarkable public discussions punctuated a media output normally distinguished for its uniformity, and this brief look hardly does justice to their scope or content. But by illustrating recurrent themes it may convey something of their flavor and provide a glimpse of the evident mood of rethinking among an influential segment of Polish society. At the least the existence of such sentiments shows that an important social stratum harbors aspirations for a more active political and economic role for the country in East and West. Both are identifiable features of Gierek's revised foreign policy.

A Retrospect

Within the limits established by Poland's subordinate membership in the Warsaw Pact community and fixed largely by its dominant Soviet ally, Poland has played an active (if sporadic) role in lobbying on behalf of its own security interests. Specifically Polish concerns have had a prominent place in the Warsaw Pact's changing and coordinated "European security" strategy. In the campaign for a multilateral security conference, which it revived in 1964 and earlier, Poland's object has been to obtain recognition of its western border or to counter developments or trends in East or West that could compromise its own political-diplomatic position on the border issue or on the legitimacy of its claim to the former German territories. It is through the prism of the unsettled territorial question that Polish leaders have viewed the policy shifts of their East European allies as well as changes in Western policy that would actually or potentially strengthen West Germany's hand in contesting the issue.

The first such initiative was the Rapacki Plan for a denuclearized zone in Central Europe, introduced in the United Nations General Assembly in the autumn of 1957. "Proceeding from the interests of Polish security and détente in Europe and having coordinated its action with the other member countries of the Warsaw Treaty,"[10] the original Rapacki Plan was intended in large measure to prohibit West German access to nuclear weapons or their emplacement by NATO on FRG territory. Subsequent variations of the

proposal set forth in response to the lack of interest in
the West demonstrated Poland's determination to enhance the
acceptability of its plan. A second variant in November
1958 proposed a simple freeze on nuclear weapons in the
zone as a first stage, to be followed later by their complete elimination. The Polish pursuit of this plan--fully
consonant though it was with Soviet objectives and apart
from its obvious propaganda value--revealed the genuineness
of Warsaw's anxiety. The various plans were stymied by,
among other things, the inability of the Poles to come to
grips with the key problem of inspection.

    Gomulka reiterated the Rapacki Plan in September 1960
at the UN General Assembly session, and in March 1962 a
third variant was submitted by Poland to the 18-nation Permanent Committee in Geneva. In December 1963 the "Gomulka
Plan" expanded the nuclear freeze by calling for nonaggression pacts between NATO and the Warsaw Pact and the "elaboration of a system of measures capable of eliminating the
danger of sudden attack."[11] Concrete talks were suggested
at which the now-related issue of "the normal development
of international economic cooperation" would be discussed.
The Gomulka Plan was conceived to frustrate the implementation of NATO's plans for a multilateral nuclear force (MLF)
and with it the nuclear arming of the Bundeswehr. At the
same time this Soviet-approved plan was indicative of more
than the simple distribution of roles within the Warsaw
Pact. As if to justify its keen interest in European security, Poland's championship of such proposals was explained by noting that its "wartime experiences and proximity to Germany" gave it a "particular interest in the
solution of this problem."

    The sequel to these Polish efforts and their lack of
success was the revived call by Poland, in 1964, for a European security conference (an idea originated by the USSR
in 1954), a project through which Poland hoped to achieve
more multilateral guarantees of its security. The broader
appeal and applicability of this proposal would, it was
hoped, provide a diplomatic platform by means of which Poland and the other Warsaw Pact states could circumvent
West Germany and NATO and press individual appeals in Western capitals. Although Western skepticism prevailed, Warsaw could report by 1966 that its energetic campaign for
European security had borne fruit. In an interview with
Trybuna Ludu,[12] Foreign Minister Rapacki pointed to Denmark
and France as two countries where "a meeting of minds"
existed on European security issues. In this context he
cited a consensus on the prevention of nuclear prolifera-

tion in Europe, recognition of the two sovereign German
states (the "touchstone" of European security), and recognition of existing European borders. Poland's ostensible
diplomatic successes on these issues had yet to be regis-
tered in any concrete agreement.

This was also a period in which the Western policy
pursued by Poland within the framework of "European security" sought to exploit the "contradiction of political interests existing between West European states and the United States,"[13] in particular the visible fissures that had
opened up over American policy in Vietnam. "In the view
of our party," said Gomulka, "the crisis in the policy of
U.S. imperialism in the world and the development of the
European situation open new possibilities for all communist
and workers' parties and all progressive forces in the efforts to achieve relaxation and normalization of relations,
and in the struggle to construct collective security in
Europe."[14] Gomulka's suggestion that West European states
could be drawn into ventures that were not in their national
interests could of course have applied with equal logic to
Poland itself.

Despite Warsaw's engagement in Western diplomacy, Polish foreign policy in this period was essentially one di-
mensional, in that it was concerned with strengthening its
hand among its Eastern allies in defense of its western
border. This was the era of the so-called Iron Triangle,
of strong Polish commitment to the entire political-territorial status quo. After 1965 Poland had abandoned an earlier bilateral flexibility vis-à-vis West Germany in favor
of a more general, multilateral European settlement.
Spurred by the Rumanian defection and possible misgivings
over Soviet intentions, Poland sought to bolster its own
claims by giving equal priority to making common cause with
its allies, above all the GDR.[15]

A landmark speech by Gomulka in May 1969 (in which he
proposed the conclusion of a bilateral treaty with West
Germany in which Bonn would recognize the finality of the
Oder-Neisse border) signaled a revision of Polish priorities. This shift was the result of a change in Soviet policy toward Western Europe that was embodied in the Budapest
Appeal on European Security of March 1969. The proposal
was interpreted by some as anticipating Soviet moves toward
détente, which in their effect might compromise Polish interests.[16] It showed that "an effective Polish foreign
policy has to concentrate on influencing developments in
the West and not simply on defending the frontier of socialism on the Elbe,"[17] an observation as relevant now as when
it was made.

The point to be made in this brief retrospective discussion of Polish foreign policy is that its center of
gravity has been determined by an overriding concern about
the western border. Similarly, the Polish demand for a
European security conference in the past has been ancillary
to the demand for West German recognition of its territorial
integrity. These 25-year-old guiding axioms have now been
realized and, as a result, have lost their preoccupying
hold on Polish perspectives. The CSCE, long viewed as a
vehicle for bringing these narrower Polish security objectives to fruition, has therefore taken on an expanded relevance.

New Priorities: Old Restraints

On 5 December 1970 West German Chancellor Willy Brandt
journeyed to Warsaw to sign the historic treaty that recognized Poland's territorial integrity within its existing
frontiers. This milestone in Polish-West German relations
closed an important chapter in Poland's postwar search for
security. Other related objectives have also fallen into
place, above all the Basic Treaty between the FRG and the
GDR, which provides for the political separateness of the
second German state. The CSCE promises to ratify the agreements already reached on the European status quo. Now
that the bases for Poland's national security have been
provided, the main issue is to translate these gains and
the new circumstances into a greater role for Poland in
Europe. As one writer has phrased it:

> We are faced with a completely new situation in
> which Poland's pro-Russian course is no longer in-
> compatible with other international associations.
> At present the Polish-Soviet alliance is helpful
> to us in expanding relations with other countries.
> . . . Our participation in the Eastern bloc pro-
> vides us with an opportunity to achieve a Polish-
> German reconciliation and to revive ties with our
> traditional friends in the West.[18]

If the treaty with Bonn has succeeded in diminishing
the nation's feeling of psychological and strategic insecurity, it has also altered Warsaw's concept of and approach to national security. In the past the uncertainty
generated by the unsettled border issue dictated that near-
myopic attention be given to maintaining the common Warsaw

Pact approach and to ensuring that the border issue remained
an integral feature of Soviet diplomacy. This accomplished,
Polish planners find themselves in a setting in which a
new, but still realistic, emphasis can be placed on national
interests. The question, therefore, is to what extent the
evolution of a more stable European situation will encourage a shift in Polish priorities.

As suggested above in the discussion of Poland's national objectives and international role, and as reflected
in the activization of Polish foreign policy, the Gierek
leadership's domestic ambitions call for Poland to play an
expanded role in Europe. If this is to be realized--for
example, if the oft-expressed desire to acquire Western
technology and other scientific and economic benefits on a
grand scale is to be fulfilled--the defense and extension
of Polish interests must ·be tended in the West as well as
the East. Moreover, the effectiveness of an invigorated
emphasis on the Western side of this equation will depend
on Poland's strength, vitality, and influence in the East.

It cannot be too strongly emphasized, however, that
the prospects for a more significant international role,
East and West, will be governed in large measure by the
interdependent factors of domestic political stability and
economic progress. The escutcheon of Gierek's leadership
is his ambitious, and thus far successful, blueprint for
the country's economic development and industrial modernization. The party's revised attention to the consumer econ-
omy--inspired by the spontaneous outburst of worker dissatisfaction in December 1970--has already produced significant, tangible benefits for a population grown restive after long years of hardship under Gomulka's policy of com-
pulsory austerity. But while the importance of these economic achievements should not be underestimated, they represent short-term gains and are the direct product of a
massive infusion of loans and credits, primarily from the
Soviet Union (which in 1971 provided a loan of at least
$100 million in convertible currencies, while the Comecon
International Bank for Economic Cooperation granted Warsaw
a special expansion of credits[19]), and of the exploitation
of existing reserves. A headlong policy of investment in
the present five-year plan, for example, accounts for an
80 percent increase in investment outlays over the 1966-70
period; a precipitate expansion of imports from the West
has produced a dangerously large trade deficit.

These high-risk ventures mean that the Gierek leadership has mortgaged the longer-term economic future of the
country. At the same time, they illustrate the intimate

connections among Poland's internal development plans, the
search for the credits and technology on which they depend,
and a successful process of détente that will ensure the
political preconditions for procuring them. One representative opinion ran as follows: " . . . A program of fundamental economic and social transformation . . . a constant, tangible increase in the prosperity of the population, and more complete . . . fulfillment of its material
and cultural needs [is a program that] can only be implemented under conditions of détente and expanding international cooperation.[20] Indeed, the emphasis on the need to
create the requisite institutional basis for this is perhaps the most oft-heard theme in official pronouncements
on the meaning of European security. The corollary is the
clear recognition that Polish foreign policy should serve
the nation's internal development. As _Trybuna Ludu_ phrased
it on 2 November 1973: " . . . The main objective of our
foreign policy is to coshape the conditions of détente and
take maximum advantage of them for the sake of developing
the Polish state and nation."

The Special Importance of the GDR

If new imperatives are evident in Polish policy vis-
à-vis the West they are also to be felt in its ties within
the communist system, above all, thus far, with the GDR.
Gierek has traveled to East Berlin on three occasions since
Gomulka's demise. Far more than courtesy calls, these
visits pointed to a new pattern of diplomacy, cooperation,
and political interests in the "special relationship" between the two northern socialist partners. The third summit meeting took place in June 1973. Emphasizing its uncommon importance, _Trybuna Ludu_ commented on 21 June 1973:
"In terms of the splendor and accompanying atmosphere accorded to Edward Gierek and the Polish delegation [the
visit] can only be compared with [the recent one] of Brezhnev to Berlin; there is nothing strange in this, since,
next to the Soviet Union, Poland is the most important ally,
and an increasingly important economic partner, of the
GDR."

The new importance of the Polish-GDR alliance found
more concrete expression in a joint document entitled "Consolidating the Friendship and Deepening the Relations Between the Polish People's Republic and the German Democratic
Republic." This charter of mutual interests and intentions,
termed by Gierek "the third important document [in the his-

tory] of our mutual relations" (after the Zgorzelec Treaty
of 1950, in which the GDR recognized the Oder-Neisse boundary, and the alliance treaty of 1967), was all the more
striking because no similar document existed between other
Warsaw Pact states. The declaration set down the broad
principles that would guide the expansion and deepening of
ties and stressed the importance each country attached to
support of the other's international position. In this connection, albeit implicitly, one passage of particular importance stressed the "strict and consistent implementation" of bilateral agreements concluded with the Federal
Republic of Germany, which acknowledged existing borders
and guaranteed territorial integrity, and of the four-power
agreement on Berlin, which codified the city's status, and
pledged that both states would act to "firmly counteract
any possible attempts to undermine the existing political
and territorial realities in Europe."[21] This revealed the
joint conviction that a common position is as important in
maintaining the status quo as it was in achieving its recognition. As Gierek himself commented, "there exists between our countries a coincidence of interests and a political interdependence."

These agreements seemed clearly to reflect the relatively greater incentives with which Warsaw and East Berlin
approach their bilateral ties, in comparison with the total
matrix of links within the Warsaw Pact community. Closer
bilateral ties are something the USSR can only welcome,
since unity between the GDR and Poland, given traditional
differences and historical antagonisms, is one very important key to unity in the entire bloc. But the will to
tighten relations probably also reflects perceptions of national interest in a period when the dynamic of Russia's
Westpolitik has engendered a somewhat more fluid international setting. In obvious pursuit of its specific interests, the Soviet Union has set an example for its allies
with regard to the extension and protection of national interests. Such considerations have contributed to the new
vitality in Poland's foreign policy vis-à-vis both East
and West.

If a dominant consideration in international policy
for both Poland and the GDR prior to the codification of
the European status quo was maintenance of the undiluted
support of the USSR, and one another, for this objective,
the policy imperative now is the elaboration of a pattern
of ties that will underwrite these gains. To the extent
that the strength of either's future diplomatic position
toward Bonn depends upon uncompromising support for the

other's interests and goals, this results naturally in a
drive to expand the platform of genuinely common interests
wherever possible. This is of course only one factor among
many, but it is an important one that serves to impose a
distinguishing character of Polish-GDR ties, in contrast
to those between some other allied states. It lends a
natural and additional impetus to relations in the political, economic, and ideological spheres and--if a sincere
will to overcome the remnants of popular resentments exists
--in promoting tourism and travel as well.

Poland's Place in Europe:
A New Balance?

Until the treaty with West Germany the bifurcation of
Europe was a necessary, if not altogether desirable, factor
in maintaining the bifurcation of Germany--a principal guarantee of Polish security. With the division of Germany now
formalized, Poland has shown a keen interest in ending the
schism of Europe as a means of legitimizing the pursuit of
its interests and objectives in the West, and of creating
the conditions that will induce and condone such a course.
The Polish concept of security foresees a "Europeanization
of Europe" with the CSCE as its main agent.[22] This is far
more than a propaganda ploy designed to hasten the expulsion of the United States from Europe (although there are
undertones of this); it might also be understood as a eu-
phemism for the "Europeanization of Poland." In the words
of one well-known Polish commentator, "We desire to continue
along the road of cooperation with all European nations,
and will do so regardless of their sociopolitical systems,
because we are an integral part of Europe, and anything
that happens there is of concern to us."[23]
A healthy sense of proportion is exhibited in much of
this opinion, which acts as a corrective to any tendency
to exaggerate possible changes in Polish foreign policy:

> We nod our heads with compassion when we hear bab-
> blers proclaim that we have been called to act as
> a center, a main cog, in Central European construc-
> tion, with branches East and West; these are fairy
> tales. . . . We have earned the right to partici-
> pate in politics, especially European politics,
> whose results lead to an economic and cultural
> rapprochement among the nations. . . . This is ob-
> viously our policy, and it is nonsense to imply

that anyone is playing the role of a go-between
in this area. . . . We start from the tenet that
the major powers in this world possess enough
megatons to involve everyone [in a holocaust],
yet--without the participation of small and medium-sized states--they cannot cope with the
task of straightening out all the world's problems and turning toward constructive cooperation.[24]

In another commentary this sense of independent
achievement as a result of the West German treaty and aspirations for a greater role are carefully tempered:

We do not overestimate our own, Polish, possibilities. Realistic foreign policy is one of the
positive and durable achievements of the Polish
revolution. We have both feet on the ground.
But we are not inclined to underestimate the importance of Poland in the world, or what we can
accomplish in the international arena, in keeping with the sane, patriotic aspirations of the
Polish nation.[25]

The course of Polish foreign policy in the post-Stalin
era has been shaped basically by two complementary factors:
the limits established by Poland's subordinate place in
the Warsaw Pact community, and the consistent, essentially
Polish, initiatives designed to extend and secure national
interests within the permissible framework. There can be
little doubt that these will remain the axes of Poland's
foreign policy. The challenge now is the less one-sided
pursuit of Polish interests.
The European balance that will encourage such a situation is, in Polish thinking, to be calculated on the basis
of states rather than the existence of blocs.[26] This means,
above all, overcoming the restraints of a European system
that perpetuates the existence of two antagonistic blocs.
As one politician put it recently in discussing Poland's
role and interests in European security, "the idea of the
reintegration of Europe is finding a very favorable climate."[27] The logic of the Polish position is that many
appear to see the nation's security, in a broader sense,
in a new balance of East-West interests and influence.
Furthermore, if a new European equilibrium is to emerge
based less on force and the paralytic tension of antagonistic positions, the country, in the eyes of one of its lead-

ing spokesmen, will have a key role to play as a "stabilizing element in Europe" because of its "unique" position in
the Warsaw Pact alliance: "Thanks to our geographical location, to our economic and military strength, we represent
the second most powerful nation in the socialist camp."[28]
The most effective outlet for Poland's stabilizing influence
would be found in an expanding network of bilateral ties in
which the accretion of mutual interests would serve as a
stabilizing factor in European politics. It should be
clear that this attitude is one that marries "European security" and Polish national interests, or in which the pursuit of "European security" is the framework for realizing
Polish national interests, including the development of
ties with the West.

At all events, an expanded role for Poland makes necessary a critical appraisal of any moves in the West (and
in the East as well) that might negatively affect Poland's
ability to play this expanded role. The criticism that
arises most frequently concerns West European integration
and the EEC, whose further development Poland fears could
result in "an amputated Europe."[29] Poland's opposition to
a stronger West European community is fully in keeping with
the Soviet position, of course, but the motivation differs
somewhat. For the Soviets an integrated Western Europe
complicates the exercise of political influence in that
area; for Poland a closely integrated Western Europe threat-
ens relegation to a permanent position on its periphery.
The stronger the sinews of West European integration, the
more difficult it becomes for Poland to play an "independent" role, both politically and economically, in Europe.
Moreover, in some Polish eyes West European integration
strengthens the system of blocs by increasing similar pressures in the East as the result of the closing of alternative paths in the West or by making them less economic.[30]
In addition, in the critical language used in one Polish
view of community building in Western Europe, "the tendency
to develop an economic integration into a political and
military bloc [is inherent]."[31] One Polish answer to these
undesirable developments is a vague notion of "integration
on a higher level," or "second-generation integration," by
which is probably meant East-West integration.[32]

This general sketch of Polish attitudes sheds light
on Poland's interest in developing its ties with France--
relations that have been emphasized for a number of reasons.
First, France has favored a looser model of West European
cooperation, while West Germany has stressed the importance
of supranational authority and closer integration up to and

including the limiting of national sovereignty.[33] Second,
a Western Europe in which France plays a strong national
role would provide a counterweight to West German influence
in a more closely knit West European community.[34] This is
of great significance, since in the Polish view the West
German-Polish relationship (and the exogeneous factors that
impinge upon it) are of central importance for the European
balance and for the security of the continent.[35] In these
ways, therefore, French attitudes implicitly support Polish
interests and should be encouraged. This does not mean
that Poland has refused to accept the reality of West European integration but only that Warsaw seeks to influence
its development in a way that will forestall any further
dichotomization of Europe.*

CZECHOSLOVAKIA

Of all the East European states it is Czechoslovakia
that has most slowly fallen into step with the Soviet policy
of détente. The treaty normalizing relations with West
Germany was signed in Prague by the German chancellor on
11 December 1973. The initialing of it the previous June
followed an impasse of more than two years during which a
series of exploratory meetings between Czechoslovak and
West German representatives failed to establish sufficient
common ground to begin actual negotiations. From the outset Prague's condition for reconciliation was West German
recognition of "the invalidity of the Munich Agreement ab
initio with all the resulting consequences," a formulation
included (literally) in the CSSR's May 1970 bilateral
treaty of friendship with the Soviet Union. Bonn declared
its willingness to recognize the Munich pact as unjust and
immoral from the beginning and as no longer valid, but the
Husak leadership remained implacable, except that in mid-
1971 the phrase "with all the resulting consequences" disappeared from the official formulation. Subsequent contacts
demonstrated that the substance of the Czechoslovak position remained the same.

---

*As Polish Foreign Minister Stefan Olszowski put it in
a speech to the Austrian Society for Foreign Policy in
Vienna (14 June 1972): "We are not against integration, but
we are against certain EEC policies as well as those dicta
on the development of integration which lead to the deepening of separation in Europe." See also Bernard Margueritte
in Le Monde, Paris, 16 June 1972.

Here the matter rested until November 1972, when a deliberate ambiguity became noticeable in the Czechoslovak stance--or rather, at first, in the Soviet interpretation of the Czechoslovak stance. An otherwise routine communiqué issued at the end of a visit to Moscow by Bulgarian party leader Todor Zhivkov failed to mention the familiar ab initio demand. In a standard reference to the significance and desirability of West German-Czechoslovak reconciliation in the framework of European détente, the document spoke only of the necessary invalidation of the Munich Agreement. Three days later a similar formulation appeared in an article in the leading Soviet government newspaper, Izvestia, followed by more statements of the same cast by Czechoslovak party leader Gustav Husak and Foreign Minister Bohuslav Chnoupek, as well as other Warsaw Pact leaders. The conspicuous disappearance of the scrupulously adhered to previous ab initio formula (apparently under the pressure of the USSR and other East European states) led Western observers to predict that agreement would be reached in the foreseeable future.

The treaty, which, according to its preamble, states that both sides are "determined to put an end once and for all to the disastrous past in their relations," is the counterpart of Bonn's earlier treaties with the USSR and Poland. It stipulates in its most important passage that both parties regard the "Munich Agreement as void with regard to their mutual relations." This, and its accompanying formulations, eliminated the 1938 Nazi pact as a primary factor in and obstacle to bilateral relations, which can now be based not on the rather artificial legacy of the past but on more immediate concerns.

The impression conveyed by the final document is more of political reconciliation than of legal precision. Bonn proffered a political and moral condemnation of Munich, but its retroactive abrogation avoided the question of when it became invalid. In the midst of this intentional ambiguity it is clear only that invalidity commenced sometime after the inception of the agreement. These points are little more than legal curiosities, however, inasmuch as the real sense of the new treaty is, as noted by West German Foreign Minister Walter Scheel, that the Munich pact is regarded as null with regard to present relations.

Article 2 of the Bonn-Prague accord acknowledges the validity of laws promulgated under the German administration of Czechoslovak territory, that is, between 29 September 1938 and the Nazi surrender on 9 May 1945. An accompanying letter contained Czechoslovak assurances that the statute of limitations on offenses committed before 1945 expired in 1965, unless they were subject to the death penalty or were crimes against humanity. Thus the agreement preserves legal acts affecting the Sudeten Germans expelled in 1945 who are now residents of the Federal Republic, including those concerning citizenship, and precludes prosecution of such individuals. Both the treaty and its ancillary provisions are to apply to West Berlin.* The remainder of the agreement followed the pattern of Bonn's other Eastern treaties, including a pledge to refrain from the threat or use of force and expressions of respect for the inviolability of borders and territorial integrity and the mutual desire to expand "good-neighborly cooperation" in economic, scientific, and cultural relations.

In many ways the document is a tacit agreement to disagree, and its ambiguity provides the basis for varying interpretations of related issues. Article 2, for example, states that the treaty and accompanying statements do not create legal basis for any material claims by Czechoslovakia or its citizens. Czechoslovak spokesmen, however, subsequently noted that the question of reparations or financial claims remained to be solved in the course of normalization. This provoked an immediate West German rejoinder that the whole question of demands for reparations could only be clarified in multilateral negotiations about a German peace treaty. In another interesting contrast of opinion, the party daily Rude Pravo found the "main political and legal significance of recognition of the nullity of the Munich Agreement . . . in the fact that it confirms that the Czechoslovak border territories torn away by force had never legally belonged to the German Reich," thus reiterating Prague's consistent postwar formulation of the legal-territorial continuity of the Czechoslovak state. In letting stand the corpus of Nazi laws, however, the treaty implicitly acknowledges Germany's de jure hegemony. These

---

*The problem of West Berlin proved less manageable than foreseen at the June initialing. A dispute developed that did not concern the treaty directly but rather the right of Bonn's embassy in Prague (which would be established as a consequence) to represent West Berlin institutions. This disagreement involved different interpretations of the September 1971 four-power agreement on Berlin, to which neither Bonn nor Prague had been a party. The dispute in fact delayed the signing of the Prague-Bonn pact, originally scheduled for September.

imprecisions illustrate the flexibility that both sides
achieved in the interests of concluding a final agreement.
Notwithstanding its importance, the treaty can do little
more than bring the two sides a step further along the
path to genuine reconciliation. It marks a watershed in
postwar relations, but it cannot, at one stroke, remove
the historical burden of mistrust and resentment that has
characterized them. Nor does it alleviate the domestic
problems faced by a highly conservative Czechoslovak regime,
which also condition its attitude toward its West German
neighbor.

It was in fact the uncertain domestic setting in Czechoslovakia that provided the backdrop to the intransigent
approach to German reconciliation that characterized
Prague's unyielding position for some two and a half years.
And it is these internal constraints, which continue to be
felt, that may provide insights into how the CSSR will approach the broader issue of European security and its own
place in it. In contrast to the graver issues at stake in
the FRG's bilateral negotiations with Poland and the GDR--
the former seeking final claim to 25 percent of its postwar territory, and the latter recognition of its statehood
--Prague's adamant attitude on what was for it essentially
a matter of historical and legal principle appeared out
of all proportion and, at times, even petulant. Indeed,
its nonnegotiable stance on the Munich issue raised the
question of whether Prague was proceeding wholly in conformity with a Soviet Westpolitik whose paramount concern
seemed to be to accelerate the momentum of détente, or,
for that matter, in accord with the aspirations of Hungary
and Bulgaria, where only resolution of the Munich problem
blocked normalization with West Germany.* After each
unproductive negotiating session, Prague protested its
willingness to come to terms with the FRG and its enthusiasm

---

*Before the July 1972 Crimean summit of Warsaw Pact
party leaders speculation abounded that Hungary was ready
to leapfrog its northern ally in establishing ties with the
Federal Republic, and for its part Bonn expressed willingness openly to circumvent the thorny problem of normalization with Czechoslovakia in the interest of expediting the
upgrading of ties with other Warsaw Pact states. The favorable outcome for Prague of the Crimean summit, which served
notice to Bonn that Hungary and Bulgaria would only follow
Czechoslovakia in normalizing ties and restored the East
European diplomatic phalanx, settled the matter for the moment.

for the process of European security, thereby implicitly shifting the onus for the impasse to the West German side; but each false start made Prague look more like a political anomaly that threatened to delay the Soviet timetable. This danger was especially real in the period before the fall 1972 _Bundestag_ elections, when it appeared possible that the CDU/CSU would recover its parliamentary majority. Thus the prospect loomed of a West German government far less amenable to compromise than the ruling SPD-FDP coalition, a situation, one might have thought, of which the Czechoslovaks, on the urging of their Soviet mentors, would have attempted to take advantage. Throughout this period of diplomatic impasse the official declarations emanating from Prague seemed intended more as a palliative for its communist allies than an accurate reflection of the complex attitudes and motives of the Czechoslovak regime.

Perhaps nowhere in Eastern Europe has the internal situation had such a direct bearing on foreign policy during the recent period of change in East-West relations than in Czechoslovakia. The Husak regime was installed in April 1969 on the unpopular platform of extirpating the reforms that had captured the enthusiasm and support of the vast majority of the population. If the Soviet invasion of Czechoslovakia had been an accident on the road to détente, as French Foreign Minister Michel Debré put it, then the new Czechoslovak leadership remained sidetracked and faced with the exigencies of a highly unstable political setting. The backlash of reform and invasion had produced a renaissance of conservative elements within the party. The most stable element in the moderate Husak's narrow constituency was probably Moscow itself. A disillusioned and deeply alienated population presented manifold difficulties to a regime bound by its Soviet mandate and its own instincts to consolidate its position through repression and at the same time to define and hold the line against excessive reprisals.

One could hardly have expected a headlong enthusiasm for détente and European security and the active, confident foreign policy toward the West that they entailed to emerge from such domestic turmoil. It was, and to a large extent still is, far less a matter of European security than of the security of the Czechoslovak regime. Internal control and consolidation were the preconditions for the introduction of any flexibility in foreign policy. Furthermore, recovering its political and diplomatic footing vis-à-vis its Warsaw Pact allies was the more pressing concern in the CSSR's international relations.

Not surprisingly, such considerations have generated an ambivalence, not to say a defensiveness, in the official Czechoslovak attitude toward a number of issues related to European security. This is evident, for example, in the particularly zealous manner in which Prague embraced the bloc-wide campaign based upon the theses that peaceful co-existence is in no way synonymous with ideological coexistence. Perhaps only the East German regime has publicized more widely than Czechoslovakia the postulate of ideological and cultural Abgrenzung. This affinity is significant because it reveals the particularly sensitive reaction of both to the unsettling effects that "ideological penetration" could have on the maintenance of a highly orthodox domestic order.* To some extent all the Warsaw Pact states have subscribed to this thesis; there are, however, perceptible degrees of difference. Even in comparison with its more reticent socialist allies Prague sees less place in a European security system for more permeable borders that would, in the Western view, mitigate ideological differences by permitting cultural and ideological cross-fertilization. On the contrary, an omnipresent theme accompanying its calls for a European security conference is that the institutionalizing of peaceful coexistence dictates the need for accelerated ideological struggle.

Reacting to the Western thesis that the very meaning of European security is a drawing together of both sides, one Prague commentator assessed a June 1972 speech of NATO Secretary General Joseph Luns to the West European Union as follows:

> [Luns] demanded that talks on so-called free movement be made a condition for convening the all-European conference. It is not difficult to guess what Luns means by this proposal. Primarily, it involves an effort to open wide the gates to ideological penetration of the socialist countries--

---

*Characteristic of the Czechoslovak position was the following commentary:
> It is not accidental that . . . the North Atlantic Treaty states are endeavoring to push to the forefront negotiations on the so-called free movement of ideas. To put it more intelligibly, this is an endeavor to legalize ideological and political interference in the internal affairs of the socialist countries. (Radio Prague, 23 July 1972.)

in other words, to establish altogether legal
conditions for ideological diversion against the
socialist states. Naturally such an approach in
no way promotes the convening of the all-European
conference; on the contrary it is detrimental to
it.[36]

Another area in which the Prague regime demonstrated
ambivalence is that of economic cooperation. The prospect
of economic gains to be derived from an easing of political
tension in East-West relations has until very recently
failed to evoke the same enthusiasm in Prague as it has in
other Warsaw Pact capitals. Here again, and for analogous
reasons, the Czechoslovak regime has displayed a diffident
attitude, voicing limited support in principle for increased
economic cooperation but wary at the same time of its negative political repercussions:

> Bourgeois politicians and ideologists who decide
> to attain old anticommunist goals by new "peace-
> ful" means rely on the development of commercial
> and other contacts between capitalist and social-
> ist countries to revive inside socialism the in-
> fluence of ideas completely alien to socialism.[37]

Interest is expressed in reducing the economic barriers to
expanded trade by conventional means, such as achieving
most-favored-nation status and eliminating quantitative
restrictions. Unlike Poland, Rumania, or Hungary, however,
Czechoslovakia did not until very recently press the issues
of Western credits or joint investments. (Toward the latter half of 1973 an observable, albeit hesitant, shift
seemed in motion on these issues of economic cooperation.)
In contrast to Rumania's assertion of a traditional
notion of national sovereignty and the hope that a European
security conference would codify it (thus supporting the
RSR's position vis-à-vis the Soviet Union) and the relative
inattention paid to this by the other East European states,
Prague has elaborated the concept of "socialist [read:
limited] sovereignty." As its political beneficiary, Gustav
Husak has appeared, appropriately, as its leading apologist.
In essence, according to Husak, "the sovereignty of a socialist state lies above all in the power of the working
class and the leading role of the communist party."[38] This
notion eschews "abstract" sovereignty and obliges socialist
states to act in concert in defending and preserving each
other's socialist achievements--above all the exclusive

authority of the communist party. Any diminution of or threat to the total organizational control of the party constitutes historical backsliding, and from these theoretical precepts the Soviet Union emerges in practice as history's arbiter. In the Czechoslovak case alone "socialist sovereignty" was given a legal basis, in the May 1970 treaty with the Soviet Union.

Husak's support for the doctrine, however, is more than a simple attempt to turn necessity into virtue. The elevation of "socialist sovereignty" to a principle of state is, under present circumstances, as much an important vector of the regime's power, authority, and perpetuation as it is a guarantee of Soviet prerogatives.[39] In the setting of a European security conference or in a European security "system" itself, Czechoslovakia's response to efforts to establish the traditional norms of national sovereignty as a matter of principle in international interaction can be little more than declaratory.

Relations with the Federal Republic

For Czechoslovakia, European security begins with the problem of redefining its relations with the Federal Republic of Germany,[40] a complicated process whose epicenter until recently was disagreement over the 1938 Munich pact. Parallel to the complex political, historical, and psychological ramifications of the "German question," there lies the related matter of Czechoslovak perspectives on a general European settlement. As noted earlier, the momentum of détente in East-West relations was punctuated by the inability of Czechoslovak and West German negotiators to reach agreement on the thorny issue of the Munich Agreement and its legal legacies.

In the end, of course, resolution proved to be within grasp. But one especially puzzling aspect during the two and a half years of negotiation with the FRG was the CSSR's ability to maintain its maximalist position in view of the presumed Soviet interest in settling this key issue and in the reordering of Czechoslovak-West German relations as a welcome, if not necessary, precursor to the projected CSCE.*

---

*Indeed, the Czechoslovaks themselves routinely drew attention to the important place normalization of relations with West Germany occupied in a general European settlement. Foreign Minister Bohuslav Chnoupek: "The normaliza-

The additional pressure imposed by the possibility of a change of government in the Federal Republic in the fall of 1972 (to an administration that Prague would probably consider less amenable to compromise) on the face of it increased the likelihood that all the Warsaw Pact states, and especially Czechoslovakia, would want to avail themselves of the Brandt government's receptivity in settling such issues. There was, however, no discernible pressure by the Soviets or Czechoslovakia's other allies to encourage a compromise agreement. On the contrary, the midsummer 1972 Crimean summit meeting of Warsaw Pact party leaders endorsed the familiar Czechoslovak demand, a show of support of which Prague was quick to take advantage. Official comment thereafter emphasized that the Warsaw Pact states stood firmly behind the Czechoslovaks and pointed up the importance of this multilateral support in strengthening the CSSR's negotiating position. A 20 August 1972 Radio Prague broadcast stressed that the Crimean summit has

> quite unequivocally backed our just demand that in the current talks with the German Federal Republic [the latter] accept, as a prerequisite to an agreement, that the Munich Agreement of 1938 was invalid from the very beginning.[41]

There are a number of factors that may help to explain the Czechoslovak position on the Munich Agreement. No doubt it had to do in part with perceptions of national prestige, and as a principle long ago ensconced in the country's foreign policy it came to have a certain self-evident rationale. (A reiteration of this position came from Presidium member Alois Indra, who stated that ab initio nullification was "a question of principle for Czechoslovakia and we cannot relinquish it."[42]) The matter of prestige, however, does not in itself explain the apparent inflexibility of the Prague regime.

---

tion of relations between Czechoslovakia and the GFR [sic] on the basis of the invalidity of the Munich Agreement from its very beginning is an important factor in the project of European security" (Ceteka, 4 September 1972). However, Prague studiously avoided describing the satisfactory resolution of outstanding problems with Bonn as a precondition for the CSCE, lest it put itself in the position of directly obstructing the conference and expose itself to pressure from Warsaw Pact allies anxious to avoid anything that would impede progress in this direction.

144

Another, possibly more fundamental, reason for Prague's inelastic approach may have had to do with developments in 1968. It is the officially accepted view that one of the Dubcek regime's cardinal mistakes was to adopt a too-willing attitude toward cooperation with West Germany. In reality, the attitude in 1968 was one of extreme caution and little was accomplished in this area, but the prospect that ties outside the control of the Soviet Union might be established heightened the latter's anxieties and served as the pretext for intervention. Dubcek was accused of underestimating the danger of West German encroachment and aggressive intentions, or, in Brezhnev's hyperbole, of having paved the way for tearing Czechoslovakia out of the socialist camp and delivering it to the capitalists. Given this perspective and the need felt by the Husak regime to present itself as the political antithesis of its predecessor, the revival of the hard-line position on the "German question" was understandable.

While satisfaction has been expressed at the initiatives toward détente taken by the Brandt government, a continuing campaign has been waged against the danger posed by "reactionary forces" in West Germany. The anti-German theme has been a salient and longstanding feature of official propaganda, but the thrust of the attacks has been narrowed and is now directed against what Prague has referred to as the "rightist front"; this is said to include, among other things, the CDU/CSU opposition, the Springer press, and the expellee organizations. In the past the German bogy has provided an element of negative cohesion between the people and the political elite, and has served as one of the main raisons d'etre for the close political and military alliance with the USSR. One may question what credibility it retains in the public mind in the wake of 1968 and the goodwill generated by the Ostpolitik. Nevertheless, the continued appearance of anti-German propaganda suggests that the regime is unwilling to surrender too summarily this rather outdated weapon lest it forfeit some of these presumed benefits. At the least it provides a useful prop for the Czechoslovak leadership in proceeding toward full normalization on its own terms, which will no doubt be limited and highly controlled. By its uncompromising stand the Husak regime seemed to be saying that the "German threat," if diminished, was still potentially real, and the premise of its revival must be precluded by securing the abrogation of the Munich Agreement.

Foreign Policy Prospects

The five years since Husak came to power have witnessed a single-minded effort to root out the 1968 reformist ideas and those associated with them. The domestic stability that the Husak-led party has succeeded in imposing also came to rest on an assertive, neoisolationist tendency reflected in the drastic reduction of contacts with the West and the tight control over, and proscription of, ideas that might conflict with the orthodox ideological creed on which the regime's legitimacy and its claim to power were fashioned. This political-ideological retrenchment and the proximity to a liberal past oblige Czechoslovak policy makers to consider the possible repercussions that an easing of relations with the West, the extent and effects of which they cannot completely foretell, might have on the shallow roots of domestic stability.

It is a principle generally endorsed by the Warsaw Pact countries that while détente and cooperation in East-West relations will reduce hostility in the political and military spheres, it must not be permitted to blunt the existing ideological differences. Prague, it will be recalled, has shown an uncommon attachment to the notion that the ideological struggle must on the contrary be intensified. As in the case of anti-German propaganda, this attitude reflects apprehension that reduced international antagonisms will boost the pressures for (and, indeed, hypothetically imply) domestic relaxation and increased interaction with the West. This is not to suggest that the Czechoslovak leadership would prefer the maintenance of international tensions but rather to emphasize that their reduction has created problems of political adaptation. Much as its East German counterpart, the Czechoslovak leadership regards such prospects as potentially deleterious to its ideological integrity. And like the GDR's policy of Abgrenzung, the offensive political strategy of sharpening the ideological struggle is a means of fending off such pressures and bolstering its ideological and political raison d'état. Given their present perspectives, neither has an interest in shaping a European security system that would mitigate ideological differences or relegate them to a secondary level of importance--in contrast to, say, Hungary or Poland, where there is less vested interest in ideology as a means of underwriting the government's legitimacy and power.

Turning to the question of how the Czechoslovak leadership will come to view the nation's prospects in a future framework of European security, it is safe to say that many of the domestic constraints that have governed the process of normalization with West Germany will continue to be felt in the broader context of the development of its relations with Western states. The latter prospect is, of course, the very rationale of European security, but for the immediate future, at least, Prague can be expected to embrace it with less enthusiasm than Poland or Hungary. This does not mean that because of the domestic constraints outlined above Prague's foreign policy is fixed at dead center. On the contrary, having been pulled along in the wake of Soviet diplomacy, Czechoslovakia has emerged from a period of self-imposed isolation, and many of the considerations that accounted for its reticence have been ameliorated. The treaty with the Federal Republic is but one indication of this. It reflects a foreign policy that after some three years of diplomatic quiescence has in fact assumed a more active and confident character. Husak has undertaken fence-mending excursions to Yugoslavia and Rumania in an effort to reestablish links badly damaged by their condemnation of the Soviet invasion and the subsequent consolidation. Thus far, however, he has ventured outside the communist sphere only once, and in a sense this official visit to India in December 1973 marked his debut on the world diplomatic stage. Similarly, the peregrinations of Czechoslovak Foreign Minister Chnoupek have been limited to the more familiar terrain of the communist world. For some time the attitudes that determine Czechoslovakia's Westpolitik will be mixed, with caution the touchstone. Reservations, however, will be balanced against incentives, including, above all, the expansion of economic relations with the West.

The 1968 period was instructive in that it revealed a number of the genuine economic interests of the country--most importantly the need for industrial restructuring and plant modernization as a means of improving its competitive position on the world market. These needs still exist, as does the great appeal of Western trade, economic cooperation, and credits for the import of sophisticated capital goods, and they constitute influences that no doubt generate internal pressures for increased economic contacts. One example worthy of mention is the apparent shift that has taken place in official policy toward the question of Western credits. After a long period in which the desire for Western investment credits evidenced in 1968 was condemned as revisionist, their procurement has now been officially sanctioned.[43]

The lure of recovering its prestige and international acceptability will also probably in the longer run impel the CSSR to pay greater attention to ties with the West. The more recent developments in Czechoslovak foreign policy indicate that the successful consolidation of its domestic authority has allowed the regime to shake off some of the paralytic effects of the 1968 invasion and instability. Nevertheless, for the Husak regime a basic dilemma remains (if in somewhat attenuated form)--that of preserving and extending a comparatively orthodox domestic order and at the same time establishing and regulating a more active foreign policy toward the West.

NOTES

1.   Jan Szczepanski, "The Fate of Poland and the Polish Character," <u>Zycie Warszawy</u>, Warsaw, 4 June 1970. For a detailed analysis of the entire discussion, see Michael Costello, "The Poles Look at Their Country and at Themselves," Polish Background Report/14, RFER (EERA), 16 September 1970.
2.   Szczepanski, op. cit.
3.   Ibid.
4.   Andrzej Mroczek, "The Clocks of Our Times," <u>Slowo Powszechne</u>, Warsaw, 12 August 1970. On the importance of science and technology and the link with the West, cf. also Krystyna Wigura, "July 22--the Second Start," <u>Glos Pracy</u>, Warsaw, 22 August 1970.
5.   Wieslaw Gornicki, "Can the Poles Fight Themselves Free?" <u>Zycie Warszawy</u>, 18-19 June 1972 (emphasis added).
6.   Ibid.
7.   Ernest Skalski, "Victoria Consummata," <u>Kultura</u>, Warsaw, 25 June 1972 (emphasis added).
8.   Ibid. (emphasis added); see also Ryszard Wojna in <u>Zycie Warszawy</u>, 17-18 January 1971.
9.   See, for example, Henryk Gaworski, "A Time of Hope," <u>Barwy</u>, Warsaw, July 1972; the editorial discussion entitled "A Feeling of Success or a Feeling of Defeat?" <u>Kultura</u>, 18 June 1972; the readers' letters in response to the <u>Kultura</u> discussion published in that journal on 9 and 23 July 1972; Janusz Wilhelmi, "We Are in the Majority," ibid., 23 July 1972; and Janusz Rolicki, "You Don't Have to Be a Genius," ibid., 30 July 1972.
10.   Foreign Minister Adam Rapacki, as quoted in P. Jaszunski, "Poland and the Nonnuclear Zones," <u>International Affairs</u>, Moscow, April 1964. See also Manfred Lach, "An Atom-Free Zone in Central Europe," ibid., August 1969.

11. Jaszunski, op. cit.

12. 31 December 1966.

13. See Gomulka's speech to the Karlovy Vary conference, Trybuna Ludu, Warsaw, 25 April 1967.

14. Ibid.

15. This brief sketch is based on the following articles by A. Ross Johnson: "A Survey of Poland's Relations
with West Germany, 1956-1967," Polish BR/15, RFER (EERA),
25 February 1968; "A New Phase in Polish-West German Relations (I): The Background to Gomulka's May 17 Proposal,"
Polish BR/13, RFER ((EERA), 20 June 1968; "A New Phase in
Polish-West German Relations (II): Gomulka's May 17 Proposal and Its Aftermath," Polish BR/14, RFER (EERA), 3
July 1969; "A New Phase in Polish-West German Relations
(III): A Preliminary Analysis," Polish BR/17, RFER (EERA),
14 August 1969. See also Neal Ascherson, "Poland's Place
in Europe," The World Today, London, December 1969.

16. For a discussion see Johnson, "A New Phase . . .
(II)."

17. Johnson, "A New Phase . . . (I)."

18. The Catholic writer Andrzej Micewski, "Our Place
in the Alliance," Zycie Warszawy, 26 January 1971 (cited
in Adam Bromke, "Poland Under Gierek: A New Political
Style," Problems of Communism, Washington, D.C., September-
October 1972.

19. See Michael Gamarnikow, "Poland Under Gierek: A
New Economic Approach," Problems of Communism, Washington,
D.C., September-October 1972.

20. Radio Warsaw, 8 November 1973.

21. Allgemeiner Deutsches Nachrichtendienst (henceforth
ADN), 20 June 1973.

22. Jozef Winiewicz, "The Polish Stand on Problems of
European Security," Europa Archiv, Bonn, 25 December 1971.

23. Wojna, op. cit.

24. Wladyslaw Machejek, "Has Poland Stuck Its Neck
Out?" Zycie Literackie, Warsaw, 9 July 1972.

25. Jozef Winiewicz, "A Season of Important Meetings,"
Literatura, Warsaw, 6 July 1972.

26. See the revealing exchange between the editors
of Polityka (Warsaw) and The Economist (London), published
in the latter on 18 June 1971.

27. Janusz Zablocki (member of the Sejm and vice-pres-
ident of the Znak group), in an article in the Italian
Christian Democratic daily Il Popolo, Rome, 30 November 1972.

28. Wojna, op. cit.

29. Jozef Winiewicz, "Europe, Yes--But What Kind of
Europe?" Polityka, 8 April 1972.

30. Ibid.

31. Ibid.

32. See the editorial signed "KS," _Zycie Warszawy_, 18 January 1972.

33. Poland has opposed the limiting of the sovereign independence of West European states through the EEC; cf. Winiewicz, "Europe, Yes."

34. Ibid.

35. Cf. Winiewicz, "The Polish Stand."

36. Jaroslav Galas, speaking over Radio Prague, 14 June 1972.

37. _Pravda_, Bratislava, 12 August 1972; see also _Rude Pravo_, Prague, 24 June 1972.

38. Speech to the 24th CPSU Congress, broadcast over Radio Moscow, 1 April 1971.

39. For other Czechoslovak statements see Ivan Hlivka and Michal Stefanak, "On Certain Questions Concerning the Application of Proletarian Internationalism, the Unity Between National and International Interest," _Rude Pravo_, 18-19 February 1971. For a candid statement of the Soviet view, see O. Hlestov, "The New Soviet-Czechoslovak Treaty," _International Affairs_, Moscow, July 1970.

40. For a discussion of Czechoslovak-West German relations and the issues involved in normalization, see Robert W. Dean, "Bonn-Prague Relations: The Politics of Reconciliation," _The World Today_, April 1973.

41. See also the speech by Slovak Premier Peter Colotka (Ceteka in English, 20 August 1972).

42. Ceteka in English, 7 September 1972.

43. Cf. Svatopluk Potac (chairman of the Czechoslovak State Bank), "Credit and Foreign Currency Policy in the Fifth Five-Year Plan," _Finance a Uver_, Prague, February 1972.

7

HUNGARY AND
EUROPEAN SECURITY:
HUNTING WITH
THE HOUNDS
William F. Robinson

VOICES FROM THE PAST

On Wednesday, Hungarian Foreign Minister Janos
Peter received State Secretary in the Bonn Foreign
Ministry Rolf Lahr, who has been in Budapest
since Monday.

After the negotiations, State Secretary Lahr
declared that . . . all current problems, including the establishment of Hungarian-West German
diplomatic relations, had been discussed.

According to Lahr, both negotiating partners
wish to normalize diplomatic relations. Asked
whether the Hungarian negotiating partner had set
any unattainable conditions, Lahr replied that he
had not noticed any such thing during the negotiations, although, he added, there is no doubt
that there are still important problems to be
clarified on the road to practical normalization.

> Radio Budapest, Homeland Service, 26
> January 1967, 2000 hours (10 days
> after the successful trip of an offi-
> cial West German delegation to dis-
> cuss the establishment of diplomatic
> relations with Rumania).

* * *

We most resolutely oppose West German revanchism,
as well as West Germany's aspirations to change
present frontiers, its disregard of the existence
of the GDR, and its attempts at rearmament, par-

ticularly its intention to acquire nuclear weapons. On the other hand, we would gladly further
develop our existing relations with the German
Federal Republic--including the settlement of interstate relations--on the basis of safeguards
for mutual interests and a consistent assertion
of the principle of peaceful coexistence.

> HSWP Politburo member Bela Biszku,
> speech to the National Assembly on
> 27 January 1967 (the day that Chan-
> cellor Kiesinger announced that dip-
> lomatic relations would be estab-
> lished between Bonn and Bucharest),
> Nepszabadsag, Budapest, 28 January
> 1967.

One of the basic principles of Hungarian foreign
policy has been to continually develop relations
with any country that is willing to do so on the
basis of peaceful coexistence and mutual respect
for one another's interests. An important feature of the present situation is the fact that
it is the German Federal Republic that has made
the effort to develop contacts. . . . Official
circles in Hungary are not opposed to the idea
of giving West German interests fair consideration. As a matter of fact, Hungary is also interested in improving [its] relations [with the
GFR], although we consider that such an improvement can only be based on mutual respect for each
other's interests. This means that neither country should stipulate any unrealistic conditions.

> Radio Budapest in English to Europe,
> 2 February 1967, 2030 hours (two days
> after the official establishment of
> diplomatic relations between Rumania
> and the FRG).

* * *

One can hardly err by claiming that the central
problem [of European security] is the question
of Germany. Without an acceptable settlement of
this matter, European security is inconceivable.
. . . Lately, in its public statements and diplomatic communications, the government of the German
Federal Republic has repeatedly stressed its

peaceful intentions and its desire to prove them
by settling relations with the East European socialist countries. . . . As far as Bonn's statements are concerned, it is known that deeds serve
to establish and support the credibility of words.
If the government of the German Federal Republic
truly wishes to contribute effectively to improving the European situation, it must take steps to
prove its definite break with all kinds of revanchist aspirations. There can be no two ways
about it. This implies recognition of the Oder-
Neisse frontier, renunciation of nuclear weapons
as well as of claims to so-called sole representation, and, naturally, recognition of the GDR--
the other German state. . . . What is needed is
not conjuring with words and fictitious rights,
but a serious and realistic consideration of the
true facts of Europe and the world as it has
evolved. Let them state on that basis that they
want settled relations and normalized contacts
between countries and states, that they want peace.
There will be no obstacles provided it is understood that two German states exist, each one representing itself. If the Bonn rulers do not bring
themselves to contemplate these problems more seriously, their words will go with the wind and they
they will carry home no laurels. They will merely
add to the pile of rigid and inconclusive stupid-
ities that yield political bankruptcy--a bank-
ruptcy already brought about by Adenauer's disregard of European realities.

> Janos Kadar, speech to a Budapest
> election rally, Radio Budapest, 22
> February 1967, 1630 hours (12 days
> after a meeting of the Warsaw Pact
> foreign ministers to discuss Bonn's
> Ostpolitik and its establishment of
> diplomatic relations with Bucharest).

ON LOYALTY TO ONE'S ALLY

To speak about Hungarian attitudes toward a European
security system is, in most respects, to repeat what the
Soviet Union has said about this topic. There should be
no illusions on this point, for Hungary does not and cannot
have any comprehensive program or concept regarding a Euro-

pean security conference that differs from, or may be considered an alternative to, that put forth by the USSR. The
leaders in Budapest may harbor their own private desires
concerning the outcome of such a conference, and occasionally there may be nuances of approach or differences of emphasis over details. Indeed, the Hungarians may even send
their lobbyists to argue in the corridors of the Kremlin,
and certainly--when Moscow has no particular desires on a
given matter, and there is reason to believe it will be
tolerant--the Budapest authorities are capable of launching
modest initiatives of their own. But outside these rather
narrow limits, and in regard to relations with the noncommunist world, Hungary remains a most loyal Soviet ally.

One of the clearest reflections of this fact has come
in the form of articles published in the two Hungarian
party monthlies. The first, written by First Deputy Foreign
Minister Frigyes Puja* in the September 1972 issue of Tarsa-
dalmi Szemle, was a vigorous advocacy of the Soviet government's maximalist position regarding the purposes and outcome of a European security conference. It was characterized
by a very sharp anti-American tone, a firm rejection of
Western proposals for more freedom of movement of people
and ideas between East and West, and yet a generally conciliatory attitude toward the Federal Republic of Germany.
Of particular note was the observation that the communist
countries could make progress toward European détente even
with a CDU/CSU government in power.

While there is no reason to doubt that Puja's treatment of the FRG accords with the Hungarian, as well as the
Soviet, view, it is doubtful whether Budapest shares the
anti-American sentiments and the fear of freer movement
that are strongly evident in the article. Since 1966, when
the two countries raised their legations to embassy status,
there has been a gradual trend toward normalization of
Hungarian-U.S. relations. This has been characterized by
the conclusion of agreements in August 1969, January 1970,
and October 1972, settling several of the outstanding problems at issue between the two countries, as well as by the
departure of Cardinal Mindszenty from the U.S. Embassy in
September 1971 and by the visits to Hungary of such high-
ranking U.S. government officials as Undersecretary of
State Richard T. Davis (March 1971), Secretary of State
William P. Rogers (July 1972), and Secretary of Commerce

---

*Puja became Foreign Minister in December 1973, upon
the retirement of Janos Peter.

Frederick B. Dent (September 1973). In addition, the Hungarians have actively been seeking most-favored-nation treatment from Washington and have been sending delegations to the United States in increasing numbers for the purpose of expanding economic relations.

The second article in question was written by Deputy Foreign Minister Robert Garai and appeared in the September 1972 issue of Partelet. In contrast to Puja, Garai was clearly on the defensive, for his purpose was to answer critics of the CPSU and its policy of peaceful coexistence. In particular, he was at pains to explain why Moscow had not canceled the Nixon summit meeting after the United States had mined Haiphong Harbor and stepped up its bombing of North Vietnam. Since he was, in fact, defending the growing Soviet attempts at achieving détente with the United States, it was obvious that he could not indulge in the negative assessment of U.S. policy that had appeared in Puja's article. Instead, he adopted a factual and objective tone, pointing out not only the necessity of peaceful coexistence in today's nuclear world, but also those aspects of American policy that made it possible.

The strong defense and promotion of Soviet interests that are exemplified by these two authoritative essays inevitably prompt a consideration of the motives behind Hungary's firmly loyalist position. Essentially, the reasons seem to be threefold.

First, the Hungarian leaders learned in 1956 that there is no alternative to alliance with the Soviet Union. The Western powers clearly demonstrated then and afterward that they would not intervene in any showdown between Moscow and its East European client states. This lesson, of course, was repeated in August 1968 with the invasion of Czechoslovakia, and in addition it was shown that the limits of permissible deviation on the part of a Warsaw Pact member country fell far short of open revolt or declarations of neutrality.

Naturally, in any alliance between a small and a superpower the latter will predominate, and the need, therefore, is to make a virtue out of this necessity. Hungary's success in accomplishing this is a second factor that helps to explain its close adherence to Soviet policy formulations vis-à-vis the external world, for the history of the Kadar era is the history of a mutually advantageous quid pro quo between two quite different and potentially antagonistic states. In return for reestablishing the primacy of the communist party, restoring and maintaining domestic peace, returning to active participation in Comecon and the

Warsaw Pact, and promoting Soviet foreign and intrabloc
interests, the Hungarian leadership has been given both
broad latitude in matters of internal policy and firm Soviet
political and economic support. These are not advantages
to be lightly dismissed, especially when no other course
of action promises anything but bitter consequences.

Added to these factors is yet a third--Janos Kadar's
personal beliefs and inclinations. A close study of what
is known about Kadar's life and career strongly indicates
that he has never been motivated by the desire for power
and prestige or the prospect of personal enrichment but
rather that he has been impelled by a genuine faith in the
communist movement, the party, and the Soviet Union. In a
less than perfect world, he has placed his trust in these
less than perfect instruments as the only means by which to
attain some ultimate goal that even he has yet to define
with any clarity. The point to be made, of course, is that
whatever else stimulates Hungary's consistent support of
Soviet foreign policy, it is strengthened by Kadar's belief
and determination that this is the correct and only path
to be followed.

ON NATIONAL INTEREST

Having said all this, it is nevertheless legitimate
to speculate what advantages and disadvantages Hungary might
derive from the European security conference. Even if
Budapest has ostentatiously identified itself with Moscow's
ideas on the matter, it does not necessarily follow that
it stands to benefit to the same degree or in the same way.
Nor does it mean that if left to its own devices, or at
least allowed to be partially innovative in this respect,
it would not devise certain limited goals solely on the
basis of Hungarian national interests.

One benefit that could accrue to the Hungarians is the
final settlement of the German question--that is, the legal
regulation and reasonable normalization of relations between the FRG on the one hand and the GDR, Poland, the USSR,
and Czechoslovakia on the other. The existence of tension
and suspicion between the two sides since the early postwar period, as well as the deliberate use of the German
"threat" as a political tool by the northern-tier countries,
has resulted in constraints on the interstate activities
of all Warsaw Pact members, including Hungary. Although,
for various reasons, Bucharest managed to remove many of
these inhibitions in 1966,[1] the same combination of circum-

stances has never prevailed with respect to Budapest, and the latter has thus been forced to await either a green light from the Soviet Union or a final settlement with Bonn (which, while closely connected with the CSCE, could come during or after the actual conference or even in between sessions).

One of the most obvious constraints on Hungarian behavior has been the Warsaw Pact veto on the establishment of diplomatic relations with West Germany. It is clear from Hungary's behavior in January 1967, in the wake of Rumania's daring conclusion of such ties with Bonn, that the removal of this veto is, and has since been, a definite goal of the HSWP leadership—a conclusion confirmed by North Rhine-Westphalian Premier Heinz Kuehn in July 1972, after a visit to Budapest. According to Kuehn, Hungary had a "strong desire" to establish diplomatic relations with the FRG, although it would not do so until West Germany's problems with both the GDR and the CSSR had been settled.*

Despite the fact that the Hungarians have been firm on this point, the Kuehn visit indicated that they might have been growing somewhat impatient with the Czechoslovaks' procrastination in their periodic negotiations with Bonn. Foreign Minister Peter reportedly told the premier that Hungary was hoping to establish diplomatic relations with West Germany in 1972. The unexpected talks between Janos Kadar and CPCS Secretary-General Gustav Husak in Bratislava from July 7 to 9 (two days after Kuehn left Hungary) reinforced such impressions, as did the failure of the communiqué they issued to draw a direct link between Hungarian support for Prague's position on the Munich Agreement and future diplomatic ties between Bonn and Budapest. All this led to speculation that, although Hungary was ready to support its Warsaw Pact ally, it may not have been entirely willing to let the momentum of its relations with the Federal Republic slip to the extent that the question of a diplomatic exchange with the FRG became indefinitely shelved.

---

*dpa, 5 July 1972. See also the communiqué of the HSWP Central Committee on 15 June 1972: "We want to settle and develop relations between Hungary and the German Federal Republic according to the basic principles of our foreign policy, in harmony with our allies, on the basis of the policy of peaceful coexistence, and in a way which serves our national interests." (Radio Budapest, 15 June 1972, 2200 hours; emphasis supplied.)

Nevertheless, the lack of progress on the question over the next six months did not prevent Premier Jeno Fock from once again repeating that Budapest would not establish diplomatic relations with Bonn until the FRG had recognized the invalidity of the Munich Agreement and settled its relations with the CSSR. Fock's remark was initially made at a press conference on 16 February 1973, during a visit to Czechoslovakia,[2] and then reiterated in his report to the Hungarian National Assembly on March 21.[3] Although the premier's statement represented no change in Hungary's attitude, it was the first time that this position had been elevated to the rank of official policy at the highest governmental level. Perhaps it was prompted by a foreknowledge that the Prague-Bonn negotiations were to be resumed in April and was thus designed as an attempt to bolster Czechoslovakia's position. It is even possible that the Czechoslovak authorities had promised the Hungarians that an agreement would be reached if at all feasible, and in return the Hungarians gave them their official and public support, hoping, of course, that this would help their allies gain better terms.

Whatever the effect of Hungarian backing--if, indeed, it had any effect at all--an agreement was initialed between Prague and Bonn on June 20. Shortly thereafter, at a meeting held in early July, during the first stage of the European security conference in Helsinki, Hungarian Foreign Minister Janos Peter and his West German counterpart Walter Scheel decided that talks would be held on the technical problems connected with the establishment of diplomatic relations between their two countries. Accordingly, a Hungarian delegation under the leadership of Deputy Foreign Minister Janos Nagy (former ambassador to the United States) arrived in Bonn on August 11, and negotiations began two days later. Although scheduled to last only two days, the talks actually stretched out to four, and it was obvious from the statements made during this time that a deadlock had developed over the issue of West Berlin. Specifically, the Hungarians were willing to allow the FRG to provide consular representation for West Berlin citizens in Hungary, but refused the same right for West Berlin institutions and rejected altogether the right of the Federal Republic to provide legal aid.

At first glance, and especially given the speed with which Budapest acted after the Bonn-Prague agreement, it was surprising that such a difficulty should crop up. However, at the end of July, before the negotiations began, the leaders of all the Warsaw Pact states held a meeting

in the Crimea (the third such annual session to take place).
In their broad review of international and intrabloc affairs, it was only natural that they discussed the latest
trends in West Germany's Ostpolitik and explored the ways
in which they could harmonize their own foreign policies
to best advantage. It is quite possible that a united
stand was adopted with regard to the desirability of insisting on a narrow interpretation of the FRG's right, under
the September 1971 four-power agreement, to represent West
Berlin's interests abroad. Such a hypothesis is supported
not only by the deadlock that occurred between the Hungarians and the West Germans, but also by the sudden refusal,
around the same time, of the Czechoslovak authorities to
allow the FRG to provide consular services for public institutions, including courts, under West Berlin jurisdiction.
Effectively this meant that the veto--ostensibly lifted
with the original Bonn-Prague agreement--had been reimposed.
Perhaps realizing that the issue was of relatively minor
import to begin with, and that it could not be resolved on
a strictly bilateral basis anyway, since it involved an interpretation of the four-power agreement, West Germany
eventually decided to proceed with the signing of its
treaty with Czechoslovakia before settling the problem of
consular representation. Most probably reinforcing this
decision was the very dim prospect of any Soviet intervention on Bonn's behalf. Whatever the motivation, the new
accord was signed in early December 1973, and immediately
thereafter Hungary consented to the establishment of diplomatic relations with the FRG. An exchange of ambassadors
then took place in January 1974--a full month before Czechoslovakia and Bulgaria appointed their own envoys.
    Aside from the elimination of certain restrictions in
its political relations with the United States and Western
Europe in general and with the FRG in particular, which
would seem to be a normal desire on the part of any state,
Hungary might also stand to benefit from an expansion of
economic ties with the West. During the latter part of the
1960s, in fact, this seemed to be the key area in which the
Hungarians expected results from a security conference.
This is only natural, however, since approximately 40 percent of Hungary's national income is represented by foreign
trade, and much of the success of the country's economic
reform depends upon arrangements that will channel Western
technology, know-how, and capital into the national economy
on a permanent basis. Or, to put it in other terms, the
development of Hungary's economic relations with the West

is a vital national interest, since failure in this sphere
would most probably impede economic modernization, a strategic goal of the New Economic Mechanism.

Nevertheless, further reflection on the matter prompts
at least one basic question. Since the beginning of 1969,
the number of economic cooperation agreements Hungary has
negotiated with the West has accelerated at an ever-in-
creasing rate, rising from a total of 53 concluded in the
five-year period from 1964 through 1968 to a total of 220
by mid-1972 and 300 by the end of 1973.[4] The number of
such agreements with West Germany alone jumped from 47 on
30 June 1971 to almost 100 a year later and over 150 by
the beginning of 1974.[5] In addition, more and more joint
enterprises are being established with noncommunist firms
abroad. At the beginning of 1971, there were 38 of these
companies, and by early 1974 their number had grown to approximately 60 scattered throughout 16 different states.[6]
Moreover, in October 1972 an enabling decree issued by the
minister of finance laid down the regulations for establishing joint firms on Hungarian soil.[7]

If all this, plus an annually expanding volume of
Western trade, yearly advances in the liberalization of
Western import quotas, Hungary's admission to GATT, the
creation of an increasing number of Hungarian-Western interstate committees on economic cooperation, and the floating
of bond issues on the Eurodollar market, can be accomplished
without the convocation of a security conference, what
further impetus to economic relations can possibly be expected from the CSCE itself? One answer to this might be
the political courage it could give Budapest to allow Western firms to invest directly in joint enterprises founded
in Hungary, thus giving life to a decree whose effect is
as yet uncertain. A second answer might be a more vigorous
Hungarian effort to join other international economic organizations, such as the IMF and the World Bank, in which it
has thus far had to express its interest in the most cautious terms. A third answer might be a gradual increase
in the number of countries with which Hungary conducts trade
solely on a hard currency basis (to date agreements have
been signed only with Yugoslavia, Austria, Tunisia, and
Syria). Whatever the answers, however, it is probably in
the economic sphere that Budapest stands to gain most.

Nevertheless, there is at least an outside possibility
that such potential advantages could be negated and the
CSCE turned into a net loss for most East European states.
This would occur if the conference effectively took place
on a bloc-to-bloc basis and resulted in the conclusion of

160

agreements or the establishment of institutions fundamentally regulated in terms of membership in EEC-Comecon or
NATO and the Warsaw Pact. The danger inherent in such arrangements is obvious, for the conduct of East-West relations would then be carried out primarily according to a
group principle, while bilateral endeavors would become
only a secondary and limited means of concourse between
the East European countries and their Western partners.
Since the groups involved--that is, on the Eastern side--
are dominated by the USSR, this would result in even greater
restrictions on the individual foreign policy activities
of Moscow's allies than those that existed prior to 1966.

The Hungarians certainly recognize this and are
strongly desirous of keeping at least their economic relations with the noncommunist world in the hands of their own
agencies in Budapest. The clearest and most authoritative
expression of Hungary's policy on the matter came in an interview with Finnish Radio and TV granted by Janos Kadar
during a visit to Helsinki in late September 1973. Kadar,
it should be noted, was speaking only four weeks after Comecon Secretary-General Nikolai Fadeev had approached the
acting chairman of the EEC Council of Ministers, Danish
Foreign Trade Minister Ivar Noergaard, in Copenhagen for
the purpose of opening negotiations between the two economic groups. When asked about the Hungarian view of future
Comecon-Common Market relations, the party first secretary
asserted that:

> There need not be economic relations between Come-
> con and the Common Market in their capacities as
> organizations. . . . What we require from the con-
> tacts between the two organizations is that they
> offer their member countries the opportunity to
> take a serious step forward along the road toward
> amplifying their [own] economic links and cooper-
> ation and facilitating contacts.

Despite such indications of concern on the part of the
East European states, centralized regulation of East-West
relations still seems only to be an outside possibility,
since the Western states appear determined to prevent any
such outcome, while the official removal of the German
"threat" and the proclamation of an era of détente and cooperation would unleash political forces in Eastern Europe
that would not only be antithetical to group restrictions
but also difficult to suppress aside from the application
of military means. Recourse to the latter, in turn, would

be self-defeating and destructive of the objectives for the achievement of which a European security conference has ostensibly been desired.

None of this means, however, that it is a question of all or nothing. Disadvantages can appear, and indeed have already done so, on a lower level and a more limited basis. The most obvious example has been the virtually bloc-wide trend toward a more conservative and restrictive ideological atmosphere, as well as the pledge, among the countries involved, to coordinate their activities in this area to a much greater degree than before. In fact, there now exists a complete network of bilateral cooperation agreements on either ideological or agitprop affairs covering East Germany, Poland, Czechoslovakia, Hungary, and Bulgaria, plus additional bilateral accords between Moscow on the one hand and Sofia, Warsaw, and East Berlin on the other. Except for the Moscow-Sofia pact, all these agreements were concluded in 1972-73, and they have been supplemented by an increasing number of bilateral discussions on ideological matters, more multilateral conferences on ideological and cultural themes, and more frequent nationwide meetings on peaceful coexistence and the struggle against bourgeois ideology. Clearly, this indicates not only a much greater degree of intrabloc coordination, but also an attempt to create a common defense against the influence of Western values in a period of greater East-West contact and international détente.

For Hungary, a country notable for its lack of ideological rigidity and extremism, this development could have worse repercussions than for the other East European states (with the possible exception of Poland). So far, however, it has been reflected only in the press, in public speeches, and in the "administrative" actions taken against a very limited group of social scientists and cultural personalities. Unless they are subjected to a great deal of pressure from their allies, it can be expected that the Hungarians will attempt to keep the negative effects of the current ideological campaign to a minimum.

Yet a further disadvantage that has accrued to Budapest as a result of the European security drive has been a blow to its prestige. This is ironical, for it is precisely the opposite that Hungary expected, owing to the role it has played, with Soviet blessing, ever since the publication of the Budapest Appeal in early 1969. In fact, Hungary's active participation as a liaison to the West on behalf of the CSCE has often been a source of pride to the Hungarian authorities.

For this reason, it came as a complete surprise when
the Soviet delegation to the MBFR talks in Vienna suddenly
and successfully demanded Budapest's relegation to observer,
rather than full participant, status in the troop reduction
negotiations. This means, of course, that the Soviet forces
presently stationed in Hungary will fall outside any eventual troop-reduction agreement. Reports emanating from the
Austrian capital spoke of the move as a tactic to force
the West into admitting Italy as a full participant (although the West, as is known, chose to reduce Hungary's
status instead). The reports also agreed that Budapest
had not been consulted about the Soviet gambit and was
clearly embarrassed by this disregard for its feelings on
the matter. Such conclusions were supported by the failure
of the Hungarian information media to mention the development in any way between late February and early May. Nevertheless, Hungary acquiesced without any public show of
disagreement, a fact that probably led to heavy domestic
criticism and reminders that neighboring Rumania would not
have subordinated its own national interests in such a way.
This, at any rate, is one plausible interpretation of an
article in the Hungarian party daily of 13 March 1973 ex-
tolling the maturity of those socialist countries able to
submerge their national interests for the good of the communist movement as a whole and plainly (although not by
name) criticizing the refusal of Rumania to do the same.
    It was not until May 6 that Hungarian sensitivity and
resentment had subsided sufficiently to allow some mention
of the affair in the press. Moreover, it had probably become evident that some explanation of the lengthy delay in
the MBRF talks had to be given to the public. Accordingly,
military specialist Istvan Kormendy, writing in the political affairs weekly Magyarorszag, complained that the zone
of troop reductions proposed by NATO "would mean that every
Soviet unit stationed abroad would be reduced, while the
Americans would have troops stationed in many West European
countries. . . . For that very reason, it would be rational
for Italy and Hungary to participate in the negotiations
on an equal footing: either both would be included in the
troop reduction zone, or both would remain outside it."
It was not until May 15, however--one day after the West
had acceded to the Soviet demand--that Kormendy, in a Radio
Budapest broadcast, gave a broader background to the MBFR
negotiations and supplied details of the Hungarian position,
admitting that Hungary's status had actually been the focal
point of the discussions for the previous three and a half
months. He did not, of course, disclose the Soviet role

163

in the affair, but attempted instead to make it appear as
if Hungary had supported a position that had been adopted
as long ago as the mid-1960s in the course of an earlier
proposal for armament reduction negotiations.

ON REGIONALISM

As is known from a number of sources,[8] the Hungarian
leadership has for several years endorsed the idea of Danubian cooperation, declaring that the nations located in
the Danube Basin, but particularly those in the Danube
Valley itself, share a "community of fate." This return
to favor of a Magyar concept born in the 19th century was
first announced by Janos Kadar in December 1964.[9] After
appropriate reaction to his remarks in the Hungarian press,
the subject was dropped in the spring of 1965, only to be
revived again at the Ninth HSWP Congress in November-December 1966. This time the follow-up was much more vigorous
and sustained, lasting more or less throughout 1967 and
characterized by both the statements of public officials
(notably Foreign Minister Janos Peter) and reasonably numerous articles in the daily press and the journals.

It was rumored at the time that the vigor of the revival could be partially explained by the destruction of
Hungary's hope of establishing diplomatic relations with
West Germany. That is to say, the advocacy of Danubian
cooperation was meant as a substitute for this plan,[10] and
therefore a link to European security was then built into
it. The refurbished concept was presented as a true continuation of the historical Hungarian idea, but with adjustments made to bring it into line with current political
reality. Having learned the lessons of the past, the Hungarians said, we must reject schemes that would lead to a
federation or confederation of the Danubian nations. Instead, it would be better to support the general idea of
regional cooperation and, in addition, to promote specific
multinational arrangements on a Danubian basis. The latter
would involve four states at a minimum (Hungary, Austria,
Czechoslovakia, and Yugoslavia--the core area) and six at
an optimum (thus including Rumania and Bulgaria, which
overlap the Balkan area).

According to Peter, the primary official spokesman
for this initiative, the Danubian project was eminently
suited, for political and geographic reasons, to be the
first of a series of regional ventures in Europe set up
for the purpose of implementing the policy of peaceful co-

existence in a more meaningful way. Gradually, in mosaic-
like fashion, these groupings could become the basis for an
all-encompassing European security system, whose creation
would thus be an organic development rooted in the natural
growth of lower-level economic and political arrangements.[11]

As indicated previously, the most lively advocacy of
these concepts was voiced during 1967. Although there is
no reason to suppose that they have since fallen into dis-
favor with the Hungarian government, it is nevertheless
true that they were removed from active consideration by
the authorities soon thereafter. In fact, except for two
very brief references to the Danubian idea by Peter in early
1970, there has been no mention of it by Hungarian public
officials for almost six years. Nor, for that matter, has
it been discussed in the press. Indeed, the only known
treatment of the issue since 1967 has been a book published
by the economists Gyorgy Ranki and Ivan Berend in the spring
of 1969,[12] in which the authors attempted to demonstrate,
through historical example, that the nations in the Danube
Basin were economically interdependent.*

It is possible that one of the main reasons why the
Hungarians failed to pursue their proposal was the Soviet
reaction to the events that took place in Czechoslovakia
during the spring and summer of 1968, and especially to the
speculation concerning the creation of a new Little Entente
(to include Czechoslovakia, Rumania, and Yugoslavia). The
formation of any independent alliance or group among Moscow's neighbors and allies has always been anathema to the
USSR, but the establishment of one in which a formerly
loyal ally was allegedly to participate with both the Warsaw Pact maverick and a state completely outside the Pact
framework would stimulate the most vociferous objections.
Although it is true that Bulgarian efforts to promote Balkan
cooperation have since received Soviet blessing, this is
probably because the main purpose of them is to increase
Soviet influence and presence in an area where American
power has traditionally been preeminent. Thus the USSR has
little to lose and much to gain, particularly if it succeeds
in utilizing its Balkan presence to augment its influence
in the Mediterranean and the Middle East. On the other
hand, in the Danubian area (excluding West Germany) it is
the Soviet Union that is the predominant power, and it

---

*Since the average time required for the publication of
a book in Hungary is over two years, it is probable that
Ranki and Berend completed their manuscript in early 1967.

would not want to run the risk of allowing the West to diminish that predominance by taking advantage of the "weakness" of relatively autonomous regional groupings.

Aside from Soviet objections, a further damper was thrown on Hungarian intentions during Tito's state visit to Austria in early 1967, when a Yugoslav radio commentary seemed to reject Budapest's call for regional cooperation schemes in the Danube Valley.* Faced with such obstacles, the Hungarian leadership apparently felt compelled to jettison its original proposals and adopt another approach-- one more in accord with prevailing Soviet and East European policies yet not out of tune with the kind of regional détente sought earlier.

In its most visible form this approach has consisted of bilateral, but parallel, economic arrangements with Hungary's neighbors. One example of this is local border trade, under which trade and cooperation ventures in, say, the Hungarian-Yugoslav border area are conducted apart from the annual and long-term trade agreements between the two countries and on a relatively autonomous basis. It is usually characterized by direct contact between the individual economic units involved and by the free flow of goods and services across the border. (Thus far, local border trade agreements have been concluded with Yugoslavia, Czechoslovakia, Rumania, and the USSR.) A second example is frontier planning, under which the frontier area of both sides of the border is considered a single territorial unit for purposes of economic development, environmental protection, and industrial cooperation. (Frontier planning agreements have been signed with Austria, Yugoslavia, Czechoslovakia, and Rumania.) Yet a third example is the connection of national power grids (for example, with Austria, Yugoslavia, Rumania, Czechoslovakia, and the USSR) and the existence or planned construction of joint oil and gas pipelines (with the USSR, Rumania, Yugoslavia, and Czechoslovakia). All these activities, as well as active participation in the affairs of the Danube River Commission, have helped make Hungary's border more porous and have created a greater sense of interdependence among the countries involved.

---

*"Care must be taken that certain European political circles do not entertain the view that small, neutral, or nonaligned countries of the old continent want to create a special club with narrow, special economic and political interests--for instance, in the Danubian area or elsewhere." (Radio Belgrade, 16 February 1967.)

Their effect has been augmented, moreover, by broader and
more intensive cultural exchanges, increasing tourism, and
more frequent political consultations (which have been most
striking with Austria in particular).

It should be stressed that, except for the Danube Commission, all these matters are regulated on a strictly bilateral basis. A quasi-regional effect has been created,
however, owing to the apparent parallelism of the over-all
arrangements, although it must also be said that none of
them is strictly analogous in detail. The Hungarians have
indeed shelved their regional cooperation proposals (at
least for the time being), but have found, it seems, a
reasonable substitute to carry on in the same spirit.
Should the European security conference be successful in
resolving some of the basic problems at issue, it is likely
that Hungary's bilateral activities in the Danubian Basin
would receive a welcome impetus.

NOTES

1. See Robert R. King, "Bucharest, Bonn, and East
Berlin: Rumania and Ostpolitick," Rumanian Background Re-
port/11, RFER (EERA), 18 December 1970.

2. See Lidova Demokracie, Prague, 17 February 1973.

3. See Nepszabadsag, Budapest, 22 March 1973.

4. Hungarian Exporter, Budapest, July 1973; MTI in
English, 24 August 1972; Radio Budapest, 24 August 1972,
1200 hours; Figyelo, Budapest, 19 August 1970, 1 December
1971, and 22 March 1974; Magyar Hirlap, Budapest, 4 March
1971.

5. Hungarian Exporter, August 1972 and July 1973;
MTI, 1 February 1974.

6. See Hungarian Situation Report/10, RFER (EERA), 9
March 1971, Item 5, and Vilaggazdasag, Budapest, 26 February 1971; and Hungarian Exporter, March 1974.

7. See Magyar Kozlony, Budapest, 3 October 1972; and
Hungarian SR/38, RFER (EERA), 17 October 1972, Item 4.

8. See, in particular, Charles Andras, "Neighbors on
the Danube," East-West BR, RFER (EWR), December 1967.

9. See Nepszabadsag, 13 December 1964.

10. See Andras, op. cit., pp. 62-63.

11. Cf., for example, Radio Budapest, 6 December 1966,
and Nepszabadsag, 25 December 1966.

12. Kozepkelet Europa gazdasagi fejlodese a XIX-XX.
szazadban [The Economic Development of East Central Europe
in the 19th and 20th Centuries] (Budapest: Kozgazdasagi
es Jogi Konyvkiado, 1969).

8

RUMANIA:
THE DIFFICULTY OF
MAINTAINING AN AUTONOMOUS
FOREIGN POLICY
Robert R. King

The Rumanian Socialist Republic (RSR) has been an enthusiastic advocate of European security, although for reasons that are quite contrary to those that led the Soviet
Union to favor the project. It views progress toward European security as a means of consolidating, perhaps expanding, its autonomy in foreign policy and of reducing the
possibility of Soviet interference in its internal affairs.
The Rumanians see three related benefits from the current
atmosphere of détente in Europe and in the interest in convening the Conference on Security and Cooperation in Europe.

First, the security conference will most probably produce a declaration of the principles that should govern international relations that, although not identical in wording, will be very similar in spirit to Rumania's oft-expressed view that international relations must be based
upon respect for sovereignty, equality, noninterference in
internal affairs, and mutual advantage. In making such a
declaration, the conference will give a certain international validity to these principles; the Soviet Union will
have made at least a verbal commitment to abide by them,
and this will amount to giving at least moral support to
Rumanian autonomy.

Second--a long-term benefit that Rumania hopes will
derive from the developing détente in Europe--the Soviets'
sense of security is likely to increase. As the Russians'
fear of hostile action from Western Europe declines, there
will, it is hoped, be a decline in the USSR's need to secure its Western border by demanding strict conformity to
Soviet wishes from the states of Eastern Europe. With the
Soviets feeling more secure, Rumania, as well as the other
states of Eastern Europe, could pursue policies that, while

not contrary to fundamental Soviet interests, at least take
national interests into greater consideration. The analogy
of Finland is not inappropriate in this context. Whether
an enhanced sense of security on the part of the Soviets
will produce a "Finlandization" of Eastern Europe remains
to be seen, but, if it does take place, Rumania's ability
to pursue an autonomous foreign policy would be preserved
and even expanded.

Finally, the movement to create a European security
system may well produce an expansion of both opportunities
for and interest in economic exchanges and cooperation.
In the mid-1960s Rumania received numerous economic benefits from Western states, primarily because of its foreign
policy. Recently East-West economic relations have come
to be based more on economic than on political considerations, and the Rumanians have faced growing trade and credit
repayment problems. The emphasis on East-West cooperation
is regarded by the RSR as a timely remedy to at least some
of its economic difficulties.

The importance of establishing a European security
system has increased in the eyes of the Rumanians as enthusiasm for it has grown. On the one hand, the development
of détente has to some extent improved Rumania's opportunities to follow an autonomous foreign policy, but on the
other it has led to fundamental changes in the international situation that have to a degree undermined existing
sources of support for this autonomy. Although one should
not underestimate the internal elements that impelled the
Rumanian leadership to adopt an independent course in foreign relations, a number of international factors enabled
them to do so and were exploited to this end.

Rumania's innovative foreign policy was initiated in
the early 1960s, at a time when the cold war confrontation
between the Soviet Union and the United States was still
the predominant feature of the international scene. The
East-West division was still clearly marked in Europe, and
both great powers were seeking to seduce wavering members
of the opposing alliance. The United States, and to a degree other Western powers including West Germany, encouraged the RSR's deviation and provided it with opportunities
for independent action. But thanks to the improvement in
Soviet-American relations, marked by the exchange of visits
between President Nixon and party leader Brezhnev in 1972
and 1973, America's interest in supporting a Soviet client
state's moves away from Moscow has decreased. Although
Rumania maintains its position as the East European state
with the highest proportion of trade with Western states,

economic opportunities in Rumania are still more limited
than those in the larger and more highly developed states
of Eastern Europe. The recent success of West Germany's
Ostpolitik has tended to minimize the importance of the
fact that Bucharest established diplomatic relations with
Bonn in 1967, long before the other Warsaw Pact states.
The economic concessions that this political action initially brought about are being terminated, and Rumania is
now on much the same footing as the rest of Eastern Europe
as far as Western states are concerned.

     Another factor that favored the development of Ruman-
ia's foreign policy autonomy was the Sino-Soviet conflict.
The Chinese were anxious to secure allies against the Soviet party, and the Rumanians shrewdly utilized neutrality
in the conflict to gain maximum concessions from the Soviet
Union. The vigorous reemergence of China into the international arena after its cultural revolution was accompanied
by the temporary development of closer relations between
it and Rumania. However, after Ceausescu's visit to China
in June 1971, which was followed by a period of Soviet
pressure on the RSR, Chinese-Rumanian relations entered a
quieter period. Both countries appear to have recognized
China's limited ability to support Rumania in the face of
any serious Soviet challenge. A reference by Chou En-lai
to the Chinese proverb "Distant waters cannot quench fire"
probably gave rise to second thoughts in Bucharest. Also,
the growing prominence of China in world affairs, marked
among other things by the visits of President Nixon and
Japanese Prime Minister Kakuei Tanaka to Peking, has probably led Chinese leaders to consider challenging Soviet
interests in the Balkans less important than improving relations with the United States and Japan.[1]

     The support and encouragement of Yugoslavia were also
important elements in the Rumanians' initial search for
autonomy. The RSR has closer political relations with Yugoslavia than with any other state, and Tito and Ceausescu
have also established a close personal relationship. Although the domestic policies of the two states are quite
different, their foreign policies are remarkably similar.
Recently, however, Yugoslav support for Rumania has become
somewhat uncertain. The purge of the leadership of the
Croatian republic that began in December 1971 and Tito's
attempts to reassert the authority of the party in social
and political life ushered in an era of domestic instability,
and the problem is compounded by Tito's advanced age and
his declining ability to participate actively in Yugoslav
affairs. In spite of these internal problems, however,

since the Brezhnev visit to Belgrade in the fall of 1971, Soviet-Yugoslav relations have improved. The result of all this has most probably been to create uncertainty in the minds of Rumanian leaders about how far Yugoslavia is willing to go in supporting their position.

Rumania's drive to find political support and to gain economic benefits by improving its relations with developing countries has not been highly successful thus far. The efforts to find new markets for manufactured goods and secure in return the raw materials needed for the RSR's economic development have had only limited success. Rumania's continued links with the Warsaw Pact and Comecon, the severance of which the Soviet Union is unlikely to tolerate, have precluded closer identification with the nonaligned states. Although Ceausescu has engaged in extensive personal diplomacy with the states of Asia, Africa, and Latin America, the political and economic dividends have been small.

As a result of changes in the international situation that produced those factors that previously favored Rumania's autonomous foreign policy, the current interest in European security has assumed a new significance for Rumania. At present it seems to offer the best hope of maintaining the autonomy that Rumania has achieved over the last decade. Under these circumstances the seriousness and vigor with which the Rumanians are approaching the problem of European security are understandable.

Because Soviet and Rumanian aims with regard to European security are contradictory, there have been a number of divergences in their respective approaches to the problem. Although both have been consistent advocates of a conference, the Soviet Union has been vague and imprecise with regard to guarantees of security. The Rumanians have been much more specific in spelling out the provisions that they consider essential if the security of all European states is to be guaranteed and if some states are to be prevented from interfering in the affairs of others.

Despite its different concept of the purpose of a European security system and despite important differences in outlook on some primary security issues, Rumania continues to participate in Warsaw Pact meetings and to subscribe to the various statements and declarations issued on the subject. Domestic commentary on the topic always assesses the Warsaw Pact pronouncements favorably and despite some differences describes Rumania's position as being in full accord with that of its allies in the pact. In an interview with a British paper,[2] Ceausescu specifi-

cally denied that there were any "contradictions between
how we in Rumania and the Soviet Union understand the question of achieving European security." Despite this, however, there are important differences on a number of primary issues.

THE PRINCIPLES OF INTERSTATE RELATIONS

The Rumanians have exhibited a continuing concern that
a declaration of the principles that should govern interstate relations be issued. Most of the bilateral and many
of the multilateral documents signed by representatives of
the Rumanian government or party include a statement of
such principles. Although its elements had been voiced
earlier, the most definitive Rumanian pronouncement on the
matter is contained in the well-known "Statement of the
Position of the Rumanian Workers' Party on the Problems of
the International Communist and Working-Class Movement"
issued in April 1964. Relations between countries with different social systems, the Rumanian party declared, should
be conducted on the basis of "settlement of international
controversies by negotiation, without resort to force, on
the basis of acknowledging the right of every people to
decide its own fate, of observing the sovereignty and territorial integrity of states, of full equality, and of noninterference in internal affairs." Relations among socialist states must be based on "national independence and sovereignty, equal rights, mutual advantage, comradely assistance, noninterference in internal affairs, observance of
territorial integrity, and the principles of socialist internationalism."[3] Since these principles were enumerated
in the Statement, Rumanian officials have constantly repeated them in essentially the same words.
As the campaign for a conference to deal with problems
of security and cooperation in Europe progressed, the Rumanians began to urge, as a matter of priority, the issuance
of a document to codify these principles of international
relations. As the time for the preparatory talks on the
security conference approached, the Rumanian government initiated a series of "joint solemn declarations" with various
other states to set the tone for the document to be issued
by the conference. As the process gained momentum, Ceausescu also began signing such declarations with leaders of
developing countries, and Rumania proposed to the United
Nations the adoption of an international agreement setting
forth these fundamental rights and duties. The principles

enunciated in the first documents were very similar to the generally accepted draft of principles drawn up during the preparatory CSCE talks at Helsinki, except that in addition the latter call for respect for human rights and fundamental freedoms and for fulfillment in good faith of obligations under international law. Later declarations have also included reference to international law.*

The Rumanians, however, have insisted on going beyond verbal declarations of principles and have been anxious to secure these rights in practice. A commentary in the party daily Scinteia[4] on the Helsinki preparatory talks observed that "simple recognition" of these principles was not enough; what is needed is "a solemn commitment by every state to observe these principles." Later, after the foreign ministers had met in Helsinki for the opening round of the conference, Rumanian diplomats criticized the preliminary statement of principles as "too weak" and insisted that the conference documents provide guarantees by agreeing that all states should take measures against any state that violated any of the principles, and should come to the aid of any victim of aggression.[5] The differences between Rumania and the Soviet Union in this regard are quite obvious. The Soviets have been vague and general in their proposals to the security conference sessions; the Rumanians, in contrast, have been quite specific and precise, proposing such provisions as the withdrawal of foreign troops, an end to military maneuvers, reduction of military expenditures, and creation of nuclear-free zones.[6]

---

*Joint declarations were signed during Ceausescu's visits to Belgium, Luxembourg, the Netherlands, Italy, West Germany, and Pakistan, as well as during the visits of the shah of Iran and the presidents of Sudan, Upper Volta, and the People's Republic of the Congo to Rumania. (For the texts of these declarations see Scinteia, Bucharest, 27 and 29 October 1972 and 20 January, 13 April, 23 May, and 5 and 30 June 1973.) The declarations with developing states also include such principles of particular concern to these countries as the sovereign right of a state to use its natural resources in keeping with its material interests, mutual advantage in international cooperation, and concern to promote economic and social progress in all nations. The Rumanian proposal to the United Nations was made in a communication to Secretary General Kurt Waldheim, which was made public by him on 6 November 1973.

SOVEREIGNTY AND EQUALITY

In approaching the question of European security, the Rumanians have sought to bolster their claims to sovereignty and equality by relying on the principles of international law. They have adopted almost without modification the classical international legal view of the sovereignty of the nation-state in international relations. A concise formulation of this view was expressed in an article in the party's theoretical monthly,[7] whose authors maintained that the purpose of a European security system "is to guarantee every nation's inalienable right to its sovereign and independent existence, peace, and security." They described these principles as "universal in the sense that they are equally binding on all states and protect all states to the same degree." No exception should be made for any military bloc or in the name of socialist internationalism: "What is prohibited by general international law cannot be permitted in the relations of any continent, region, or group of states with any particular state." To bolster this assertion the authors quoted "Engels's well-known view that 'true international collaboration is possible among European nations only if each of these nations is fully autonomous at home.'" In international law, any security system must "guarantee that small and medium-sized states may engage in international relations with fully equal rights, eliminating the 'right' of the strongest, the 'right' of the fist, and the law of the jungle, and establishing the role of law and 'the power of right.'" This emphatic avowal of the equality and sovereignty of every state has been a consistent theme in Rumanian foreign policy statements since the early 1960s.[8]

The Soviet Union has not denied that interstate relations must be based upon recognition of the sovereignty and equality of all states. In fact, nearly every Warsaw Pact statement has included lip service to this idea. Nevertheless, Moscow clearly relegates sovereignty to the rank of a secondary issue, while Bucharest gives it a position of primary importance. The Soviet Union and the orthodox members of the Warsaw Pact have sought to undermine the Rumanian view of international law, and, particularly since the invasion of Czechoslovakia in August 1968, East European ideologists and jurists have attempted to give a legal foundation to the Brezhnev Doctrine. Although their attempts have been countered by the Rumanians and directly attacked by the Yugoslavs, they have nevertheless tried to postulate an essential difference between relations among

capitalist states and relations among socialist states.
The former (as well as relations between socialist and
capitalist states, for the most part) are governed by the
classical principles of international law, including such
concepts as sovereignty, equality, and independence. Socialist states are fundamentally different, however, because
they have undergone a social transformation that has moved
them into a higher stage of development, and hence relations among socialist states are based on the principles
of proletarian internationalism, which include the fraternal obligation to come to the assistance of any socialist
state in which the progress of socialism is endangered by
reactionary forces. As an East German professor explained:

> The socialist sovereignty of every socialist coun-
> try includes that country's right and international
> obligation to maintain and develop its own social-
> ist achievements, and to defend the dictatorship
> of the proletariat and the social foundations of
> socialism in every other country of the social-
> ist commonwealth.[9]

Soviet apologists have not only attempted to justify the
right to intervene in the affairs of other socialist
states but also have more or less openly criticized the Rumanians for failing to accept their reasoning. One Soviet
author recently argued that for any country to oppose the
Soviet Union is "contrary to its own vital interests."
Nevertheless, there are some "who do not bother to grasp
the fact that principles of sovereignty and independence
would quickly become fiction if the real and effective aid
of the Soviet Union and other socialist countries were not
in tangible proximity."[10]
    These contradictory views are of course a reflection
of more fundamental differences. Rumania is anxious to
build up a bloc of small states that will insist upon their
sovereignty and equality in order to reach the goal of security in relation to the great powers. The Soviet Union
desires that its primacy be recognized and accepted by the
Warsaw Pact states. Although Moscow wants European security negotiations to be conducted by individual countries,
not blocs, in order to take advantage of differences among
the members of the North Atlantic Alliance, it is equally
anxious that the Warsaw Pact states accept and follow the
Soviet leadership. The justification for these opposing
positions in terms of international law and of Marxist
ideology is merely a legalistic superstructure that reflects

more basic differences of opinion. Bucharest seeks to expand and consolidate the limited autonomy it has won from
the Soviet Union, and Moscow is anxious to maintain its
control over Eastern Europe in the face of the disintegrative pressures set in motion by détente.

THE ROLE OF SMALL- AND
MEDIUM-SIZED STATES

In their attempts to have the principles that they advocate in international relations put into practice the Rumanians have sought to create a unified bloc of small- and
medium-sized states, to ensure that their interests are
taken into consideration in any security system that may
be evolved. The RSR fears that an agreement between the
great powers may be made at its expense and without its
consent. This anxiety lest other powers determine its
fate, linked with the campaign to expand its autonomy in
foreign policy, has led Rumania to emphasize increasingly
the necessity for small- and medium-sized states to play
an important role in international affairs. It has insisted
that any European security system must guarantee the sovereignty of small states and has consistently linked the
setting up of any such system with the postulate that agreement must be reached on the basis of participation by all
nations concerned. The frequent bilateral exchanges between Rumania and smaller European states (Denmark, Holland,
Belgium, Luxembourg, Finland, Yugoslavia) have provided
opportunities to reiterate this concern and to seek agreement on certain common issues. Rumanian leaders have frequently made statements such as: "lasting security can
only be achieved through joint effort; it will be the result not of an agreement reached among several states or
among existing blocs, but of an understanding among all
states on the continent on the basis of the fact that they
have equal rights."[11]

This concern for the role of small countries has understandably not met with a favorable reaction in the other
states of the Warsaw Pact. Although there had been earlier
indications that they disapproved of the RSR's position,
the invasion of Czechoslovakia and the enunciation of the
Brezhnev Doctrine marked the beginning of more general
criticism. Rumania was not the only state to express the
view that small states had an important role to play, but
it was the only member of the Warsaw Pact to do so; and
specific criticism of Rumania's position was voiced by a

number of loyal pact members. Hungary, which has occasionally taken the lead in censuring Rumania's autonomous foreign policy, has been a primary critic of its emphasis on
the role of small states. One of the most direct attacks
came in the summer of 1971, after Ceausescu's visit to
Peking. The Hungarian trade union daily published an article that explained that "the role of alliance systems has
become more important" and hence that both "small and large
countries" have "a greater opportunity to engage in foreign
political activity" within alliances. Lenin's authority
was invoked to bolster the observation that although states
were entitled to self-determination, there was also a danger that "nationalist distortions and an inclination toward
national isolation" would make their appearance.[12] The
implied criticism of Rumania was obvious.

To emphasize the role of small states and to ensure
that their interests are not ignored, Rumania has partici-
pated vigorously in the various phases of the security conference. Its delegation to the preliminary consultations
that opened in Helsinki in late November 1972 made its
presence felt on the very first day, and during the first
week of the talks Rumania was cast in the role of enfant
terrible, tenaciously maintaining its point of view in the
face of obvious Soviet and East European opposition and
perhaps less than enthusiastic support from the other states
present. During the opening ceremonies, the Rumanian delegation unsuccessfully sought recognition from the Finnish
diplomat who had been selected chairman just as he adjourned the session. The Rumanians protested this step,
and at the next session they received an apology.

This little skirmish, however, was only a prelude to
the complex problems involved in setting up procedural rules
to govern the deliberations during the preparatory conference. The chairman drew up a list of 10 such rules, which
were the outcome of discussion by the various delegations
during the first few days of the conference. The Rumanians
were insistent that decisions reached at the conference be
based on consensus rather than majority vote, and since this
was also advocated by a number of other delegations it was
agreed that decisions would be adopted on this basis--that
is, in the absence of objection by any delegation.

The Rumanians reportedly wanted to see the chairmanship rotated among the participating states, but acceded
to the desire of the other delegations to have a Finnish
chairman throughout. The question of the vice-chairmanship, however, did give rise to differences. The original
proposal was that a vice-chairman, or an "acting chairman,"

would be selected if the chairman could not preside at any session. The Rumanians insisted that the vice-chairmanship should rotate, and also that the chairmanships of any working groups that might be established to deal with particular problems also be rotated. This proposal was not particularly welcomed by many of the delegations, who felt that rotating chairmen for the working groups would lead to inefficiency and would slow down the progress of the consultations. The Rumanians, however, were adamant. They later insisted that the location of the various phases of the conference also be rotated, and in both cases their demands were acceded to, primarily because of their tenacious insistence.

The Rumanians consider having both chairmanship and location rotate "an expression of the equality of rights of states and of the participation of all in the organization and development of the proceedings of the conference."[13] They have stressed that the principle of rotation, which is now being reflected for the first time in an international conference, "is a significant contribution to the development of international practice."

The major point of disagreement that the Rumanians raised at the beginning of the preparatory talks was related to the first point in the draft of the procedural rules,[14] which stated: "All states attending shall participate on the basis of complete equality and independence." While insisting upon the equality, sovereignty, and independence of all participating states the Rumanians wanted to go one step further and have the rule specify that participation would be "irrespective of a country's membership in any military alliance." It was this demand that provoked the greatest opposition.

The Soviet delegation stated that it could not see the legal significance of the Rumanian wording, and the Bulgarian, Czechoslovak, East German, Hungarian, and Polish delegations expressed the opinion that there was no reason to include the formulation. In contrast to the strong opposition of the Warsaw Pact states, most West European states and Yugoslavia were apparently willing to go along with the Rumanian wording in order to achieve consensus on the procedural regulations.

Despite the refusal of the Soviet Union and the other Warsaw Pact states to accept its demand, Rumania remained adamant. Finally, however, the Rumanians themselves proposed a compromise formula--that the consultations would "take place outside the framework of military alliances." The Soviet Union and other states accepted this, and it was included in the version of the rules that was ultimately adopted.[15] The Rumanians' unyielding insistence that their demands be accepted was based on the view that the conference must recognize the rights and role of small- and medium-sized states in international relations, and must not become an occasion for great powers to decide the fate of smaller nations. While certain of the small states in Western Europe were unwilling themselves to take such a stand, many apparently applauded the Rumanians for doing so. Interestingly enough, despite the universal opposition of the Warsaw Pact states to the Rumanian proposals at Helsinki, the differences were played down in the East European news media, probably in order to avoid escalating the confrontation and creating the impression that the USSR was insisting upon conformity among its East European client states.

MILITARY ISSUES AND DISARMAMENT

Because of its concern that a European security system ensure it a continuing opportunity to pursue its autonomous foreign policy, Rumania has been anxious to move beyond merely securing a commitment on the part of all European states to observe certain principles in foreign relations. One of the RSR's primary aims has been to establish limitations on the ability to use force against other states through some kind of agreement in conjunction with a security system. The Rumanians have argued, logically enough, that "while the principle of abstention from force is an essential legal bastion of security, elimination of the instruments of force--the armaments--is its material guarantee."[16] While preventing the USSR from resorting to force is the principal consideration, the approach has been to seek general agreements that apply to all states. This avoids a direct Soviet-Rumanian confrontation over the issue, since the Soviet Union has at least agreed in principle to limit the use of force. Also, if all states accept practical limitations on their ability to use force, the Soviets' feeling of insecurity should decrease, and European opinion may pressure the USSR into accepting an agreement.

The simultaneous dissolution of both NATO and the Warsaw Pact in the context of a wider security agreement has been a move consistently advocated by Rumania. The Soviet Union and its allies stated in the treaty that established the Warsaw Pact in 1955 that their military alliance exists only to counter the NATO alliance and will be dissolved as soon as the Western alliance ceases to exist. The Warsaw Pact states have emphasized or played down the idea of dissolution of blocs as their assessment of the international scene required. Generally, however, their interest in the issue seems to be related primarily to its propaganda value, rather than to a sincere commitment to abolishing military alliances. In the declaration on European security issued in Bucharest in 1966, the Warsaw Pact member states, including the USSR, called for "simultaneous dissolution of existing military alliances" and their replacement by a "system of European security."[17] This proposal has been reiterated in numerous documents and commentaries on European security, although it was played down increasingly as prospects for a security conference brightened. Despite its even-handed phrasing, however, the Soviet Union has consistently said that the first moves toward dissolution ought to be taken by NATO, with the implication that the Warsaw Pact will follow suit afterward. At the conference of European communist parties at Karlovy Vary in 1967, Soviet party leader Leonid Brezhnev called upon "Communists and progressive forces" to work for the dissolution of NATO, and proposed that the members of the Western alliance accept neutrality "as an alternative to participation in this military-political grouping."[18]

The Rumanians have been more consistent and apparently more sincere in their advocacy of the dissolution of both military blocs; in fact, the proposal was incorporated into the April 1964 "Statement."[19] It has since become customary to link the reduction of tension and the encouragement of a climate of détente to the elimination of blocs--as, for example, when Ceausescu told the 10th Rumanian party congress in August 1969, "In the first place, the liquidation of military blocs, both the aggressive North Atlantic bloc and, simultaneously, the military Warsaw Treaty, would greatly benefit the cause of security and peace in general."[20]

Although the Rumanians continue to cite military alliances as a threat to security and peace, they have also criticized them as an infringement of the sovereignty of the member states. The division of the world and of Europe into hostile political and military blocs was declared "not only an incentive to the armaments race but also an obstacle to the full exercise of their functions as sovereign, independent states by the natural subjects of international relations, the sovereign nations."[21] Recently the calls for the simultaneous dismantling of military alliances have perhaps not been repeated as frequently as they were earlier, but nevertheless Rumanian commentary upon European security continues to insist upon their dissolution.[22]

A comment by Polish Foreign Minister Olszowski during his visit to Vienna in June 1972 may indicate the current attitude of orthodox members of the Warsaw Pact on the elimination of blocs. During a lecture on European security to the Austrian Foreign Policy Society, he stated that Poland would not suggest the immediate dissolution of existing military blocs but would instead advocate the establishment of a new security system based upon their existence. If Olszowski's comment reflects the views of the Soviet Union and other Warsaw Pact states, the differences between Rumania and its allies may widen, particularly since Bucharest considers this to be an important security issue.

In addition to demanding the liquidation of military blocs, the Rumanians have for years consistently listed a number of related military measures that will contribute to the creation of a climate of security and détente. These include negotiations to reduce the size of national armies, the elimination of all foreign military bases, the withdrawal of all troops within their own national borders, and the cessation of military maneuvers on the borders of other states.[23] Quite obviously, such proposals are directed against the "peace-loving" Soviet Union (which has troops stationed in East Germany, Poland, Czechoslovakia, and Hungary), as well as against the "aggressive" North Atlantic Alliance (which stations American, British, and French troops in West Germany). The demand that military maneuvers on the borders of other states be discontinued first appeared only at the time of the invasion of Czechoslovakia, but it has become a standard demand since that time. The proposals that foreign military bases be eliminated and that all troops be withdrawn within their national borders were contained in the Warsaw Pact's Bucharest declaration of 1966. Although Soviet statements refer to these proposals on occasion, they do so less frequently and with less conviction than do Rumanian commentaries.

Rumania has also linked European security with general, or at least European, disarmament. Although this is not the place to enter into detailed discussion of Soviet-Rumanian differences over general disarmament, it should be said that Rumania has been an active participant in the disarmament talks in Geneva and has proposed a number of resolutions on this topic to the General Assembly of the United Nations. In this connection it has followed the policy it considers to be in its own best interest, and frequently its views have differed from those of the Soviets. Nor have Rumanian spokesmen been above criticizing the Soviet Union, as well as the United States, for failing to make any substantial progress toward disarmament.[24]

Also related to both disarmament and European security are Rumania's proposals that a denuclearized zone be created in the Balkans. On the one hand the growing movement toward some type of European security arrangement gives Rumania a favorable opportunity to advance its Balkan proposals, and on the other the creation of a nuclear-free zone and the furthering of multilateral cooperation in this region are factors that would contribute to European security.*

MUTUAL FORCE REDUCTION TALKS

The Rumanian position on the question of mutual force reduction in Central Europe has accorded with the positions it has taken on other issues related to European security. Consistent with their concern that the security of Europe be guaranteed by steps toward disarmament and practical limitations on the use of force, the Rumanians have been anxious to have the question of reducing the size of armies dealt with in conjunction with the general talks on European security. They have also been quite anxious that all European states participate in such talks. This insistence upon including all states in the military discussions is related to the desire to enhance the role of small- and medium-sized states in international affairs and to have the equality, sovereignty, and independence of all states recognized. There also appears to be some fear that a bloc-to-bloc confrontation would result in agreements that would favor the Soviet Union and the United States but that would not consider the interests of countries like Rumania. The Rumanian position was expressed in specific terms by Ceausescu on the eve of the preparatory talks in Helsinki,[25] and just a week after a number of the NATO states had proposed to the Warsaw Pact states, excluding Rumania and Bulgaria, that talks on mutual and balanced force reductions start.

The Soviet Union had different motives for favoring the talks on mutual force reductions, which led to certain areas of difference and others of agreement with the Ruman-

_____

*See Chapter 10 for more on this topic.

ian view. The Soviets have been anxious to secure general political statements of principle on European security that will encourage both détente and a weakening of America's strength in Europe with as little commensurate reduction of their own strength as possible. Hence they favored separating discussion of military matters from the general discussions on European security, in order to prevent their caution at the former from obstructing progress at the latter. In order to slow down the force reduction talks and perhaps to induce unilateral American reductions, the Soviet Union favored including as many states as possible in these talks. The interest in encouraging French participation, which appears to have been the thrust of Brezhnev's talks with Georges Pompidou in Minsk in January 1973, apparently sprang from this concern.

The Rumanian desire to participate in the talks and the Soviet desire to expand their scope led the Soviet Union in January 1973 to suggest, in response to an earlier NATO proposal, that additional states, including Bulgaria and Rumania, be drawn into the talks. Once the preliminary discussions began in Vienna, the Rumanians finally accepted a kind of observer status in the discussions because of strong objections on the part of NATO to the participation of states other than those directly involved in the areas to be affected by force reductions. During this initial period the Soviet Union continued to advocate that Rumania participate as a full member. Although it accepted observer status, the RSR continued to express the view that all interested states should be able to express their views at the force reduction conference.[26]

Later developments in the Vienna preparatory talks aroused further Rumanian dissatisfaction. Among the events that caused particular concern were the sudden decision to change Hungary's status at the negotiations from participant to observer, the tendency to restrict discussion to full participants, and the unwillingness to accord observers the right to make proposals. The decision to exclude Hungary from the zone to be covered in the force reduction negotiations was probably a source of major concern to Rumania, since Soviet troops are still stationed there. The first signs of Rumanian irritation were contained in a series of articles published in the party daily Scinteia (on 9, 12, 13, and 14 May 1973). The essential point was that all nations, large or small, have the right to be consulted and to participate, on equal terms, in the processes of negotiation and decision making on issues of concern to themselves in particular and to the international

community in general. No single state, <u>Scinteia</u> said, has
the right to make decisions on behalf of other states, and
all states have the right to be kept informed so that no
decisions detrimental to their security interests can be
made in Vienna.

That these articles were in fact directed at the great
powers because of their conduct at the force reduction
talks was made clear by Rumanian delegates in Vienna.[27]

ECONOMIC, TECHNOLOGICAL, AND
CULTURAL COOPERATION

In addition to the problems related to security there
is the question of cooperation among European states, which
was the second major item on the CSCE agenda proposed by
the Warsaw Pact conference on security and cooperation.
The primary area of concern for the Warsaw Pact states is
the expansion of trade and of economic, scientific, and
technological cooperation. Both the Soviet Union and Rumania have enthusiastically encouraged this aspect of détente in Europe, each for its own reasons. The USSR is
anxious to take advantage of Western technology and research
in order to strengthen its economy and enable it to compete
with Western enterprises on a more equal basis. (The desired effect would be to make Soviet goods more advanced,
which the Soviet Union hopes would, among other things,
strengthen its economic ties with Eastern Europe.) The
Rumanians, on the other hand, see the general expansion of
trade and economic-technological-scientific cooperation as
providing a new opportunity to revitalize their own attempts
to expand trade with the West and thus reduce their dependence upon their fellow Comecon states.

In recent years the Rumanians have encountered increasing difficulties both in their domestic economy and
in foreign trade. The shift in the orientation of trade
toward the West initially resulted in substantial benefits
to the Rumanian economy. Not only was Rumania getting more
advanced Western goods, but Western states, West Germany
in particular, were willing to extend it generous credit
terms, primarily for political reasons. Although these
Western credits were responsible for a large portion of
Rumania's economic growth, they have also exacerbated Rumania's domestic economic problems, since repayments have
recently begun to fall due and meanwhile West Germany and
other West European states have made it clear that they
would not "purchase" improved relations with the states of

Eastern Europe by continuing to extend generous credit
terms.*   At the same time, like most other East European
states Rumania has been having difficulty in marketing its
manufactured goods in the West, and therefore exports are
not expanding as expected.   Under the circumstances Bucharest has found it necessary to reach economic agreements
with the Soviet Union and to increase its participation in
Comecon to an extent that it would probably have preferred
to avoid.   These moves did not indicate a change in Rumania's
basic economic policy of diversifying its trade partners
and relying less on trade with its Warsaw Pact allies but
rather the fact that economic realities have required certain adjustments.

As a result of these economic problems, Rumania has
taken a number of steps to reduce its trade deficit: it
has adopted new legislation permitting the establishment
of cooperative economic ventures, 49 percent of whose capital can be owned by private Western companies, with which a
number of agreements have already been reached for the establishment of such companies; it has concluded a number
of agreements on economic cooperation with less-developed
countries; it became the first Warsaw Pact state to deal
officially with the European Economic Community, when it
requested and was granted general trade preferences; it
has sought recognition as a developing country, in order
to gain the trade benefits that developed countries extend
to this group of states; and it has sought, thus far unsuccessfully, most-favored-nation treatment by the United
States.   For Rumania, therefore, the European security and
cooperation campaign represents a new opportunity to revive
its drive for greater economic links with the West.   Although the ultimate goals of all-European economic-technological-scientific cooperation sought by the Soviet Union
and Rumania are divergent, the views on the need for such
cooperation and on how to achieve it are close.[28]

The Soviet and Rumanian positions on other areas of
cooperation are even more similar.   The Rumanians, like

---

*During his state visit to West Germany in June 1973
Ceausescu reportedly sought a long-term, low-interest credit
of 300-400 million Deutsche marks and most-favored-nation
status for Rumania's exports.   The West Germans apparently
were unwilling to grant the former request and unable to
grant the latter, since their trade policy is now under the
jurisdiction of the Common Market.   (See the Frankfurter
Allgemeine Zeitung, 28 June 1973.)

the Soviets, are in favor of cooperation in the areas of "education and art . . . hygiene and public health, protection of the environment . . . traffic in and consumption of drugs, alcoholism, and crime."[29]

However, when it comes to such issues as the free flow of information, ideas, and people, the Rumanians, like other members of the Warsaw Pact, have been much less eager to encourage cooperation. Thus far they have not become involved in the bilateral ideological agreements that have been negotiated between the other Warsaw Pact states, probably because they object to the anti-Chinese overtones of most of the agreements and because they may wish to emphasize and maintain their autonomy in foreign affairs. But this does not imply that Rumania is ideologically less vigilant or orthodox. Although some of the more repressive effects of the cultural-ideological campaign launched by Ceausescu in July 1971 have been mitigated, cultural life remains severely restricted and exchanges with non-Rumanians are carefully regulated. Any expansion of contacts with West Europeans will probably be carried out only under close party control.

HOPES AND HAZARDS

Rumanian-Soviet differences on the question of European security and cooperation are a function of differences in underlying goals and objectives, and they only become apparent when the two states' over-all foreign policies and the implications of these policies are being considered. In statements by Rumanian and Soviet leaders and commentaries in the mass information media, the two states are in at least formal agreement on most issues relating to European security. Rumania has been careful to express its views by stressing some parts of Warsaw Pact declarations and ignoring others.

The numerous statements on the subject that appeared in both countries earlier did not go into specific detail regarding the matters at issue. In the past the West European states' insistence that certain preconditions be fulfilled before a security conference was convened made explicit statements of position unnecessary, but the situation has changed. Now that the conference is well under way, it has become necessary for all states to consider and express precisely what they desire and will accept, and during the sessions of the conference that have been held thus far it has become apparent that there exist certain elements of strain in the relationship between Moscow and Bucharest and that more are likely to appear.

The decisions of the security conference will be a major element in determining the future system of international relations in Europe and will thus have a major effect on Soviet-Rumanian relations. On questions of such moment neither side will be willing to compromise on important issues. In the past Rumania's relations with the Soviet Union have followed a pattern of confrontation followed by a period of "consolidation" in which tension has eased but no substantial concessions have been made to Moscow; a period of consolidation has been in turn followed by another confrontation. Relations between the two countries are currently in the consolidation stage, following the confrontation that was provoked by Ceausescu's visit to China in 1971. Another phase of confrontation could come on the head of the security conference.

If their relations do become strained over the issues of European security, Bucharest would seem to be in a relatively strong position. The Soviet leaders have indicated a serious interest in holding a successful security conference. They have been willing to make important concessions on Berlin and to risk alienating East Germany. They have personally committed themselves to détente, and hence they are most unlikely to rescind these concessions and forfeit the goodwill they have built up just in order to force Rumania to conform its foreign policies to Soviet wishes. This is particularly true since Rumania is unlikely to move much beyond the positions it has maintained for the last several years. If the Rumanians manage a new confrontation with Moscow with the same skill they have shown in the past, they could well be successful in resisting Soviet pressure.

It is perhaps not an exaggeration to say that Rumania's autonomy in foreign policy depends on the outcome of the security conference. To a great extent, however, that outcome will be strongly influenced, if not determined, by Soviet-American relations, by the Warsaw Pact and NATO, and by the larger nations of Western Europe. Although the Rumanians are aware of this, they have certainly not been fatalistic about their future. The vigor and energy with which they have defended their interests have earned them the admiration of many. But diplomatic skill and daring are not enough; economic and political realities suggest a somewhat gloomier prognosis for Rumanian autonomy. Economic considerations have already forced the RSR to make long-term commitments for Soviet raw materials. Thus far the Soviet Union has provided a more welcome market for Rumanian manufactured goods than have Western states. Attempts to expand trade relations with the West have encountered problems despite initial successes, and the alternative of securing raw materials and a market for manufactured goods in developing countries has been less successful than hoped. Politically, the international conditions that favored and permitted the evolution of Rumanian autonomy--the cold-war confrontation, the Sino-Soviet dispute, the proven viability of the independent Yugoslav model--have for different reasons become less propitious. Unless the security conference produces major shifts in the Soviet attitude toward Eastern Europe (which is most unlikely), the maintenance of an autonomous foreign policy will become increasingly difficult.

And this policy, while no doubt approved by the majority of the population, has not been institutionalized. For most of the last decade it has been identified with and controlled by one man--Nicolae Ceausescu. Although the bulk of the party membership probably accept Ceausescu's continuation of the foreign policy initiated under Gheorghe Gheorghiu-Dej, there are probably also many in the party who question its wisdom or value. There are certainly some who, for emotional or ideological reasons, would favor better and closer relations with Moscow. There are also others who would probably favor economic reforms along the lines of those being carried out in Hungary. Since the Soviet leaders are not likely to tolerate both experimentation with the economic system and autonomy in foreign policy, they would give priority to economic issues. A change of party leader would probably bring about an improvement in relations with the Soviet Union.

Even if Ceausescu remains head of the Rumanian party for some time there may be internal pressure for a shift of emphasis in foreign policy. After his eight-nation African tour in March-April 1972 there were reports of criticism of his personal diplomacy as being high in cost and low in benefits. The internal economic problems which Rumania faces are serious. Continual reorganizations plus the continuing demand for high investment have produced strains. For the population, the party's policies have brought about some improvement in the standards of living; however, investment in consumer goods is low, and the problem of food supply has been aggravated by the agricultural policies. Under these circumstances the popular appeal of an autonomous foreign policy may well lose some of its luster, and consequently the emphasis accorded it may also decline.

188

NOTES

1. For a discussion of these problems in Rumanian-Chinese relations see Robert R. King, "Rumania and the Sino-Soviet Conflict," Studies in Comparative Communism 4 (Los Angeles, Winter 1972): 373-393.
2. The Sunday Times, London, 10 October 1971.
3. Scinteia, Bucharest, 26 April 1964.
4. 14 May 1973. See also Scinteia, 9 September 1973.
5. See, for example, the Reuter dispatch from Helsinki, 6 July 1973.
6. Cf. Rumanian Foreign Minister Gheorghe Macovescu's speech in Helsinki (Scinteia, 5 July 1973) and that of Soviet Foreign Minister Andrei Gromyko (Pravda, Moscow, 4 July 1973).
7. Nicolae Ecobescu and Edwin Glaser, "European Security and International Law," Lupta de Clasa, no. 3 (Bucharest, March 1972). Ecobescu is a deputy foreign minister and Glaser a leading specialist in international law.
8. Articles supporting the Rumanian view of sovereignty on the basis of international law include D. Tinu, "European Security Can Only Be Built on the Basis of the Principle of Sovereign Equality for All States," Scinteia, 25 October 1973; Sergiu Celac, "Toward Full Affirmation of the Principle of Equality in the Law of States," Lupta de Clasa, no. 10 (October 1971); Constantin Lazarescu, "National Sovereignty, Socialist Internationalism," ibid., no. 3 (March 1971); and Constantin Vlad, "Internationalism, National Sovereignty, and Patriotism," ibid., no. 4 (April 1970). Two extended treatments of the Rumanian view are Gheorghe Moca's Socialismul si Suveranitatea de Stat [Socialism and State Sovereignty] (Bucharest: Editura Politica, 1972) and his Suveranitatea de Stat: Teorii Burgheze Studiu Critic [Sovereignty of the State: A Critical Study of Bourgeois Theories] (Bucharest: Editura Politica, 1973). Although in the latter book Moca criticizes a number of American scholars who suggest limitation of sovereignty his vigorous assertion of it as a principle applicable to the socialist state affirms the Rumanian rejection of limitations on state sovereignty from any quarter.
9. Herbert Kroeger, Horizont, no. 43 (East Berlin, October 1969). For similar Soviet arguments see Pravda, 26 September 1968, and K. Ivanov, "Lessons for the Future," International Affairs, no. 10 (Moscow, October 1968).
10. Sh. Sanakovey, "The Socialist Countries in the Struggle for Security in Europe," Mezdunarodnaya Zhizn, no. 3 (Moscow, March 1972).

11. *Scinteia*, 26 July 1971.

12. Tamas Palos, "Small Countries--Big Policy," *Neps-zava*, Budapest, 20 August 1971.

13. Interview with Valentin Lipatti, Rumanian ambassador to Finland and chief of the Rumanian delegation at the multilateral preparatory talks, *Lumea*, Bucharest, 21 June 1973.

14. The text of these draft rules was released by Reuter on 24 November 1972.

15. The final text of the procedural rules was released by Reuter on 28 November 1972.

16. Ecobescu and Glaser, op. cit.

17. "Declaration on Strengthening Peace and Security in Europe," *Pravda*, 9 July 1966.

18. Ibid., 25 April 1967.

19. *Scinteia*, 23 April 1964.

20. Ibid., 7 August 1969.

21. Ecobescu and Glaser, op. cit.

22. See, for example, *Scinteia*, 27 April 1972, and Constantin Mitea, "The Idea of European Security in Light of Practical Actions," *Lupta de Clasa*, no. 2 (February 1972).

23. See, for example, the commentary in *Scinteia* on the eve of the Helsinki meeting (30 June 1973), and Foreign Minister Gheorghe Macovescu's address to that gathering, as reported in ibid., 5 July 1973.

24. For Rumanian commentaries on disarmament that are also related to the question of European security, see *Scinteia*, 21 September and 20 November 1971, 4 and 17 March and 23 June 1972, and 26 September 1973, and *Romania Libera*, Bucharest, 5 September 1973.

25. In a speech to the Rumanian Central Committee plenum of 20-21 November 1972. See *Scinteia*, 21 November 1972. See also *Era Socialista*, no. 6 (14) (Bucharest, November 1972), p. 32.

26. See the Rumanian delegation's statement accepting observer status as released to APA/Vienna, 14 February 1973.

27. *Arbeiterzeitung*, Vienna, 20 May 1973, and Ager-pres, 28 June 1973.

28. For statements on the Rumanian position on economic, technical, and scientific cooperation, see Nicolae Belli and Marian Chirila, "European Security and Economic Collaboration," *Lupta de Clasa*, no. 2 (February 1972); Costin Murgescu, "European Security and Economic Cooperation," *Era Socialista*, no. 19 (October 1973); *Viata Econom-ica*, Bucharest, 4 February 1972; and *Scinteia*, 11 October and 1 November 1973.

29. Mitea, op. cit. See also *Scinteia*, 19 October 1973.

YUGOSLAVIA:
IDEOLOGICAL CONFORMITY
AND POLITICAL-MILITARY
NONALIGNMENT
Slobodan Stankovic

The desire of the Yugoslav leaders that the European security conference should be successful is sincere, and they have energetically worked toward that end. Their objectives, however, differ in a number of respects from those pursued by the other states in Eastern Europe. Yugoslavia's singular concerns are a function of two factors: first, the country's unique position as a friend of the Soviet Union and the Warsaw Pact states on one hand and of the United States and the countries of Western Europe on the other; and second, its geographical position.

Yugoslavia is a state ruled by a communist party, but it has chosen to pursue its own independent path and rejects ideological tutelage from the Soviet Union. At the same time it maintains a policy of nonalignment in foreign affairs, in that it rejects superpower hegemony and does not belong to either of the European blocs. This policy, however, is limited to military and political matters; the Yugoslavs have specifically excluded ideological nonalignment. (This has created certain practical problems, since the Soviet Union's insistence that ideological conflict must continue in all spheres tends to undermine the Yugoslav policy of military and political nonalignment.)

Yugoslavia is in a critical geographical location. The Balkans, traditionally a major European trouble spot, continue to exhibit elements of instability. A local conflict could well pose a serious threat to Yugoslav security, since both the Soviet Union and the United States are linked through military alliances with Yugoslavia's neighboring states, Albania maintains close ties with China, and all are seeking to increase their influence in the area. In addition, Yugoslavia's proximity to the Middle East and

the eastern Mediterranean places it on the periphery of a
highly volatile area in which both superpowers are deeply
committed.

Further complicating the Yugoslav search for security
is its complex and problematical internal situation. The
serious national, economic, and political divisions that
are now giving rise to domestic difficulties impose certain
limits on Yugoslav foreign policy and tend to invite external interference. Hence the Yugoslavs anxiously seek to
prevent any agreement or disagreement between the two superpowers from having an unfavorable influence on their own
internal developments, and at the same time they are anxious
to prevent any domestic political, economic, or ideological
crisis from being used as a pretext for foreign intervention
from any quarter. A complicating factor is the imminence
of President Tito's departure from the scene. The Yugoslav
leaders are engaged in a race with time, since the ensuring
of a greater measure of domestic and international stability is more likely to be achieved if Tito's considerable
influence can be used in the process.

There appear to be three primary and related aims in
Yugoslavia's position on European security: to secure the
commitment, in deed as well as word, of the European states
to a declaration of principles that will preclude interference in Yugoslavia's internal affairs and provide the most
favorable circumstances for the continuation of the policy
of nonalignment; to ensure a greater degree of regional
security in the Balkans and the eastern Mediterranean; and
to prevent, via international and internal measures, any
action against Yugoslavia on the part of the superpowers
and to keep the security conference from becoming a bloc-
to-bloc confrontation that would ignore Yugoslav interests.

In the opening phase of the CSCE in Helsinki, Yugoslav
Foreign Minister Milos Minic submitted a declaration from
the Yugoslav government setting forth the principles that
should be observed in international relations. They ran
as follows:

1. recognition of the sovereign equality of all
    states; respect for the rights inherent in sover-
    eignty
2. abstention from any threat or use of force
3. recognition of the inviolability of frontiers
4. recognition of the territorial integrity of all
    states
5. resolution of all conflicts by peaceful means
6. noninterference in the internal affairs of other
    countries

7. respect for human rights and basic freedoms, in-
    cluding the freedom of thought, conscience, and
    religion
8. recognition of the equal rights of nations in gen-
    eral and of the right of self-determination in
    particular
9. cooperation among states
10. faithful fulfillment of international legal obli-
    gations[1]

These principles relate primarily to international relations, but they also reflect domestic needs and concerns.
It is clear from the commentaries on them that the Yugoslavs interpret them in a very specific and narrow fashion.

The principles of the inviolability of frontiers and
territorial integrity reflect concern for the problem of
regional security, which is given high priority in Yugoslavia. The Yugoslav-Bulgarian dispute over Macedonia is
the most immediate reason for Belgrade's insistence on
preserving the territorial status of all countries, and not
only those in Central Europe. "Changes in the balance in
the south or the southeast," said one Yugoslav political
analyst, "can easily upset the precarious balance in the
center and set it in motion. It is not easy to define
the main element of stability or security in Europe, but
it may be true that one of the weakest spots in the structure is the situation in the Balkans."[2] Shortly before
the Helsinki conference of foreign ministers started, the
same analyst wrote: "Even if a bilateral [Soviet-American]
agreement concerning Central Europe has been reached, the
fact remains that certain quarters are warming up illusions
about the revision of frontiers; in this respect some not
altogether peaceful campaigns in the southeastern part of
Europe are occasionally launched."[3] The highly emotional
question of Macedonia is the most inflammable issue in
Balkan politics, and Belgrade and Sofia have been unable
to resolve it despite repeated attempts and apparent goodwill on both sides. The insistence that Balkan security is
linked with the broader issue of European security is an
important Yugoslav concern. (See Chapter 10, on the Balkan
aspects of European security.)

Yugoslavia's interest in regional security, however,
has extended well beyond the Balkans. The fear of a great-
power confrontation in the unstable Middle East (a fear
that appears to be justified in light of the most recent
outbreak of hostilities in that area) has led the Yugoslavs
to insist that the two superpowers and the security conference be forced to deal not only with Europe but also with

a broader area, preferably a Europe enlarged by the Mediterranean countries, and that all be permitted to participate in deciding questions that affect their destinies. This idea was reiterated by Tito in a major speech at the nonaligned summit in Algeria on 6 September 1973, when he said: "Yugoslavia has always emphasized--and we did so in Helsinki as well--that Europe cannot become an island of tranquillity and prosperity in the middle of an ocean of instability and poverty. Europe's security is inseparably linked to the independence, security, and general prosperity of all nations." And he continued: "The security of Europe has, for instance, been closely linked to the situation in the Mediterranean, where the consequences of the Middle East crisis have been directly felt."[4] Although the Yugoslav proposal that the Mediterranean countries and their problems be dealt with at the CSCE has not yet been accepted, the latest Middle East conflict has underlined the close connection between European security and the problems of this area.

The fear of collusion between the United States and the USSR has been the consistent motivation behind Yugoslavia's attitude toward the security conference. As noted above, its nonaligned position has led the country's leaders to focus much of their foreign-policy activity upon preventing any agreement or dispute between the superpowers from adversely influencing Yugoslavia's own internal or external policies and on preventing an internal crisis from being used as a pretext for foreign intervention. As a result the Yugoslavs have been more vocal than other small European states in insisting that the CSCE must take into consideration the interests of small states as well as those of the superpowers.

Although the Yugoslavs are anxious to prevent the security conference from becoming a bloc-to-bloc affair, their concern appears to be with the superpowers themselves rather than with the blocs they lead. Yugoslav analysts explain that international activity does not necessarily involve a bloc as a whole but often consists of "individual action by the superpowers." In certain sometimes very important foreign political matters Moscow and Washington act without their allies (or at least some of them), and other individual members in each of the blocs also at times act independently of the leading powers.[5]

This reduction of the role of the blocs as such in international politics and the strengthening of divisive tendencies within them have, according to the Yugoslavs, given rise to special relations between the superpowers

that are more complex than in the past, when they were generally confined to confrontation. Today they take the form
of confrontation, competition, or cooperation, each of
which takes on a different aspect, depending on the situation.

Yugoslavia's fear for its own security is heightened
by the confrontation between the United States and the
Soviet Union in the Mediterranean and the Middle East, which
"makes the southeastern part of Europe significantly less
stable." Competition between Washington and Moscow in the
military field is regarded as undesirable, particularly
should the two superpowers try to extend their spheres
of influence (which in the long run would lead to new con-
frontations). But even cooperation between them, although
considered "the most constructive element in bilateral relations," is, in the opinion of Yugoslav observers, imbued
with "potential dangers, both for the future of any further
evolution of international relations and for the interests
of the remaining countries."[6]

It is difficult to understand precisely what the Yugoslavs regard as the solution to the problem posed by the
prevailing bipolar structure in Europe, even though they
continue to emphasize that détente has helped to transform
this structure gradually into a new system of relationships.
They maintain that the final goals must be the removal of
all barriers dividing the two blocs in Europe and the introduction of "really equal relationships" among European
states in place of "the existing hierarchical structure,"
which is dominated by the superpowers. In other words,
"Europe must free itself from the confrontation of the
superpowers and from dependence on their bilateral dealings,"
however well intentioned.[7] Except for claiming that this
is a "long-term goal," however, Yugoslav analysts have so
far been unable to suggest realistic measures that would
be acceptable to both the United States and the USSR. This
is particularly true when they talk about removing the
barriers dividing the two European blocs yet at the same
time paradoxically insist that ideological barriers cannot
be removed, that ideological coexistence cannot be accepted.

THE UNCERTAINTY OF SOVIET POLICY

Complicating the search for security is the problem
of Yugoslavia's relations with the Soviet Union. On the
one hand, the USSR represents probably the most serious
threat to Yugoslavia's security, but, on the other, simi-

larities in ideological outlook bring the two states together in uneasy cohabitation. The Yugoslav rejection of
ideological coexistence with "imperialist forces" is addi-
tionally complicated by the fact that Tito's ideological
coexistence with Moscow has also been deficient for the
past 25 years. Generally speaking, the Yugoslavs maintain
that the existence of the Soviet Union and other communist
countries has contributed to the survival of communist rule
in Yugoslavia in the face of "imperialist threats." They
have never forgotten, however, that they have had to face
serious threats from the Soviet Union, which has attempted
a number of times to replace Tito's "revisionist regime"
with one more amenable to its control. For this reason the
Yugoslav leaders have never concealed the fact that they
would prefer to see a different form of socialism prevail
in Eastern Europe.

In the Platform for the Preparation of Postitions and
Decisions of the 10th Congress of the League of Communists
of Yugoslavia, published in June 1973, the ideological
struggle between individual communist parties and states
was described as continuing and even worsening:

> The possibility of fresh confrontations and new
> forms of polarization cannot be excluded. Con-
> temporary trends have once again reaffirmed the
> untenability of the theory and practice that one
> single party, or one single state, or any other
> international center, can arrogate to itself the
> leading role.[8]

Hence, despite the improvement in Soviet-Yugoslav relations
that began after Brezhnev visited Belgrade in September
1971 in order to repair the strains caused by the August
1968 invasion of Czechoslovakia, the Yugoslav leaders have
no intention of abandoning their rejection of Soviet leadership.

Here again, however, the Yugoslavs are hindered by
their opposition to ideological coexistence. On the one
hand the Platform rejects all blocs, on the other it insists
that "new forms of international working-class solidarity"
must be found "which will counter the new forms of solidarity among the capitalist class."[9] This view of a socialist bloc facing a capitalist bloc contradicts the document's
attempt to portray the Yugoslav party as strictly opposed
to any bloc alignment.

In addition to holding similar views on ideology, the
Yugoslavs and the Soviets have adopted corresponding posi-

tions on certain foreign policy issues. The most prominent
example of this is their stand on the Middle East. During
the most recent hostilities the Yugoslavs gave permission
for Soviet aircraft carrying materiel to the Arab states
to use Yugoslav airspace and to refuel at Yugoslav air-
fields. Although Belgrade may expect something from Moscow in return, this action reflects the fundamental agreement between the two countries about the Middle East. The
Yugoslavs admitted that their pro-Soviet stand on this issue "has been very unfavorably received in the United
States."[10]

Although similar positions on other foreign policy
questions and a close correspondence of views on ideological issues have tended to bring Yugoslavia and the USSR
together, Soviet actions in Eastern Europe have frequently
produced major differences and have raised serious questions about Yugoslavia's security. The Soviet-led invasion
of Czechoslovakia stunned the Yugoslav leaders, and its
theoretical justification, the so-called "Brezhnev Doctrine,"
could be interpreted as permitting direct Soviet military
intervention in Yugoslavia as well. The effect of the action against Czechoslovakia created a new state of uncertainty in Belgrade. While Yugoslavia is generally regarded
as a communist state, the Soviet Union has vacillated from
time to time over whether it is a member of the "socialist
community" and hence whether the Brezhnev Doctrine would
be applicable to it or not.

Any direct Soviet attack on Yugoslavia would not only
have international repercussions but would also cement the
precarious unity among the Yugoslav nationalities. In
January 1973 Stane Dolanc, secretary of the Executive Bureau of the Yugoslav party Presidium, recalled in a television interview how "a high official from a Western state"
had questioned him about national defense in general and
the internal political dispute among the various nationality groups. Dolanc noted at the time that if anyone
should attempt to attack Yugoslavia or threaten its independence, the Yugoslavs "would ignore any differences of
opinion or conflicts and would arise as one man and unite
in the struggle against this threat from outside." The
diplomat listened carefully and then asked very politely,
"And what will happen if no one attacks you?"[11]

The fact that Dolanc raised the problem in front of
several million television viewers indicates that the Yugoslav leadership seriously considered the possibility of
both internal and external attempts by the Soviet Union
to draw the country into the Soviet sphere. Indeed, after

the events of 1968 it was the internal approach that was
Tito's greatest concern.

NATIONWIDE DEFENSE

The invasion of Czechoslovakia forcefully brought home
to Yugoslavia's leaders the inadequacy of their own defense
capabilities. The expansion of the Soviet military presence
in the Mediterranean area increased the possibility of a
great-power conflict in the Balkans, and given these circumstances Tito and his comrades decided at the beginning
of 1969 to place the country's defense on a new foundation.
Instead of relying only on a professional army, they opted
for the concept of "people's defense"--participation by the
entire population in military activities in the event of
war. In practice it meant that the defense of Yugoslavia
was decentralized and transferred to the local level.
    The February 1969 Law on National Defense proclaimed
"Nationwide Defense," the chief aim of which was to orga-
nize immediate resistance in such a way that "the enemy is
never allowed to relax, so that there is created in him a
feeling of insecurity, powerlessness, fear, panic, a loss
of faith in victory."[12] Under this law communal, local,
and republican authorities established headquarters responsible for national defense in peace and war. Every citizen
is pledged to take part in the armed defense of the country.
    In a series of lectures to the State Defense Academy
in Vienna at the beginning of 1971 the Croatian General
Srecka Manola, since dismissed because of his connections
with the purged party leadership in Croatia, described
what the Yugoslavs understand by the concept of "defense,"
a term, he said, that might possibly lead to misunderstand-
ing. "By defense," said Manola, "Yugoslavs understand not
only something of a static nature but the sum of all actions by the armed and unarmed forces of the Yugoslav peoples to protect their country's freedom and independence."
He stressed the fact that no one defense concept and no
one organizational scheme could have lasting validity.
They depend, he said, on the strategic situation, which
must be evaluated in two ways--by analyzing the foreign
political situation, and by analyzing the internal political circumstances.[13]
    Even though Tito is considered the chief architect
of "Nationwide Defense," its real promoter was General
Viktor Bubanj, Yugoslavia's chief of staff, who died suddenly in October 1972. Bubanj openly admitted[14] that even

a socialist country could become Yugoslavia's enemy, although he rejected the idea that the Yugoslavs would necessarily fight against the Soviet Union and other communist
states:

> Because of the many contradictions which exist
> between socialist countries, we have to take into
> consideration the possibility of becoming involved
> in a conflict with one of them. For us, as a so-
> cialist country, for our working people, for our
> soldiers and officers, who are educated in a spirit
> of socialist solidarity and internationalism, of
> brotherhood and friendship with other socialist
> countries, it is of extreme importance to under-
> stand correctly and explain the character and
> possibility of such socialist aggression against
> our country.

Bubanj stressed that the Yugoslav concept of Nationwide
Defense was "neither anti-Soviet, nor anti-American, nor
anti-Italian, nor anti-Albanian, nor anti-Austrian, nor
anti-Bulgarian, etc." Yugoslavia was against any aggressor
"regardless of what political ideas he holds." "We would
like to say quite clearly that we shall never accept any
policy of hegemony and force, regardless of whether such a
policy is justified by 'communist ideas,' 'socialist solidarity' or--as they say in the West--by the idea of a 'free
world.'"[15]

WILL SOVIET TROOPS BE INVITED?

Here we return to the starting point--to the question
that was asked of Stane Dolanc: "And what happens if no
one attacks Yugoslavia from outside?" The basic assumptions of the Yugoslav leaders are that the Soviet Union
and its East European allies will not use force against
Yugoslavia, but that should these states for some reason
decide to do so, as happened in the case of the CSSR, the
Yugoslavs would defend their country regardless of the
fact that the Warsaw Pact armies belong to the communist
bloc.
Here lie both the strength and the weakness of the
Yugoslav theory of defense. Ostensibly, the Warsaw Pact
armies did not enter Czechoslovakia as aggressors or invaders but as "brothers" who were "invited" and "called
on" to "help" Czechs and Slovaks threatened by imperialist

forces inside and outside the country. In other words,
the Soviets might not "attack" Yugoslavia, but they might
come as "invited guests."

In order to prevent any such possibility, Article 217
of the draft text of Yugoslavia's new constitution, now being discussed throughout the country, stipulates the following: "No one shall have the right to acknowledge or to
sign [any document legalizing] capitulation or to accept
or acknowledge the occupation of the Socialist Federative
Republic of Yugoslavia or any part thereof. No one has
the right to prevent citizens of the Socialist Federative
Republic of Yugoslavia from fighting against an enemy who
has attacked the country. Such acts are unconstitutional
and shall be punishable by law as high treason. High treason is a crime against the people and shall be punished as
a grave criminal offense." Similar clauses are also included in the new draft constitutions for Yugoslavia's six
republics. They all deal specifically with capitulation
and occupation of the country by foreign aggressors.

In January 1971 the National Assembly of the Socialist
Republic of Croatia published the draft text of the Croatian
Law on National Defense. This was the first law of its
kind in Yugoslavia. Although it was never adopted and was
dropped following the purge of top party and state leaders
of Croatia in the fall of 1971, its significance remains,
particularly in connection with the above-mentioned formulations about capitulation and occupation. Section IV of
the preamble to the Croatian Law on National Defense contained a formulation not included either in the Federal
Defense Law or in the draft texts of new constitutions.
It read: "No one shall have the right to invite an enemy's
armed forces into the country or to help enemies to carry
out any type of forcible measure against our citizens or
to collaborate with them in the political and economic
fields."[16] Apparently the now purged Croatian leaders believed that by forbidding anyone in Croatia "to invite an
enemy's armed forces into the country" they made it possible
for themselves, in advance, to disagree with any invitation
issued to "enemy armed forces" by some other Yugoslav con-
stituent republic or nationality. In other words, they
wanted all the Yugoslav republics and nationalities to be
able to decide who is "a friend" and who is "an enemy."
No doubt the Croatian formulation was made under the impact of the occupation of Czechoslovakia and the postoccu-
pation argument over whether the Czechoslovak leaders (as
claimed by the Soviets) had "invited" the Warsaw Pact troops
to enter the country "as friends and allies," or whether

these troops were guilty of "aggression" (as originally claimed by Tito and his colleagues).

By calling the would-be invaders the "enemy's armed forces" the Croatian leaders obscured their real goal of preventing the Warsaw Pact troops from repeating in Yugoslavia what they had done in the CSSR. The formulation would have been more logical and understandable if they had not specified "enemy" foreign forces but had merely said it was forbidden "to invite any foreign armed forces into the country." This would have been more in harmony with Yugoslavia's policy of nonalignment and with the Nationwide Defense system, which considers an enemy to be any potential aggressor from either East or West. It is fairly certain that if Soviet armed forces entered Yugoslavia, they would do so not as "enemies" but, as in Czechoslovakia, as "friends," "brothers," and "allies" who were invited by "healthy elements" in the Yugoslav party.

This, of course, raises the question of whether "healthy forces" exist in Yugoslavia that, after Tito's death, might request Warsaw Pact troops to enter the country. Such forces do exist in the party, in the army, and in the individual republics, but they are not strong in number. From time to time one hears references in the party leaders' speeches to pro-Western "anarcholiberals" and to "Cominformist elements." For several years there has been no talk about pro-Soviet party members, but mention has been made of "Stalinists" or "Cominformists" who (at least in theory) are not even supported by the Soviet Union. Still, a great majority of party members probably favor the Soviet Union. Most of the pro-Soviet forces are to be found among those groups who were persecuted between 1948 and 1955, when a general anti-Soviet policy was being pursued in Yugoslavia. As far as the situation in the army is concerned, opinions vary. The army leaders, however, would probably do everything possible to maintain the integrity of the Yugoslav state.

THE DOMESTIC DIMENSION

In the present era of détente Tito, who for years took advantage of the East-West confrontation, has suddenly found himself in an atmosphere in which it is no longer possible to play off one bloc against the other. Any such attempt today would be interpreted as a cold-war action.

During the era of confrontation many of Yugoslavia's political and economic weaknesses were obscured by its assertive and independent foreign policy, which on the one hand made both the country and Tito popular throughout the world but on the other caused the Yugoslav leaders to ignore the deteriorating internal situation. In the altered international atmosphere, however, Yugoslavia's many domestic weaknesses suddenly became glaringly apparent, and to people not familiar with the real domestic situation it seemed as if the deterioration had taken place overnight.

Tito, no longer in a position to profit from confrontation, felt constrained to take two important steps. First, he had to come to an acceptable arrangement with Moscow, which, in fact, he apparently did during Brezhnev's visit to Yugoslavia in September 1971. Second, he had to introduce internal changes. Decentralization and democratization in party as well as state affairs had to be halted, and an attempt was made to establish stronger central party and state control. This, of course, was difficult to do, since the party and state leaderships in the six republics and the two autonomous provinces had acquired a considerable degree of independence over the years. It had become the practice to speak of Yugoslavia not as a federal state but as a federation of states, and an attempt to federalize the party was under way. Under the changed circumstances Tito came to regard as his most important task the strengthening of the central party and state leadership. In December 1971 he began his campaign, moving first against the Croatian and then against the Serbian party leaderships, both of whom had enjoyed a great deal of autonomy. The others (particularly in Macedonia and Slovenia) were on the way to achieving the same degree of independence, but they had proceeded more cautiously, waiting first to see how things would turn out in Croatia and Serbia.

There are two major problems that the party and its leaders have not been able to solve. One is the conflict among the Yugoslav nationalities, and the other is that of reconciling party ideology with the self-management system.

Two kinds of nationality problem have been discernible in Yugoslavia since 1945. The first has existed since the creation of the Yugoslav state after World War I, when a number of nationalities were bound together in a single state despite the fact that for centuries they had been subject to widely differing forms of cultural influence and political rule. Prior to and during World War II these national differences were intensified and gave rise to major problems. This traditional aspect of the nationality question remains a source of instability in contemporary Yugoslavia and will continue to be so for some time.

202

The second aspect of the nationality problem is of an ideological or, as many party members put it, a bureaucratic nature. Various communist groups carry on their ideological battles under cover of the nationality question. The real problem is not that the individual national groups are unable to reconcile their differences and merge into a "Yugoslav nation," but rather that the members of the "leading elite" (the communist party) are involved in a bitter, internecine ideological struggle that to a certain extent seems to take on national overtones. One might almost conclude that at the present stage the upsurge of nationalism is less the cause of the present crisis in party and state than a consequence of it. The result is that a struggle against nationalism inside the party has become necessary.

SELF-MANAGEMENT VERSUS THE PARTY

As a result of the development of the self-management system, contradictions have evolved between party theory and the realities of the system. The party members in factories and on the local level have found themselves in an impossible position. The principle of democratic centralism obliged them to implement decisions reached by party bodies outside the factory, but inside the factory, where they were supposed to lead nonparty workers, they did not feel bound by its decisions. This resulted in estrangement between workers and the party, a conflict that was identified by Milovan Djilas 20 years ago as a basic contradiction within the Yugoslav system: an attempt to carry out a genuine liberalization in a one-party dictatorship sets in motion forces that ultimately come into conflict with the dictatorship.

How can the hierarchical system, obligatory for any party organized on the Leninist principle of democratic centralism, be harmonized with the self-management system, which rejects all hierarchy? How can this harmony be achieved in a society in which bureaucratic centralism has given way to bureaucratic polycentrism? How should one reorganize a party that is not only the main source of bureaucracy but is supposed to engender unity in the working class within the framework of a "market planned economy?" In spite of Yugoslav claims that the conditions for viable economic activity have been created, the market applies its own rule-of-thumb measurement to these conditions, and "owing to the differing technical decisions made in the

various branches of the economy and in the various factories
within any one branch, new inequalities are continually
being created."[17]

If one attempts to build up the system of self-management under such circumstances one runs into real social
contradictions. While on one hand the bourgeois class has
been eliminated by revolutionary means, the economic conditions for the existence of classes remain. Also, under
workers' self-management, despite ideological claims to the
contrary, the worker does not manage as long as he produces.
He is, in fact, only a nominal self-manager; in practice
he is still a wage-earner. He does not regard the manager
of his enterprise as someone who is serving him and the
common cause but rather as a new exploiter in altered form.
A rapid transformation of individual motivation has resulted from the fact that an individual can obtain anything
for which he can pay, and there has been a general reorientation away from common social and collective goals toward
personal, family, and microsocial ones, which has resulted
in a conflict between individual and collective interests.
The former are promoted by the market economy; the latter
are promoted by the party, the press, and the other mass
media, which preach "socialist awareness" and criticize
"individualism."

One of Yugoslavia's leading Marxists, Professor Predrag
Vranicki of Zagreb, who is also an editor of the contro-
versial philosophical bimonthly Praxis, said in a lecture
in August 1973 that the important goals of socialism were
not to be achieved by strengthening the political sphere.
Until now the working class has not been historically prepared to take such a process to the extreme, he stated, and
the political avant garde of the working class, the party,
had neglected to prepare them to do so. When one under-
takes to experiment, priority must be given to practice,
which, however, must retain the theoretically formulated
essentials.[18]

In Yugoslavia the new forms of self-management were
intended to gradually eliminate the traditional ruling
structure of the state. But self-management was not to
assume traditional political forms; the state would have
to change into the political instrument of the new self-
management forms.[19] This meant that the party, whose dictatorship had so far been conducted through the state,
would have to relinquish its monopoly in order to adjust
to self-management. In effect it would have to wither
away, an idea suggested at the sixth party congress in November 1952--a congress that is now fiercely attacked even

204

by Tito. Its leaders have not been willing to see the Yugoslav party die out, and they are doing their utmost to stop
any such trend.

THE PROBLEM OF TITO'S SUCCESSION

These are the circumstances under which Tito is trying
to resolve the crucial problem of his succession. A decisive factor in this connection is the army, since any successor or successors must have its support. In the period
of internal turmoil that has engulfed Yugoslavia since December 1971 the armed forces have come to play a more prominent role in any considerations of post-Tito politics, and
the hard line Tito has adopted since then, while no doubt
motivated by concern to reduce the serious internal tensions,
has also been designed to preserve the party's primacy.
To this end he suggested that the Yugoslav army should, if
necessary, intervene. At a reception in Sarajevo in December 1971 he said: "The task of the army is not merely to
defend the territorial integrity of the country, but also
to defend socialism when we see it in danger and when it
cannot be defended by other means."[20]
On another occasion he warned that he would never allow "anyone else to come and establish peace and order for
us," emphasizing in this connection that he "would rather
resort to the ultimate means," that is, to the Yugoslav
army.[21]
Tito's concept of the role of the army has been given
a certain ideological justification: "Our armed forces
have both internal and external functions--i.e., functions
that are in accord with the Marxist concept of the role of
the military force in the transitional period and with the
actual needs of our society at a given level of development."[22] Although its internal function is expected to become of secondary importance with the strengthening of the
self-management system, the fact that the country has been
subject to increasing internal instability in the last
several years makes the army an important internal factor
as well. Moreover, it is quite clear that the army's ability to resist foreign invaders is conditioned by the
strength of the country's internal fiber. As Croatian
General Manola explained: "When the internal tensions
within a society grow beyond a certain point, the ability
to resist external dangers diminishes. We know this from
earlier experience with national unity." He then added
that "an attack on an independent state does not always

have to be motivated by the desire to win strategic advantages over the other side. The very independence of a state can have dangerous effects on a bloc."[23]

This indirect reference to the Soviet Union seems appropriate in light of the latter's exploitation of three sensitive spots in its efforts to generate internal difficulties. The three, all nationality issues, involve the Serbian minority in Croatia, the Albanians in Kosovo, and the Yugoslav-Bulgarian dispute over Macedonia.

Although the military is likely to play a major role in determining the successor to Tito, other factors and forces will also be important--the party, the state bureaucracy, the various republics and autonomous regions representing the different nationalities. Tito is anxious to make the succession as orderly and smooth as possible and has taken various steps to ensure this. Initially he thought collective bodies representing the various forces within the country would be the best solution, but at the Ninth Congress of the League of Communists of Yugoslavia in March 1969 he unexpectedly proposed the establishment of a party Executive Bureau, which was subsequently created. In September 1970 he again surprised his fellow countrymen by announcing, in a speech in Zagreb, that "a sort of collective presidency of Yugoslavia" would be created to include "the best people from the individual republics." Their task would be to replace him as chief of state and thus enable him to devote his time to other matters.*

Although Tito was obviously trying to prevent a repetition of the "Rankovic case"** with his proposals for collective party and state bodies, few people in Yugoslavia have much faith in this type of solution. The 23-member State Presidency with Tito as its head as "president for life" has become a colorless forum whose routine activities have little effect upon Yugoslav politics. Tito, who oc-

---

*On the very day that Tito made his proposal of a collective presidency, a Belgrade weekly ran the following motto for the week on its front page: "The Bigger the Head, the Bigger the Headache."

**It may be recalled that before 1966 Tito at one point publicly designated Aleksandar Rankovic as his successor, but Rankovic, with the secret police and the party organizational apparatus in his hands, later grew impatient at Tito's longevity and tried to force a solution of the succession during Tito's lifetime. For this he was purged in July 1966.

cupies the three most important posts in the country--president of the republic, president of the party, and supreme military commander--has never been able to delegate enough of his power to a collective body, such as the State Presidency, to give it any real authority.

As problems with the various collective bodies have become apparent, focus has again shifted to finding an individual who can replace Tito. Developments in Yugoslavia over the last few years suggest that the person or persons who succeed must fulfill the following conditions: first, he must not be a Serb, because the non-Serbian nationalities could interpret such a move as an attempt to achieve "greater Serbian hegemony"; second, he must nonetheless have Serbian support; and third, he must also have the support of the Yugoslav army.

Thus far only one top party leader in Yugoslavia seems able to meet all three requirements: 63-year-old Edvard Kardelj. Certain actions by Tito over the past two years suggest that he would like to see Kardelj as his successor, but Stane Dolanc, a Slovene like Kardelj and currently secretary of the party's Executive Bureau, is also a strong contender.

The cases of Georgi Malenkov in the USSR (whom Stalin slated in advance as his successor), of Lin Piao in China (whose succession was even incorporated into the party constitution), and of Aleksandar Rankovic (whom Tito once named as his successor) demonstrate, however, that in communist states an heir apparent to a charismatic leader is by no means certain to succeed. The evidence suggests that communist leaders have not been particularly successful in hand-picking their successors, and moreover, in a multinational state based on decentralized administration and the self-management system, appointing a "one-man successor" in advance contradicts the very spirit of the system itself.

In the final analysis, however, it is clear that whoever succeeds Tito will not be able to survive without the support of the army. After Tito's death the armed forces could well emerge as an independent political force in an effort to prevent a possible civil war. The army is the one organization in Yugoslavia that is not constructed along self-management lines, and thus it has not suffered the erosion and loss of cohesion that have taken place in other institutions. Moreover, its leaders have never concealed the fact that they regard preventing the disintegration of their country as their most important duty, whether the threat to unity is internal or external. Thus if Yugoslavia's economic and ideological problems cannot be solved before Tito's death the likelihood of military intervention is bound to increase.

Because Yugoslavia's domestic tensions are so significant and have such a profound impact upon its foreign policy, they affect its attitude toward European security to a much greater extent than is the case with the other states of Eastern Europe. In addition to its domestic instability, the geographical location of the country, in the Balkans and on the periphery of the Middle East, creates conditions under which security is an important preoccupation. The possibility that the Soviets might take military action or intrigue with internal factions is an additional source of uncertainty. Moreover, this concern to ensure the independent evolution of the state is complicated by Yugoslavia's unique, and in some respects contradictory, policy of political-military nonalignment and ideological commitment to communism. Despite these problems, however, the Yugoslavs have realistically appraised their situation, and, provided it follows lines roughly approximating their expectations, they see in the security conference the best opportunity for securing their independent future.

NOTES

1. Borba, Belgrade, 6 July 1973.
2. Leo Mates, "The Balkans and European Security," Survival, no. 3 (London, May-June 1973), p. 117.
3. In Komunist, Belgrade, 4 June 1973.
4. Borba, 7 September 1973.
5. Ljubivoje Acimovic and Vladimir Glisic in the quarterly Medjunarodni problemi, no. 3 (Belgrade, 1972), p. 51.
6. Ibid., p. 52.
7. Ibid., p. 55.
8. Borba, 15 June 1973, special supplement, p. 29.
9. Ibid., p. 30.
10. Milika Sundic, speaking over Radio Zagreb, 11 November 1973.
11. Borba, 31 January 1973.
12. Ibid., 6 June 1970.
13. Oesterreichische Militaerische Zeitschrift, Vienna, March-April 1971.
14. In a book entitled Doctrine of Victory (Belgrade: Narodna Armija, 1972), p. 35.
15. Ibid., p. 42.
16. Vjesnik, Zagreb, 11 January 1971.
17. Nase teme, no. 12 (Zagreb, December 1966).

18. _Politika_, Belgrade, 24 August 1973.

19. _Sueddeutsche Zeitung_, Munich, 15-16 September 1973.

20. Radio Zagreb, 22 December 1971, 0615 hours.

21. _Borba_, 20 December 1971. See also Tito's speech of 22 December 1971 in _Politika_, 23 December 1971.

22. _Socijalizam_, no. 1 (Belgrade, January 1973).

23. _Oesterreichische Militaerische Zeitschrift_, March-April 1971.

10

EUROPEAN SECURITY AND
THE PROBLEM OF
BALKAN SECURITY

F. Stephen Larrabee

The movement toward the reduction of East-West tension that has accelerated with the preparations for the security conference has had a distinct echo in the Balkans. Increasingly over the last several years all Balkan governments have begun to address themselves to the problems of greater regional cooperation and security. To a great extent this concern has been an outgrowth of developments in Central Europe, and in particular of the improved relations between the two superpowers, but it has also had its decidedly regional aspects. Historically, the Balkans have been one of the most combustible areas in Europe and the frequent focus of great-power confrontation. Its conflicts have seldom remained localized but have invariably drawn one or another of the dominant powers into a vortex.

This was particularly true in the 19th century, when Russia and Austria-Hungary vied for control of the Balkans as Ottoman power in the region began to decline. The incendiary mixture of Balkan nationalism and great-power chauvinism served to earn the area a well-deserved reputation as the "powder keg of Europe." While in the latter half of the 20th century the focus of great-power rivalry has shifted somewhat, the Balkans have still remained an area of volatile politics--as the Greek civil war, the Stalin-Tito dispute, the Albanian-Soviet rift, the Cyprus question, periodic flare-ups of polemics over Macedonia, and the several military interventions in Greece and Turkey bear witness.

This legacy of political instability and great-power intervention has left an indelible mark on the consciousness of the region and has given the various countries involved a strong interest in exploiting the present climate of improved East-West relations to enhance security and co-operation within the Balkans. Moreover, this desire to exploit the present movement toward détente has been given a sense of greater urgency by several other developments. First among these is the fact that the Middle East has now become the prime area of great-power confrontation. Within this framework the Balkans, which have traditionally been regarded as the "gateway to the Mediterranean," have been cast in a new light, especially in the eyes of the Soviet Union, whose interest in the Mediterranean has increased with its emergence as a bona fide naval power and the expansion of its presence in the Middle East.[1] Both factors have served to increase Moscow's interest in preventing the emergence of a power vacuum in the Balkans that might be exploited by a rival.

Second, there has occurred a revival of traditional nationalism that has manifested itself in the desire for greater national autonomy on the part of many Balkan states, both aligned and nonaligned, as the fervor of the cold war has begun to wane. This reemergence of nationalism has been particularly strong in those states that fell into the Soviet sphere of influence after World War II. There nationalism has tended to have an increasingly anti-Soviet edge and has led to increasing friction between the Soviet Union's desire to retain its hegemony and maintain close, preferably cliental, relations with these states and the desire on the part of the former "satellites" to increase the scope of their autonomy. This tension, moreover, seems likely to increase rather than decrease in the future and has given the search for greater regional security a particularly strong impetus.

Third, and related to the above, has been the deepening of the Sino-Soviet split and its tendency to spread to other areas. This has increased the Soviet concern that the Balkans, where China already has a bridgehead in Albania, might become the focus of Chinese incursions aimed at further undermining Moscow's already fragile position.* An increase in Chinese influence in the Balkans would not only further erode Soviet influence in the area but would probably have repercussions elsewhere in Eastern Europe and thus open up a Pandora's box that the Soviet Union

_____

*One Soviet-inspired article in Magyar Hirlap (Budapest, 13 August 1971) charged that Chinese diplomacy in the Balkans had an anti-Soviet bias and warned of a "Tirana-Bucharest-Belgrade axis" supported by Peking.

would prefer to keep closed. Soviet concern regarding Chinese incursion into the Balkans was particularly well illustrated at the time of Rumanian party and state leader Nicolae Ceausescu's trip to Peking in June 1971, followed as it was by the visit of Yugoslav Foreign Minister Mirko Tepavac. Soon after Ceausescu's return home Rumania (and later Yugoslavia) came under increased Soviet pressure, which involved maneuvers on Rumania's borders and a campaign of escalated criticism in the East European press.[2] As the summer wore on a virtual war of nerves was waged, in an effort to warn both countries, but particularly Rumania, of the dangers of further rapprochement with Peking. While Chou En-lai's remark late in the summer that "distant waters cannot quench fire"[3] seemed to put both Balkan states on notice that Chinese aid--for the time being at least-- would be limited to verbal support only, nonetheless the strong Soviet reaction to Ceausescu's visit is indicative of the potential instability inherent in the deepening of the Sino-Soviet split and the emergence of China from its diplomatic isolation.

FUTURE SOURCES OF INSTABILITY IN
THE BALKANS

The problem of regional stability has also come to concern the various Balkan states with greater urgency because there exist a number of unresolved problems in or on the periphery of the peninsula that could heat up at some future date to engulf not only the Balkan states but the superpowers as well in a dangerous conflict. One of the most important of these "trouble spots" is the so-called "southern flank," involving Turkey, Greece, and Cyprus. Here problems of foreign policy overlap with, and are complicated by, problems of internal development. Not only do both Turkey and Greece have longstanding traditions of deep-seated animosity toward one another but both are societies in transition, suffering the growing pains caused by a rapid postwar change of traditional ways of life. As a consequence both societies have been increasingly susceptible to domestic upheaval and political instability over the last decade.

While the recent military interventions in the political life of Turkey and Greece have temporarily mitigated the outward manifestations of this instability, they have hardly removed their underlying causes, which lie deeply embedded in the conflict between Byzantine and Ottoman traditions inherited from the past and the requirements of a modern democratic state. In both countries alien Western institutions were grafted onto systems that lacked the infrastructure that existed in the advanced Western countries from which the institutions were borrowed. These institutions have not been able to develop strong enough roots to withstand the dislocations brought about as a result of the accelerated economic and social changes that have taken place in the past decade or so. At present both societies seem to be facing what Samuel Huntington[4] has termed the "primary problem of politics"--the tendency of economic and social change to outpace political change. Under such circumstances military regimes generally tend to be better at seizing power than at carrying out long-range programs of political modernization, and thus it seems probable that both countries will continue to be plagued by a significant degree of political instability for some time to come.

Such instability could have significant foreign policy repercussions for countries that occupy such important strategic positions in the Mediterranean. While both Greece and Turkey are firmly wedded to NATO, Moscow has been quite successful in exploiting both strains in Ankara's relations with Washington (originating in the American intervention in the Cyprus crisis of 1964) and West European antipathy toward the Greek regime to improve its relations with Ankara and Athens. The long-term Soviet goal seems to be to nudge both countries further from the NATO alliance,[5] but Moscow would undoubtedly welcome any situation that would reduce the effectiveness of either country as a NATO partner.

The fall of the Papadopoulos regime in November 1973 has done little to discourage whatever hopes Moscow entertains regarding improvement of its position in the Mediterranean. The coup that toppled George Papadopoulos bears witness to the degree to which Greece remains plagued by deep-seated political instability, which is likely to manifest itself again no matter what form of government evolves. While it is too early to say exactly in which direction the Gizikis-Androutsopoulos government will move, the present army-backed regime gives little indication that it intends to return the country to democratic rule in the near future. This is likely to lead to a further isolation of Greece from the European community. Moreover, there has been a noticeable rise in anti-Americanism, especially in traditionally pro-U.S. sectors of society, as a result of what was perceived as tacit U.S. support for the Papadop-

oulos regime. This feeling has been reinforced by the significant increase in the U.S. military presence in Greece
under a U.S. Navy home-port agreement signed last year.
While this anti-Americanism is not widespread it is on the
upswing and could become an important factor in the future
should the new, strongly nationalistic Greek regime begin
to take a more independent stance, as it has given some indications of doing.

Such a situation is given particularly ominous overtones by Greece's strategic position in the Mediterranean
and the threat of a renewed Cyprus crisis. Instability in
Athens could encourage the Enosis forces to intensify their
struggle, and while the Greek government has tried hard to
avoid a direct confrontation over Cyprus and has generally
shown considerable restraint on the issue, passions still
run high. For this reason the situation remains a highly
volatile one and a government in Athens beset by increasing
internal instability might find it necessary to come to
terms with the adherents of the now-deceased General Grivas.
Such a situation would increase the pressure on the defiant
Cypriot president, Archbishop Makarios, to turn toward Moscow for help—something that, despite the Kremlin's encouragement, he has so far been reluctant to do. The potential
interaction of the Cyprus issue with Soviet-American rivalry
in the Mediterranean and Near East regions makes the prospect of a renewed crisis in Athens or Nicosia particularly
dangerous. Either would pose an important threat to Balkan
security.

THE APPROACH OF THE POST-TITO ERA

Yugoslavia, touching as it does upon seven states, can
justifiably be called the heart of the Balkans, and any
change in its position would inevitably have some effect
on the policies of bordering states. While Belgrade has
managed with remarkable success to pursue a policy of nonalignment, the approach of the post-Tito era has thrust
Yugoslavia back into the forefront of Soviet, and Western,
concern and has led many observers to wonder whether the
Yugoslav experiment will be able to survive its architect,
or, if it does, what form this survival will take. This
question has been given all the more urgency by the sense
of permanent crisis that has beset Yugoslav society over
the last few years. While Tito's purges of the Croatian
and Serbian leaderships, as well as his calls for greater
party control and a return to a more doctrinaire brand of

communism, have stemmed the most immediate disintegrative
impulses, they have done little to remove the underlying
causes of the crisis, which involve fundamental problems
of economic and administrative policy as well as deep-seated
historical antagonisms.[6] These threaten to become more
acute once Tito has departed from the political stage.

To a great extent Yugoslavia has been Tito's personal
creation. It was the force of his personality that molded
the system and prevented a further proliferation of centrifugal forces. "No institution, not even the army," as Croatian leader Vladimir Bakaric has noted,[7] "has as much prestige as Tito." In times of crisis--such as when Rankovic
was ousted in 1966 or during the Croatian student strike in
December 1971--Tito has acted as the archetypal "heroic
leader" who comes to the fore when change can no longer be
delayed and there is a widely felt need for direction from
above.[8]

The problem is that such charismatic authority is in
itself essentially unstable and transitory. By its very
nature it stands opposed to institutional authority. Its
final success depends on its transformation into something
more stable than charisma. The key question concerning the
post-Tito era, therefore, is whether in the short time remaining Tito can transform his personal authority into some
sort of institutionalized political authority that will survive him, or whether his departure will plunge Yugoslavia
back into the political instability that characterized the
interwar years. To date Tito has been the prime moderator
of social conflict and the guarantor of the unity of the
Yugoslav state. It is not quite clear what institution
(if any) will, or can, perform that function once he has
retired.

Should the succession crisis serve to regenerate many
of the disintegrative tendencies that have plagued Yugoslavia over the last few years and that are deeply embedded
in the present Yugoslav system, the resultant instability
could pose a much greater threat to Balkan and European security than could the Cyprus issue. It is hard to believe
that such instability would not encourage the Soviet Union
to renew pressure for a reorientation of Yugoslav policy
along lines more subservient to its own. And it is equally
difficult to envision a weak, unstable Yugoslavia as being
able to resist such pressures.

Moscow already appears, in fact, to have begun pre-
paring the groundwork for such an eventuality. Since Brezhnev's visit to Belgrade in September 1971, which signaled
the advent of a new phase in Soviet-Yugoslav relations, the

Kremlin has intensified its efforts to improve relations with Yugoslavia, particularly in the economic sphere (for example, Moscow recently granted a 1,300-million-dollar credit for the development of Yugoslavia's power and metallurgical industries). While the Yugoslavs have been quick to deny the frequent Western speculation that the loan implies a return to the Soviet orbit, it appears probable that Moscow hopes that this economic aid and its own involvement in the Yugoslav economy can be used to political advantage once Tito has left the scene. Moreover, the visit paid to Belgrade by Kosygin in late September 1973 has done little to allay Western suspicions regarding Moscow's long-term goal.

It seems clear that a post-Tito Yugoslavia wracked by economic difficulties and increased nationality tensions would turn the Balkans into a potential battlefield for a power struggle between two, if not three, major powers. The United States, which has supported the Yugoslav attempt to forge its own path independently of the USSR with both financial and military aid for the past 25 years, would be unlikely to remain aloof if increased Soviet pressure were exerted on a weak, fragmented Yugoslavia. And it is even possible that China would seek to exploit an opportunity to outflank the Soviet Union. Such a situation could once again turn the Balkans into a potential powder keg and would be particularly ominous in light of the volatile situation in the Middle East.

THE RUMANIAN-SOVIET CONFLICT

Another source of instability in the Balkans, although one far less dangerous than those already mentioned, is the conflict between Bucharest and Moscow over the independent nature of Rumania's foreign policy. Since 1964, when the differences first began to attract the serious attention of Western observers, the conflict has evolved from a one-dimensional dispute over economics to a multidimensional rift involving a whole host of issues: the command structure of the Warsaw Pact; Rumania's neutrality in the Arab-Israeli war; Rumania's reservations regarding the signing of the nonproliferation treaty; relations with West Germany; the Soviet intervention in Czechoslovakia; and, most recently, approaches to the EEC.

To date the Rumanian leadership has pursued a policy of calculated risk and has refrained from pushing the Soviet leadership over the threshold of tolerance. That this

216

threshold has not yet been crossed has been largely due to
the fact that Rumania has threatened only one of what Fritz
Ermarth aptly termed the three fundamental dimensions of
Soviet policy in Eastern Europe--internationalism, security,
and legitimacy.* Soviet "security" interests have not been
fundamentally threatened because Rumania, unlike Czechoslovakia, does not border on West Germany, and thus its geographical position in southeastern Europe is not of crucial
strategic importance. Second, Ceausescu's own brand of
national communism has avoided the political pluralism that
threatened the Leninist party-state system in Czechoslovakia
and with it the Soviet view of "legitimacy." Thus only the
principle of "internationalism" has been violated, and this,
while disturbing to the Soviet Union, has not proved so in-
tolerable or unmanageable as to provoke Moscow into incur-
ring the risks and costs entailed in preserving it.

Yet as Eastern Europe--and the West--were to learn in
1968, the threshold of Soviet tolerance is a vague and sub-
jective line, which can be crossed unwittingly. Moreover,
it is ultimately in Moscow, not in Bucharest, that the
threshold is defined. So far Rumania has displayed an as-
tute sense of the limits of possible deviation, and the
Soviet Union has displayed a corresponding regard for the
costs of intervention. The key question, however, is whether
the restraint that has characterized the relationship to
date will continue to be shown in the future. The risk
that one or the other of the two antagonists will at some
time overplay its hand or back the other into a corner is
not so minimal as to be discounted. Against the background
of 1968 there is enough doubt to justify regarding the Rumanian challenge as a potential source of instability in
the Balkans.

THE MACEDONIAN DISPUTE

Lastly, security in the Balkans is threatened by the
continued failure to resolve the Macedonian question, a

---

*See his "Internationalism, Security, and Legitimacy:
The Challenge to Soviet Interests in East Europe 1964-1968"
(Rand Corporation Memorandum 5909 PR). In Ermarth's framework, "internationalism" refers to the relations among communist states; "security" to the preservation of the prevailing East-West balance of political power; and "legitimacy" to the monopoly of power by the communist party within
the individual East European states.

perennial source of discord between Bulgaria and Yugoslavia.
The Macedonian question has a long and tortuous history
that precedes the establishment of communist rule in either
country, but since the end of World War II the dispute has
centered around the ethnic origin of the Macedonians. Although the Bulgarians have been willing to accept Macedonia
as an integral part of the Yugoslav federated state and
have disclaimed any territorial ambitions in regard to
Yugoslav Macedonia, they have been unwilling to recognize
a separate Macedonian nationality. The polemics have often
been stimulated by seemingly obscure points of history and
linguistics, but Belgrade has tended to regard these "historical debates" as little more than disguised forms of
irredentism, despite repeated Bulgarian denials, which could
be used by later generations to raise a claim against the
Yugoslav state. For this reason periodic flare-ups of the
issue have contributed to sharp deterioration in relations
at various times in the past[9] and still, despite some recent efforts to resolve the issue, remain a source of tension in the Balkans.

In actual fact the Macedonian issue might be dismissed
as of relatively minor importance if it were not for the
prospect of increased nationality tensions within Yugoslavia
once Tito has left the political stage and the fact that
the Soviet Union has tended to use the issue as a way of
putting pressure on Yugoslavia through its Bulgarian proxy.
Since Brezhnev's visit to Belgrade in September 1971 the
polemics have subsided markedly, and the issue appears to
have taken a back seat to the present Soviet desire for
improved relations with Belgrade. Yet the Macedonian question has by no means been resolved. A resurgence of nationality tensions could tempt the Soviet Union to revive
the polemics, and the issue could become an important bargaining chip in relations with Yugoslavia in the post-Tito
era. Moscow is well aware of how deep the age-old currents
of nationalism in the Balkans run, and unless the Yugoslavs
somehow succeed in forcing resolution of the issue very
soon it could, as so often in the past, become a catalyst
of further turmoil in the Balkans.

EFFORTS TO ACHIEVE GREATER
REGIONAL COOPERATION

Despite the various political alignments within the
Balkans and the existence of a number of outstanding problems between individual states, there have been a notice-

ably heightened desire for more cooperative relations within the Balkans and greater recognition that the fates of the various Balkan states are closely linked. The fact that throughout history local conflicts have invariably tended to draw in the other Balkan states as well as some of the great powers has contributed to the emergence of this growing regional consciousness. The prime motive force, however, has been the reduction in East-West tension over the last several years.

Of all the Balkan states Rumania has proved to be the strongest and most persistent advocate of Balkan cooperation, both bilateral and multilateral, and it has been largely on Bucharest's initiative that the issue of Balkan security has gained increased attention. Rumania's interest in Balkan cooperation is not new; it can be traced as far back as 1957 when, as part of Khrushchev's effort to reduce tensions with the West, Rumanian Premier Chivu Stoica addressed messages (later to be known as the Stoica Notes) to Albania, Bulgaria, Greece, Turkey, and Yugoslavia proposing a conference aimed at promoting Balkan détente. More recently, however, Rumania has sought to stress the idea of turning the Balkans into a "zone of peace." In June 1970, for instance, it sent notes to other Balkan countries suggesting multilateral conferences and increased cooperation, and a note to the secretary-general of the United Nations calling attention to Rumania's interest in broadening interstate relations in the Balkans and turning the area into "a nuclear-free zone of peace and peaceful coexistence."[10] Since then Rumania has put forward a similar proposal on numerous occasions, and in July of 1972, at the Rumanian National Party Conference, Ceausescu proposed a meeting of representatives of the Balkan states to discuss economic, political, and cultural cooperation and the creation of a permanent body to further economic cooperation.[11]

At the same time Bucharest has pursued a policy designed to improve relations with "all states regardless of their social system." Relations with Bulgaria have improved as a result of the signing of a treaty of friendship and cooperation in November 1970 and two more recent meetings with Bulgarian leader Todor Zhivkov in August and September 1971. The return of the Rumanian ambassador to Athens in July 1968 (he had been absent since the coup in April 1967) marked the beginning of an improvement in relations with Greece, which is highlighted by the visit of former Foreign Minister Corneliu Manescu to Athens in June 1971.

Finally, relations with Yugoslavia have developed to the point that the two countries, as one Yugoslav commentator noted, "hold identical views" on most international issues.[12]

In effect Rumania's Balkan policy has been a corollary of its general policy on European security. Both have sought to emphasize the principles of "sovereignty, integrity, and independence," in an effort to offset Soviet hegemony and loosen the bonds imposed by bloc obligations. Support for regional solidarity based on turning the Balkans into a "zone of peace" serves to place greater constraints on any attempt by Moscow to enforce the "Brezhnev Doctrine" and increases Bucharest's freedom of action. In this regard the greater cooperation between Yugoslavia and Rumania in the last few years has been quite significant. Since the invasion of Czechoslovakia in August 1968 there has emerged a growing awareness of the degree to which Rumania and Yugoslavia share common interests despite the very different nature of the internal order in each country, and this has led to a more or less tacit alliance between the two. Each has tended to regard threats to the other, veiled or open, as indirect threats to its own security. This interlinkage was well illustrated by the tension engendered in the Balkans during the summer of 1971 by Yugoslavia's sharp reaction to Soviet-inspired attacks on Rumania.

How long this solidarity will continue is a moot point. Although both countries have a strong interest in forging closer bilateral relations and supporting Balkan-wide cooperation, which works against Soviet hegemony, recent developments in Yugoslav politics, both domestic and foreign, have raised a number of questions regarding the direction in which Yugoslavia is likely to move once Tito departs. While reports in the West have perhaps exaggerated the degree of Yugoslavia's rapprochement with the USSR, nonetheless it is clear that the improved climate of relations--symbolized in particular by Tito's visit to Moscow in May 1972 (his first in four years) and the receipt of a large Soviet credit in September of the same year--is bound to affect Rumania's position. Closer Soviet-Yugoslav collaboration deprives Rumania of an important ally, undermines regional solidarity, and in the end infringes heavily upon Rumania's own freedom of maneuver.

Yugoslavia and Rumania have not been the sole supporters of Balkan security, however. Since 1968, when Greek Foreign Minister Panayiotis Pipinelis proposed a "code of good conduct" as the basis for relations among Balkan

states, Greece has given high priority in its foreign policy
statements to the concept of Balkan security. In November
1972, for instance, Deputy Foreign Minister Aninos Kava-
lieratos raised the issue during an official visit to Rumania, stressing Greece's desire to turn the Balkans into
a "zone of peace, good-neighborliness, and fruitful cooperation."[13]

For Greece such calls for greater Balkan cooperation
serve to counterbalance, if not offset, its increased isolation from Western Europe. In its foreign policy the
Papadopoulos regime, despite its anticommunist rhetoric,
has been more influenced by realpolitik than by ideology.
Growing Western antipathy to the military dictatorship has
provided Greece with a strong impetus to expand its trade
with Eastern Europe and cultivate better relations with all
Balkan countries. Today, in fact, relations with Bulgaria
and Rumania are better than with many of Greece's NATO allies. Particularly significant for Greece's Balkan policy
was the establishment of diplomatic relations with Albania
in May 1971, which ended a technical state of war between
the two countries that had existed since 1940.

Albania, too, has been caught up in the winds of change
sweeping across Europe into the Balkans. The invasion of
Czechoslovakia, and most recently China's decision to seek
rapprochement with the United States, have forced Albania
to begin to move out of its shell and increase its contacts
with the outside world. Over the last few years there has
been a noticeable "opening to the West,"[14] which has sought
to offset Albania's (largely self-imposed) isolation. The
area where this has borne the greatest fruit has been the
Balkans, and the most dramatic manifestations of this "new
look" in foreign affairs has been the improvement of relations with Yugoslavia, which in the space of three or four
years have changed from uncompromising hostility to neigh-
borly cordiality.

The main consideration that prompted Tirana to reconcile its longstanding differences with Belgrade was fear
of Soviet aggression. The Albanians have come to see
Balkan cooperation as a bulwark against this, and in April
1969 they even pledged assistance to Yugoslavia in case of
a Soviet attack.[15] This, together with Albanian party
leader Enver Hoxha's admission that the Albanian minority
in Yugoslavia had made progress in achieving equality,[16]
set the basis for a gradual improvement that culminated in
the establishment of diplomatic relations in February 1971.
At the same time Albania has moved to normalize its relations with Bulgaria (which had deteriorated since the re-

call of diplomatic representatives in July 1968) and in May 1971 established full diplomatic relations with Greece. These moves were all designed to increase Tirana's security by offsetting its isolation and counterbalancing its ties to Peking, which have been subjected to increasing strain since China's rapprochement with the United States began.*

DIFFERENCES IN APPROACH TO
BALKAN SECURITY

While all countries generally supported efforts toward greater Balkan cooperation as the preparations for the European security conference moved into the final stages, differences in approach to the problem of Balkan security have become more evident. Rumania has sought to link this issue to the larger one of European security, in the apparent belief that security in the Balkans can only be achieved with the cooperation of the two superpowers. Ceausescu, in fact, has urged that the superpowers should formally express their willingness to guarantee the independence of the area,[17] apparently with the aim of committing the Soviet Union to a policy that would minimize opportunity for the application of the Brezhnev Doctrine in the Balkans as well as at eliciting a commitment on the part of the United States to guarantee Balkan sovereignty and integrity --primarily Rumania's.

The Yugoslavs, on the other hand, have feared that this might lead to a "new Yalta" in the Balkans and have tended to argue that the less the superpowers interfere the better are the chances for greater independence and sovereignty.[18] They would prefer to see the superpowers allow the Balkan countries a free hand in settling their own affairs and so Belgrade has displayed skepticism toward Rumanian calls for multilateral cooperation. For the time being the Yugoslavs seem to prefer to table the issue and to await the outcome of the European security conference before proceeding further. Moreover, Belgrade strongly feels that there can be no security in the Balkans until,

---

*In an apparent reference to the Chinese decision, Hoxha warned at the sixth party congress that "it is not possible to use one imperialism to oppose the other," and said that the Albanians consider the struggle against imperialism a "double" one that is "one indivisible whole." (Radio Tirana, 2 and 4 November 1971.)

as one writer has put it, the area is "freed from the bal-
last of obsolete nationalist ideas"[19]--that is, until the
Macedonian issue is resolved. As long as the Bulgarians
continue to maintain that Macedonians are ethnic Bulgarians,
the Yugoslavs feel there can be no meaningful security in
the Balkans.

      Greece, while in general it supports Rumanian proposals
for Balkan security, has taken a somewhat ambiguous position
on the issue of multilateral cooperation, although the Greek
position remains flexible in the main, because the concept
of a "neutralized " Balkans is an important trump that can
be played against Western criticism of the Greek military
regime. Bulgaria, on the other hand, has rejected multilateral cooperation entirely. In apparent response to
Ceausescu's proposals at the National Party Conference in
July 1972[20] that a multinational body of Balkan representatives to promote further Balkan cooperation be set up and
that a meeting of Balkan representatives be arranged, Bulgarian Premier Stanko Todorov noted that "in spite of the
favorable atmosphere prevailing in the area of the Balkans,
one must be satisfied with strengthening bilateral relations
and concentrate the main effort on the European cooperation
and security conference being held in Helsinki."[21] Bulgaria's firm rejection of all multilateral initiatives has
led many observers to suspect that Sofia, as so often in
the past, is acting as a mouthpiece for Moscow. This view
is given all the more credibility by the apparent Soviet
squelching of a Bulgarian suggestion, in the spring of 1971,
that an all-Balkan security conference be convened.[22]

BULGARIA AND BALKAN SECURITY

      Bulgaria's rejection of multilateral cooperation in the
Balkans provides a convenient moment to consider Sofia's
role in the Balkans in greater detail. Many observers would
perhaps question whether, in light of Bulgaria's reputation
as Moscow's staunchest ally, there is justification enough
to devote much attention to this question. It should be
remembered, however, that "national perspectives" are often
latent and are not always reflected openly in official com-
muniqués. Moreover, if the history of communism in the
Balkans has demonstrated anything, it is that nationalism
constitutes a strong centrifugal force that has often ex-
ploded quite unexpectedly to engulf every Balkan state to
one degree or another, and Bulgaria, as the abortive coup
in 1965[23] bears witness, has not been entirely immune. In

light of this, and of the fact that Sofia's role has generally been neglected in other analyses of East European
perspectives on European security, it may be worth taking
a closer look at what effect the question may have on future Bulgarian policy.

For Bulgaria, as for most Balkan countries, European
security is first and foremost a question of Balkan security. While Bulgaria has traditionally been only a marginal
actor in European politics, it has played an important, if
not always constructive, role in Balkan affairs. Balkan
conflicts have played a paramount role in determining its
history, and over all it has not fared very well as a result of them. Thus Bulgaria's fortunes are as intimately
linked as those of any other Balkan state to the question
of Balkan security, and it seems apparent that if Sofia is
ever to leave the political backwater in which it has spent
so much of its past it must be through cooperation with
Bulgaria's Balkan neighbors rather than in conflict with
them.

In considering Bulgaria's role in and contribution to
European and Balkan security, however, one must recognize
the present centrality of Bulgaria's relationship to the
Soviet Union. Sofia's link with Moscow, as the draft program adopted at the last (10th) party congress in April
1971 aptly put it, is the "cornerstone" of Bulgaria's domestic and foreign policy.[24] In effect it means that the
relationship with the Soviet Union defines the boundaries
of what is realistically possible and is the overriding
consideration in the way in which the Bulgarian leadership
defines its national interest. However, over the last few
years Sofia's ties with the USSR, rather than loosening as
has been the tendency elsewhere in the Balkans, have been
strengthened as a result of a policy of increased economic
integration with the Soviet economy.* This has served to
circumscribe Sofia's room for maneuver even further; at
present Bulgaria could hardly pursue a more independent

---

*The policy of integrating the two economies more
closely was first announced by Todor Zhivkov at the July
1968 Central Committee plenum and later amplified at the
September 1969 plenum, when Zhivkov noted that Bulgaria
intended to "move gradually toward joint planning in a number of branches" with the Soviet Union. Since then it has
been formalized in a series of sweeping economic agreements
signed in May 1968 and August and November 1970.

policy along the lines of that followed by Rumania or Yugoslavia, even should it so desire. Its economy is so tightly linked to that of the Soviet Union--close to 60 percent of its trade is with the USSR alone and another 20 percent with the other Comecon nations--that any attempt to move too far from Moscow would have serious economic consequences.

Yet whatever the political liabilities, Bulgaria's relationship with Moscow has been extremely profitable economically. Bulgaria has received more economic aid than any other East European country, and this has helped it to industrialize at a much more rapid pace than would otherwise have been possible.* Moreover, the chronic economic difficulties suffered by Rumania and Yugoslavia owing to the balance-of-payments deficits run up by large imports from the West have demonstrated the dangers threatening small Balkan countries that attempt to expand their trade with the West. Lastly, even if Bulgaria wished to expand its trade with the nonsocialist world, the West European market for Bulgarian goods is severely limited and Sofia lacks the hard currency to pay for many Western goods. For these reasons Bulgarian policy in the near future is likely to continue to be strongly influenced by the country's close ties with Moscow.

At the same time, however, a greater stabilization of the status quo in East Central Europe as a result of the CSCE might tend to make the Soviet Union feel more secure about its interests in Eastern Europe. This could have important consequences for all the East European countries, Belgrade included. It could mean that the limits set to freedom of action would be expanded and that, without jeopardizing its ties with Moscow, Sofia could begin to pursue a more autonomous policy.

The area where this would be most likely to have an effect is the Balkans. Here, moreover, there are precedents

---

*The extent to which the Soviet Union has been willing to underwrite Bulgarian industrialization is clearly illustrated by the fact that by 1967 more than 130 large industrial enterprises constructed with Soviet aid were producing 85 percent of all Bulgaria's ferrous metals output, 95 percent of its nonferrous output, 55 percent of its chemical manufactures, 70 percent of its electrical goods, and 100 percent of its shipbuilding output (see Rabotnichesko Delo, Sofia, 10 May 1967). In the same year it was estimated that there were 5,000 Soviet specialists in Bulgaria (see Politicheska Prosveta, no. 8 (Sofia, August 1967).

for a more autonomous policy. On rare but not insignificant occasions in the past Sofia has sought to take advantage of the coincidence of Soviet policy objectives and its own more "national" ones to assert itself, though diplomatically. In 1957 and 1959 Bulgaria was one of the staunchest supporters of the Stoica Notes, which were part of a general Warsaw Pact campaign to promote European security and called for a Balkan summit meeting to discuss differences and pave the way for general détente in the region. Most noteworthy in this connection was the Bulgarian proposal, offered by Zhivkov in an address to the National Assembly in December 1959, that Greece and Bulgaria reduce their military forces to the minimum needed to guard their borders. Zhivkov repeated this offer at the September 1960 session of the UN General Assembly, along with a proposal for "the transformation of the Balkans into the first area to implement the idea of general and complete disarmament."[25] The Bulgarian proposal went further than anything suggested at the time even by the Soviet Union, although it seems highly unlikely that it was made without Moscow's assent.

The most important example of Bulgaria's attempt to pursue a more independent policy without antagonizing Moscow, however, came in 1965-66, in the wake of Khrushchev's fall, when the Soviet leadership was preoccupied with the problem of internal consolidation. Bulgaria seized this opportunity to assert itself diplomatically, and again it was in the Balkans that this had the most noticeable effect. Relations with Greece, which had begun to improve in the summer of 1964 with the signing of a number of agreements, became steadily better. Serious efforts, which met with considerable success, to improve relations with Rumania began after the death of Rumanian leader Gheorghiu-Dej. Most noticeable was the improvement in relations with Yugoslavia, which was highlighted by Tito's first visit to Sofia in 18 years. These steps were also paralleled by a remarkable but brief flirtation with Bonn.

While the period of initiative was short lived and hardly constituted a challenge to Moscow, it did illustrate the direction in which Bulgaria could move and that the precedent and potential for a more active national policy do exist. Moreover, in recent years Sofia has once again begun to pursue an active Balkan policy. Not only has it sought to improve bilateral relations with all its neighbors but it has also emerged as a strong advocate of the Rumanian proposal to turn the Balkans into a "zone of peace, cooperation, and security."* This campaign to improve relations in the Balkans has been highlighted by a new 20-year treaty of friendship with Rumania (November 1970); an agreement with Turkey providing for the establishment of consular relations and expanded scientific and cultural exchanges (September 1970); and an accord with Albania reestablishing diplomatic ties.

As a result, relations with Rumania at present are more cordial than at any time in the last decade, and relations with Greece have warmed to a point where it is difficult to imagine that less than 10 years ago both countries were still officially at war. In fact, in March 1971 Bulgaria submitted an eight-point plan for economic cooperation that was the most comprehensive ever put forward to Greece by a communist country.

Most significant, however, has been the improvement in relations with Yugoslavia as a result of a switch in Bulgarian policy on the Macedonian question that began soon after Brezhnev's visit to Belgrade in September 1971. The Yugoslavs began to detect "a different and incontestably more correct" approach,[26] than had been taken previously, and this new "objectivity," according to a Yugoslav paper some months later,[27] was "a significant contribution to the efforts to create a more favorable climate for the development of friendly, good-neighborly relations." While the issue still continues to spark occasional sharp responses on the part of the Yugoslavs, the level and frequency of polemics has definitely subsided, and this deescalation has been matched by increased contacts at a high level, the most recent being a visit by Stane Dolanc--the secretary of the Yugoslav Party's Executive Bureau and often mentioned as a possible successor to Tito--to Sofia in February 1973 to confer with Todor Zhivkov.

BALKAN SECURITY IN WIDER PERSPECTIVE

As the recent subsiding of the Macedonian polemics has once more illustrated, tranquillity in the Balkans is to a

*Zhivkov backed the idea of a zone of peace in his speech to the 10th party congress in April 1971 (BTA, 20 April 1971), and in a speech on 25 June 1971 (Radio Sofia, 25 June 1971). Since then the call has become increasingly insistent.

great degree contingent upon factors outside the Balkan region itself. Throughout history the dominant world powers have played a paramount role in Balkan affairs, and no matter what develops out of the CSCE it seems likely that in the final analysis Balkan security will probably depend as much, if not more, upon the interests of the superpowers as it will upon the desire for better relations on the part of the Balkan states themselves.

Of all the powers Russia has perhaps the longest and most enduring interest in the Balkans. Involvement in that area has been a persistent theme of Russian foreign policy for over two centuries, and with only occasional lapses Russian leaders, both Soviet and tsarist, have regarded the region as essential to their definition of national interest.[28] With the expansion of Soviet naval power in the Mediterranean and the growth of Soviet-American rivalry in the Near East Moscow's interest has increased. As a consequence, over the past several years the Soviet Union has sought to improve relations with all Balkan states. A limited rapprochement--discussed in greater detail earlier --has been effected with both Yugoslavia and Rumania. Ties with Bulgaria have been strengthened through a program of close economic integration of the two economies, in an effort to keep Sofia strongly wedded to its traditionally strong pro-Soviet orientation. Only ties to Albania have eluded efforts at improvement.

On the southern flank, Soviet diplomacy has also made significant inroads in improving relations with Turkey. Turkish foreign policy has traditionally been wary of Moscow but at the same time has attempted to maintain correct relations. Stalin's attempt after World War II to revise the Montreux Convention of July 1936, which regulates use of the Dardanelles and his demand that three northern Turkish provinces be ceded to the Soviet Union put a severe strain on relations. As the fervor of the cold war has waned, however, Ankara's desire to establish a more balanced relationship with Moscow, together with Turkey's continuing resentment over U.S. policy toward Cyprus, has given the Soviet Union an opportunity to improve relations with Ankara. To a degree Turkey has reciprocated, in the hope of gaining greater diplomatic leverage on the Cyprus issue, although in the last few years the tempo of improvement has slackened somewhat.

Historically Turkey has always occupied a special role in Russian diplomacy because of the straits issue, and at present better relations with Ankara are a key component of Moscow's Balkan policy. The Kremlin's long-term goal seems to be to lure Ankara into a more neutralist position, which might eventually facilitate a revision of the agreements on the straits, a consideration of growing importance now that the Middle East has become the prime trouble spot in world politics.[29] In any conflict there, especially one into which the superpowers were drawn, Turkey would play an important role, and good relations with that country would be an important asset to the USSR.

Soviet relations with Greece have undergone less improvement but nonetheless remain quite correct. Soviet censure of the Greek junta has been surprisingly mild; rather than criticizing the antidemocratic nature of the Greek regime Moscow has concentrated its attacks on Greece's ties with NATO and its dependence on Washington and at the same time has sought to exploit Western criticism of the Papadopoulos government to encourage Greece to loosen its ties with NATO and move toward a more neutralistic stance. In this regard calls for Balkan cooperation play an important role.

The Soviet Union, however, is not the only power with a strong interest in the Balkans. Moscow has had to contend with increased diplomatic activity on the part of the United States, and, to a lesser but still not insignificant extent, of China. Over the last several years the United States has succeeded in repairing some of the deterioration in its relations with Turkey that followed in the wake of the 1964 Cyprus crisis. At the same time--at least temporarily--Washington's position in Greece improved with the decision by the Papadopoulos government to grant the United States home-port facilities. Relations with Bucharest have perhaps undergone the greatest improvement, since the United States has sought to take advantage of Rumania's desire to conduct a more autonomous policy vis-à-vis the Soviet Union. In the summer of 1969 President Nixon paid a visit to Rumania, the first by an American president to an East European country, which was followed by Ceausescu's visit to the United States the following year. Lastly, Washington's enduring interest in the fate of Yugoslavia was signaled by Nixon's visit to Belgrade in the fall of 1970 and Tito's visit to the United States in the fall of 1971.

In its Balkan policy the United States has been motivated by concern to offset any increase in Soviet hegemony that might lead to a shift in the balance of power in the Mediterranean region. It has thus supported the efforts of both Yugoslavia and Rumania to conduct policies independent of Moscow. Despite this, however, the American policy toward these two Balkan states is basically different. Washington would clearly regard any attempt by Moscow to pressure Yugoslavia, which has followed a policy of non-alignment for over 25 years, as more serious than any attempt to reduce the scope of Bucharest's autonomy. Rumania is a member of Comecon and the Warsaw Pact, whereas Yugoslavia is not, and Bucharest is generally conceded, tacitly if not openly, to fall within the Soviet sphere of influence. An effort by the Soviet Union to pressure Yugoslavia into altering its present nonaligned course, on the other hand, would probably meet with strong resistance from the United States, because it would upset the status quo in the Balkans and might eventually tip the balance of power in the Mediterranean area as well.

In recent years a third factor has come to play an increasingly important role in Balkan policies: China. Yet despite the intensity of Soviet fears about the emergence of a Belgrade-Tirana-Bucharest axis supported by Peking, China's interest, as Chou En-lai warned, is still limited, and is likely to remain so for some time to come. To a great extent its activities in the Balkans to date have been a counterattack aimed at offsetting Soviet attempts to "contain" China, such as the USSR's call in 1969 for an Asian collective security system and its recent conclusion of a treaty with India. Thus, as Moscow has attempted to move into China's backyard, China has in part responded by moving into Moscow's. At present China needs as many allies or, as G. P. Hudson has termed them,[30] "benevolent neutrals," as possible in order to divert or restrain the Soviet Union, and therefore has an interest in strengthening the position of any power that is in conflict with the Soviet Union. Thus, it has a stake in promoting and supporting nonalignment and regionalism in the Balkans. Regardless of its recent diplomatic assertiveness, however, China is not yet a superpower but rather a medium-sized one whose primary concern is regional rather than global.

CONCLUSION

During the past half decade two contradictory trends have manifested themsleves in the Balkans: on one hand, there are a number of issues--among them the Cyprus dispute, the Macedonian polemics, the disintegrative tendencies in Yugoslavia, and the Rumanian search for greater independence --which have served to increase the possibility for both regional and global insecurity; on the other, there has

been a noticeable effort on the part of all Balkan states
to improve relations and work toward greater regional cooperation. The key question is which of these contradictory
tendencies will prevail in the future.

Balkan politics have traditionally defied prediction,
and it would be foolhardy to attempt to forecast the future
with any degree of precision. One can at least outline the
possible alternatives and their implications, however.

One of the most important factors that will influence
future Balkan developments will be the outcome of the talks
on European security and troop reductions in Helsinki,
Geneva, and Vienna, and this is why the Balkan states have
been so intensely concerned that their interests be represented at these talks. Should the talks serve to remove
some of the sources of tension that have crippled East-West
relations over the past two decades, as it is hoped they
will, this could reduce the tendency of the superpowers to
treat the individual Balkan states as pawns in a global
chess game and might also lead to a loosening, or at least
a gradual change in the structure, of the present system of
alliances. Either development could serve to promote a
trend toward greater flexibility in the conduct of foreign
policy on the part of the Balkan states as well as spur efforts to achieve greater regional solidarity. At the very
least, the consideration of alternative methods of ensuring both individual and regional security would be facilitated.

At present most alternative concepts seem premature.
The time may not be at hand to abandon present alliances,
but this need not imply that in the future others may not
become more attractive. The road from the present state
of improved commercial ties to a regional security system
is, of course, long and filled with imponderables. Yet
throughout the 20th century, despite the repeated hostilities that have pitted one Balkan state against the other,
the desire for some sort of regional grouping or federation
has persistently reemerged. The proposed forms of such a
grouping have varied, but the durability of the concept at-
tests to its strength.[31] Under certain circumstances the
present fledgling efforts at greater cooperation could serve
as a basis for the realization of this long-held goal.

Yet should the talks in Helsinki, Geneva, and Vienna
only serve to move the center of confrontation further to
the south--as many Balkan states fear may unfortunately be
the case--then it is clear that security in the area would
be lessened and the maneuvering room of the Balkan states
would become even less than it is at present. Given the

legacy of unsolved problems and the potential instability
that still exists, such a situation might indeed help to
turn the region into a European powder keg. For this reason the Yugoslavs have strongly insisted that the problem
of European security cannot be separated from the problem
of Mediterranean security. The renewed outbreak of the
Arab-Israeli conflict in October of 1973 only served to
strengthen their argument.

In the final analysis, of course, much depends upon
events outside the Balkans, in particular the extent of
future conflict or cooperation between the two superpowers.
Both the latter have a strong interest in preserving stability in an area lying on the periphery of the Middle East.
Instability in the Balkans would only tend to make the
Mediterranean more unstable, which in turn would reflect
upon the situation in the Middle East. Thus Balkan security,
perhaps more than at any other time in the past, is today
an important aspect of the whole question of European secu-
rity--as much for the superpowers as for the Balkan states
themselves.

NOTES

1. For a further discussion of Soviet policy in the
Balkans, see F. Stephen Larrabee, "Changing Russian Perspectives on the Balkans," Survey 18, no. 3 (London, Summer 1972).

2. For a detailed analysis of the campaign see F.
Stephen Larrabee, "Neue Entwicklungstendenzen auf dem
Balkan," Europa Archiv, Bonn, 10 March 1972.

3. Vjesnik, Zagreb, 28 August 1971.

4. In Political Order in Changing Societies (New
Haven, Conn.: Yale University Press, 1968), p. 5.

5. See Udo Steinbach, "Neuere Entwicklungen in den
politischen Beziehungen zwischen der Sowiet Union und der
Tuerkei, Griechenland, und Zypern," Osteuropa, Stuttgart,
July 1973.

6. For a detailed analysis of these problems and their
implications for the post-Tito era, see Victor Meier, "Die
Sackgasse der Spaet-Titoismus," Osteuropa, July 1973, and
John C. Campbell, "Insecurity and Cooperation: Yugoslavia
and the Balkans," Foreign Affairs 51, no. 4 (New York,
July 1973).

7. In an interview with Harry Schleicher published
in the Frankfurter Rundschau, 17 December 1971.

8.   See Stanley Hoffman, "Heroic Leadership: The Case
of Modern France," in Lewis Edinger, ed., <u>Political Leadership in Industrialized Societies</u> (New York: John Wiley &
Sons, 1967), p. 123.
9.   For a detailed analysis of recent ups and downs
in the polemics see F. Stephen Larrabee, "Bulgaria's Politics of Conformity," <u>Problems of Communism</u>, Washington,
D.C., July-August 1972.
10.   Agerpres, 13 June 1970.
11.   <u>Scinteia</u>, Bucharest, 20 July 1972.
12.   Drogoljub Vujica, writing in <u>Politika</u>, Belgrade,
14 November 1971.
13.   Radio Bucharest, 28 November 1972.
14.   See Peter R. Prifti, "Albania's Expanding Horizons,"
<u>Problems of Communism</u>, January-February 1972.
15.   <u>Zeri i popullit</u>, Tirana, 11 April 1969.
16.   Ibid., 19 September 1970.
17.   Victor Meier in the <u>Tages Anzeiger</u>, Zurich, 16
August 1973.
18.   Ibid.; see also the <u>Corriere della Sera</u>, Milan,
17 August 1973.
19.   Ljubomir Radovanovic, "Balkan Cooperation," <u>Review
of International Affairs</u>, Belgrade, 5 May 1973.
20.   <u>Scinteia</u>, 20 July 1972.
21.   Bulgarska Telegrafna Agentsia (hereafter BTA), 28
March 1973.
22.   Carl Buchalla in the <u>Sueddeutsche Zeitung</u>, Munich,
23 April 1971.
23.   For a detailed analysis of this bizarre incident
see J. F. Brown, "The Bulgarian Plot," <u>The World Today</u>,
London, June 1965.
24.   BTA, 13 March 1971.
25.   Radio Sofia, 28 September 1960.
26.   <u>Nova Makedonia</u>, Skopje, 25 January 1972.
27.   Ibid., 5 March 1972.
28.   For a discussion of Russian interest in the Balkans during the tsarist period see Ivo Lederer, "Russia
and the Balkans," in Ivo Lederer, ed., <u>Russian Foreign Pol-
icy</u> (New Haven, Conn.:   Yale University Press, 1962).   For
the more recent period see Larrabee, "Changing Russian
Perspectives."
29.   Steinbach, "Neuere Entwicklungen."
30.   In <u>Problems of Communism</u>, Washington, D.C.,
November-December 1971.
31.   For a detailed history of earlier efforts at Balkan
unity see L. S. Stavrianos, <u>Balkan Federation, A History of
the Movement Toward Balkan Unity in Modern Times</u>, Smith Col-
lege Studies in History XXVII (October 1941-July 1942).

Whatever the divergent interests and perceptions that
have emerged in the context of détente, and that appear to
be leading toward greater diversity in both domestic and
foreign policies among the East European states, their impact will be tempered by influences external to Eastern
Europe as well as by forces within the area. The crucial
factor in determining the degree to which divergencies are
permitted to develop in Eastern Europe is, of course, the
interaction between these states and the Soviet Union. A
successful security conference will probably bring enhanced
self-confidence and a greater sense of security to the Soviet Union, with the possible result that Soviet leaders
will interpret less rigidly their need for conformity in
Eastern Europe. Regardless of the success of the security
conference from the Soviet perspective, however, Eastern
Europe will remain an area of fundamental concern.

For Eastern Europe itself, perhaps more important than
the development of a new relationship between the USSR on
the one hand and Western Europe and the United States on
the other will be the internal evolution of Soviet society
and institutions, which détente may encourage. A Soviet
leadership that is more responsive to the needs and concerns of its own population and interest groups is likely
to be more sympathetic to the divergent interests of the
East European governments and parties.

The dynamics of domestic development in both the USSR
and Eastern Europe offer a contradictory and highly complex
picture. On the one hand a quarter century of communist
rule in Eastern Europe has produced certain important
transformations that are unlikely to be reversed regardless
of what happens in the Soviet Union or in the international
sphere. The precommunist elites have been eliminated, and
the postwar generation has grown up knowing no alternative
to the present system. Ruling elites with their own vested
interests have evolved that are anxious to perpetuate the
status quo. Many of the economic and social changes that
communist rule has introduced have to a degree achieved
popular acceptance, and as a result a certain stability
has been achieved in the region in the sense that external
challenges are less of a threat to the existing order.
At the same time, the attractiveness of Western states for
the peoples of Eastern Europe has shifted from the areas

234

of ideology and politics toward economics. The East Europeans would like to achieve the economic efficiency, the
high standard of living, and the advanced technology enjoyed in the West.

Paradoxically, the economic and social progress
achieved in Eastern Europe, which is in large measure responsible for the degree of popular acceptance of communist
rule, has created conditions likely to lead to increased
social conflict in the decade ahead. The countries in the
area are facing problems similar to those confronting less
developed countries in other parts of the world. The instability and disorder in the third world are due, in the
words of Samuel Huntington, to "the lag in the development
of political institutions behind social and economic
change."[1] The communist leaderships have devoted a large
proportion of their countries' resources to economic development, and despite certain distortions and inefficien-
cies that this process has introduced, economic growth has
been significant. A social and cultural transformation
has also been effected under party direction, and the
changes that have resulted from these policies--urbaniza-
tion, industrialization, increased literacy, the expansion
of education, the proliferation of mass information media--
have broadened political consciousness and increased political demands. Although most of the states in Eastern Europe still have not reached the level of developed industrialized nations, their socioeconomic progress has been
impressive.

At the same time, however, in the respective countries
the communist party and the political institutions it di-
rects have failed to keep pace with these deeper social and
economic changes. The party is structured to mobilize the
population for the transformation of society, but has not
yet adapted itself to administer efficiently the complex
system it has created. Both the economy and society have
developed to the point where decentralized decision making
is necessary, but the party continues to be highly centralized and autocratic. The system is still geared to the
creation of large investment funds, which are channeled
into the development of heavy industry, although the returns on such investments are dwindling. Although growing
pressure to raise the standard of living has forced increased investments in light industry, the system is not
geared to respond to consumer demand.

The reluctance to adapt to socioeconomic changes which
the party itself has produced is the result of various
complex factors. The party bureaucracy has developed a

certain vested interest in maintaining intact the system
that is the source of its perquisites. In Eastern Europe
any attempts to alter the system in any fundamental manner
also raise questions and fears in the minds of the Soviet
leadership. Reluctance to change stemming from bureaucratic
self-interest and Soviet hegemony is in turn bolstered by
ideological arguments that favor the maintenance of the
status quo.[2]

EUROPEAN SECURITY AND DOMESTIC CHANGE

The impact of détente and of the movement toward European security upon Eastern Europe will have to be assessed
in light of the prospects for the continuation, and probably the intensification, over the next decade, of the social conflict that results from the discrepancy between
economic and social development and monopolistic political
authority, and to some extent from a "revolution of rising
expectations" with regard to the standard of living. Expanded East-West economic-technological relations, more extensive personal contacts, and the freer flow of informa-
tion--all of which in one form or another will probably
emerge from the security conference--will further the economic development and modernization of Eastern Europe.
Even economic relations are difficult to isolate, however,
and increased contact on purely technical issues will have
a certain spillover, at least among the technocratic element of the population, in raising questions about political and economic administration. This in turn could increase pressures to adjust the East European systems.
One must not forget, however, that much can be done
to counter these pressures. The leaders of Eastern Europe
have been aware of the hazards of increased human contacts
and have vigorously sought to limit East-West intercourse
to that officially under government control. These questions of increasing contacts among peoples are the major
issues in the CSCE's so-called "Basket Three," and they
have provoked significant differences between the East and
West European states in Helsinki and Geneva. In a further
attempt to limit the effects of freer contacts, the East
Europeans have undertaken a massive ideological campaign
with the intention of fortifying their populations against
the pernicious effects of exposure to Western ideas and
economic and political views.
Social unrest is not confined to Eastern Europe; it is
characteristic of all societies undergoing the process of

social, economic, and political development. In Eastern
Europe, however, internal social conflict is, to use Adam
Bromke's term, "externalized,"[3] in the sense that it becomes
an issue in relations with the Soviet Union. Maintaining
communist-party rule on the Soviet model in Eastern Europe
is a primary factor in legitimizing Soviet hegemony in the
area, and any threat to this type of party rule is seen as
a challenge to Soviet interests, as was the case in Czechoslovakia in 1968.[4] The USSR has exhibited a certain willingness to tolerate variations in the internal systems of
the East European states--witness the significant differences between the Hungarian and Bulgarian systems of economic management--but nevertheless the spectrum of acceptable deviation is narrow.

To enforce its hegemony the Soviet Union can ultimately
rely upon force, but in an era of détente this would certainly be counterproductive as far as relations with the
West are concerned. The use of force against an East European state would certainly set back any hope of détente.
The fact that the Soviet leaders were willing to pay a
price, in terms of the immediate relationship with the
East German leadership, by agreeing to concessions and compromises on issues relating to Berlin and West Germany reflects a measure of their commitment to détente. Also, as
East-West economic relations expand, the USSR's stake in
perpetuating détente will grow. With each step toward relaxation, the cost of intervention in Eastern Europe climbs.
This does not mean that a decision to use force could not
ultimately be taken, but it does suggest that, as the price
of intervention rises, the threshold for intervention may
also be raised, giving the East European states somewhat
greater latitude in dealing with their internal problems
and perhaps also in their foreign policy.

In dealing with the possible effects of détente there
are two external factors which must also be considered:
China and Western Europe. Both have the potential to exert
influences that could affect both internal social developments and the external pattern of relations in Eastern Europe. In examining these two influences, however, it must
be kept in mind that the Soviet Union considers its vital
interests to be involved.

CHINA

From the Soviet perspective, China's influence on
Eastern Europe holds two dangers, the first ideological,

the second political. The ideological threat stems from
the Marxist-Leninist model that the Chinese claim to represent. The specific attributes of a Chinese model are difficult to spell out, the more so since Peking's policy has
varied considerably over time, ranging from a stridently
militant to a rather relaxed line in both domestic and
foreign policy. If the occasion requires, the peculiarities of the Chinese variant can be broadly interpreted, and
the details of the model are less significant than its existence. Thus far, with a few short-lived exceptions (the
Bulgarian "great leap forward" in 1958, for example), none
of the East European states except Albania has accepted the
Chinese model. This does not mean, however, that Chinese
ideology has not had an influence in Eastern Europe. Within
many East European parties ultraleftist or Maoist factions
exist and have been publicly criticized. A faction in
exile supported by China and Albania launches propaganda
attacks from Tirana on the Polish party. Hungary, too,
has been concerned with a radical leftist movement.[5]

Soviet concern about the possible attractiveness of
Peking's brand of Marxism-Leninism is reflected in attempts
to firm up the ideological cohesion of Eastern Europe. One
aim of the ideological campaign that is now under way is to
counter this attractiveness. After the Crimea conference
between East European party heads and the Soviet leaders
in July 1973, a much harsher anti-Chinese line became apparent, and the calls for a conference of world communist
parties that began to be heard in late 1973 appear to mark
a renewed Soviet effort to excommunicate Peking from the
movement in order to diminish the appeal of the Chinese
model. There is little possibility that a pro-Chinese faction will gain control of one of the East European parties,
but the Chinese, by their devotion to a different variety
of Marxism-Leninism, have the potential of remaining a
source of factionalism that might foster certain imbalance
in the East European parties. They represent a potential
ideological fifth column with which the Soviet Union must
be concerned.

The Chinese also pose a political threat to the Soviet
Union. Their search for influence among both communist and
noncommunist states on the USSR's western frontier is the
most immediate danger, but in the long run, as China comes
to play an increasing role in world affairs, its challenge
to Soviet influence in other areas will become sharper.
The People's Republic of China is far removed from Europe,
and its primary concerns in foreign policy are understandably oriented toward Asia. Nevertheless, the PRC's growing

role as a world power and the importance of Europe in world politics imbue events on that continent with considerable importance in Chinese eyes.

China's present policy vis-à-vis Europe has three main aims: to seek better relations with the states of Eastern Europe; to seek improved political and economic relations with the states of Western Europe and to encourage European unity; and to engender doubts about the success of the European security conference. Probably because the most favorable response has come from them, the PRC's approaches to Eastern Europe have focused upon the dissident states. Albania has been a close ally for well over a decade, and in the last few years relations with Rumania and Yugoslavia have also become much more friendly. China's approaches to the other East European states have been largely unsuccessful and have been limited to moderate efforts to improve bilateral economic relations and not entirely successful efforts to improve interstate (as opposed to interparty) relations. Success has been greatest in the Balkans, but the threat to the other Warsaw Pact states has also been a source of concern to the Soviet leaders, and their campaign to counter Chinese influence and strengthen the ideological cohesion of the East European states reflects the potentially disruptive effect the Chinese can have. It is the USSR that is behind the propaganda that pictures the Chinese as seeking to disrupt the unity of the socialist camp. The most vigorous effort to do this was made in the summer of 1971, shortly after Rumania's President Ceausescu and Yugoslavia's Foreign Minister Tepavac had paid state visits to China. The Chinese were accused of "seeking to drive a wedge between the socialist countries"[6]--a theme that has frequently been repeated since that time.

China's efforts to improve relations with Western Europe have also been stepped up recently. In the new surge of international contacts that followed the end of its Cultural Revolution, China exchanged ambassadors with all West European states except Portugal and Ireland. Among foreign ministers who have paid recent visits to Peking are Walter Scheel of West Germany, Sir Alec Douglas-Home of Britain, Maurice Schumann of France, and Guiseppi Medici of Italy, and the late French President Georges Pompidou and former British Prime Minister Edward Heath have been received in Peking. Economic relations with Western Europe have also undergone significant intensification. In addition to entering into bilateral economic relations with a number of its members, the Chinese have negotiated directly with the EEC, and it seems probable that official recognition will be accorded that organization. In fact, in a conversation with Medici, Chou En-lai expressed approval of the EEC and urged its member states to work for political and military, as well as economic, union.[7] Paradoxically, the PRC leaders have on the one hand expressed qualified approval of the North Atlantic Alliance and on the other encouraged West European states to maintain their individual military preparedness in order to preserve their independence from the superpowers. These actions, and particularly the favorable treatment of the EEC and NATO, have provoked numerous Soviet criticisms of Chinese policy.

In addition to seeking improved relations with all European states and, at least verbally, encouraging West European efforts to achieve unification, the Chinese have been highly skeptical of the movement toward European security. In his address to the United Nations General Assembly in October 1972, Deputy Foreign Minister Chiao Kuan-hua called the CSCE "the European insecurity conference" and insisted that until the two opposing military alliances are disbanded and foreign troops withdrawn "European peace and security are still under threat."[8] The Chinese have indicated their own reservations about the conference mainly by selective reporting and emphasizing similar doubts voiced by others. The Chinese news agency's report on the first-stage meeting of foreign ministers[9] noted that "some ministers expressed a desire for détente in Europe, but were very much afraid that they might be deceived by the superpowers and get false détente instead of real security." The brief excerpts from the speeches of various foreign ministers provided by Hsinhua were chosen to stress these doubts, and the Soviet foreign minister's insistence on a conference declaration renouncing the use of force, opposing interference in internal affairs, and respecting the sovereignty of other countries was juxtaposed with a Soviet spokesman's assertion that these principles "would not apply to such acts as the armed Soviet invasion of Czechoslovakia." Chinese criticism of the security conference has provoked a flood of coordinated attacks on Peking in Soviet and East European news media.

Related to the Chinese leaders' attitude toward European security is their position on Germany. They apparently choose to see German reunification as a distinct possibility. Foreign Minister Scheel was reportedly told by Chinese Foreign Minister Chi P'eng-fei that the present "abnormal situation" in Germany could not continue indefinitely, and that the right of the German people to reunification could not be permanently refused.[10] These views, however, provoked a vigorous East German response that overstated the vague support the Chinese have given German unification.[11] The PRC's obvious interest in keeping the German issue alive is based on a desire to encourage instability on the Soviet Union's western frontier, since resolution of the German problem has been at the root of Russia's concern about security in Europe since the end of World War II.

Its attitude both toward the German question and toward European security has led the Soviets and East Europeans to accuse China of seeking "to prevent final recognition of the results of World War II, including the inviolability of borders as they currently exist."[12] This accusation brings to mind the claims of the Chinese against Soviet territory, including that voiced by Chairman Mao Tse-tung in 1964, when, in an interview with a group of Japanese socialists, he observed that "the places occupied by the Soviet Union are too numerous" and denounced the USSR's retention of the Kuriles and Mongolia. He then commented, in regard to the situation in Eastern Europe: "[The Soviets] have appropriated part of Rumania. Having detached part of East Germany, they drove the local inhabitants into the western part. Having detached part of Poland, they incorporated it into Russia, and in compensation gave Poland part of East Germany. The same thing happened in Finland."[13] This attempt to raise sensitive issues between the Soviet Union and the East European states must continue to haunt Soviet leaders.

The Chinese policy of seeking to undermine Soviet influence in Eastern Europe, encouraging a stronger, more united Western Europe, and disparaging the security conference is naturally related to the Sino-Soviet conflict and to Chinese fear of the Soviet Union. The policy is more complex, however, than the calculation, as expressed in simple form by a Bulgarian commentator, that China opposes European security "because a normalization of the situation in Europe would untie the Soviet Union's hands in Asia."[14] The Chinese are only too well aware that their own influence in Europe must, for geographical reasons, remain limited. In their perspective, however, Europe--particularly a united Western Europe--is an important element in the multipolar world that is evolving from the realignments and readjustments presently taking place. A strong Europe, with a strong Japan and a strong United States, would provide China with greater maneuverability vis-à-vis the Soviet Union.

What effect Chinese policy is likely to have on the evolution of Eastern Europe is difficult to assess. As

has been obvious with regard to its attempts to expand its
influence in the Balkans, the distance factor has limited
China's opportunities, and the Chinese leaders, as well as
those of Rumania and Yugoslavia, seem to recognize this.
From the Soviet perspective, China is not so much a direct
threat to Soviet interests in Eastern Europe as an indirect
one. If the USSR is required to become more involved in
Asia because of Chinese challenges there, the East European
states may be able to bargain their support of the Soviet
Union for greater autonomy in the conduct of their own foreign and domestic policies.

WESTERN EUROPE

     Changes in Western Europe over the past decade have
had an important impact upon Eastern Europe, and the Western half of the continent will influence developments in
the East to an even greater extent in the future. During
the 1960s its sustained high levels of economic growth and
rising standard of living and the evolution of the European
Economic Community have given Western Europe a new importance in East European eyes. But expanded economic relations with Western Europe inevitably entail a certain increase in political and social influences from the West.
The isolation of the East European states from developments
affecting their Western neighbors has never been complete,
but the acceleration of the scientific-technological revolution has made such isolation both less possible and less
desirable.
     The evolution of the European Economic Community will
be a major factor in influencing the evolution of Eastern
Europe during the coming decade. In the past East European
and Soviet officials have preferred bilateral trade arrangements with the West European states, and the East
European states have for the most part succeeded in circumventing the EEC. With the transfer of policymaking com-
petence to community--that is, supranational--level, Western integration is bound to affect, if not define, the con-
glomerate of political and economic changes within the respective Eastern and Western communities, as well as the
pattern of interaction between them. Since 1 January 1973,
trade agreements between EEC countries and Comecon member
states have had to be negotiated by the Brussels Commission, although bilateral trade agreements entered into before that date may continue until 31 December 1974.

In the past, however, the political undertones of
trade with the East have divided the EEC and impeded the
formation of common positions. According to some, the EEC
members are still divided, and are determined to continue
taking essentially unilateral approaches in trade with the
communist countries. Although technically. speaking the
EEC was to begin negotiating with Eastern Europe as a bloc
on trade agreements after 1 January 1973, EEC member governments have shown that they have little intention of honor-
ing this commitment fully. France and West Germany in particular, with their strong political interest in Eastern
Europe, have been especially unwilling to delegate negotiating power to the EEC Commission in Brussels. The 10-
year bilateral cooperation agreements signed by Germany
(May 1973) and France (July 1973) with the Soviet Union,
and the economic exchanges for which they will provide a
framework, are considered by many in the EEC as a means of
circumventing the commission's authority over bilateral
trade, an authority that in any case still remains to be
defined. Such agreements certainly appear to violate the
spirit, if not the letter, of EEC regulations, and they
could stunt the growth of supranational authority.

The Comecon states have increasingly indicated a
greater willingness to deal with EEC institutions in economic matters. Soviet party Secretary-General Brezhnev admitted in early 1972 that the EEC was a fact of life that
would have to be dealt with.[15] At the same time, the Soviet
and East European assessment of the European Economic Community has evolved in such a way as to open the door to
contacts. Western economic integration, in the Eastern
view, has gained a certain legitimacy and a greater degree
of detachment from political and military integration;
from the same point of view, progressive forces within the
EEC are becoming increasingly averse to the American presence in Europe. In August 1973 the secretary-general of
Comecon met unofficially with EEC officials in Copenhagen
in what promises to be the first of a series of meetings.
Already there are signs of concern among some Comecon members, however, about that organization's suitability as an
instrument for dealing with the EEC. Rumania, which approached the EEC directly in a successful bid to receive
generalized preferences for its trade with the community,
has explicitly voiced misgivings about having Comecon
handle economic relations with the EEC. Like other East
European states, including Hungary, the RSR fears that if
Comecon deals with the EEC on behalf of its member states
the interests of the smaller states will not be taken fully

into consideration. And in view of the economic dispropor-
tion between the Soviet Union and other East European
states, such fears may not be unfounded. At the same time,
however, one can argue the reverse--that the bargaining
position of the individual East European states with the
EEC would be improved by joint action.

The primary impulse behind Eastern Europe's new willingness to deal with the EEC is economic. In the opinion
of West Europeans, however, political as well as economic
motivations are apparent. Since the foreign policies of
the West European states have in recent years been regional
rather than global in orientation, their political concern
to improve relations with Eastern Europe is likely to continue. There are strong pressures to circumvent multilateral control of economic relations between the EEC states
and the East European countries, but West Europeans are
becoming increasingly aware of the need for integration if
they are to safeguard their own destiny in a world of superpowers, although the reaction to the most recent Middle
East conflict and the concomitant oil crisis emphasized
the limited degree of integration achieved thus far. The
further progress of West European integration may be a factor
that will permit and even encourage expansion of relations
with Eastern Europe; a united Western Europe would be in a
stronger position to encourage economic cooperation with
the Eastern states. With a unified and growing economy en-
compassing all of Western Europe and an increased capacity,
through integration, to develop and utilize advanced technology, Western Europe will exercise greater influence in
relations with both the Soviet Union and its East European
allies. On the other hand, if France and West Germany insist upon maintaining strong bilateral ties with the East,
West European influence could be divided and weakened.

Western Europe's relations with the United States suggest certain possible parallels with the relationship between Eastern Europe and the Soviet Union. Just as a
greater sense of security in Western Europe has encouraged
the expression of differences within the North Atlantic
Community, so the security conference and, in particular,
the FRG's acknowledgment of the political-territorial status
quo in Central Europe, have provided new opportunities for
East European differences to come to the fore. The consequences in Eastern Europe, however, are potentially more
serious. Differences within the Atlantic alliance have occurred on the level of interstate relations, and they are
likely to remain at that level. Within the Warsaw Pact,
on the other hand, the differences are likely to have con-

244

sequences not only for interstate relations (as has already happened to some extent in the case of Rumania) but also for the domestic political systems of these states. The insistence that the domestic political systems conform to the Soviet model is less likely to avoid challenge in the future. The "West German revanchist" threat has lost much of its credibility in Eastern Europe, and the threat of American imperialism becomes less believable as the United States implements the Nixon Doctrine and in view of the disarray in NATO. The evolution of the internal political and social systems in Eastern Europe is potentially very significant, since it will have repercussions on the relationship of these states to the Soviet Union and on their general foreign policies. The Soviet reaction to these developments will be conditioned by the internal evolution in the Soviet Union and the effect of détente on Soviet foreign policy assessments.

A basic assumption in this volume is that the process of détente has begun and will continue and that in this context greater divergency of interest among the East European states is not only possible but also very likely. This basic assumption, however, may not prove to be correct. Projections of this nature cannot take into consideration the unforeseen variables that may arise, and the first flush of excitement over détente may obscure the continued existence of serious obstacles to further progress. In fact, the latest round of hostilities in the Middle East has raised a new series of questions in this regard. As U.S. Secretary of State Henry Kissinger has observed, détente is not divisible; it is not possible to have détente in Europe and confrontation in the Middle East. The euphoria that surrounded Brezhnev's visit to the United States in June 1973 was dissipated by the resumption of hostilities between Israel and its Arab neighbors less than four months later. The tone of Soviet propaganda on the Middle East has perhaps been less strident than in the past, and U.S. government spokesmen have said that the policy of improving relations with the Soviet Union prevented escalation of the crisis to the point where the superpowers would become directly involved. Détente is certainly a new factor in Soviet and American foreign policy calculations, but the basic relationship between these two states has not fundamentally changed.

Perhaps the hopes and elation engendered by Nixon's and Brezhnev's exchange of visits, the intial phase of the CSCE, and the success of West Germany's Ostpolitik were unjustified, and the Middle East crisis has only served to

bring expectations into line with reality. This is not to
deny that concrete benefits may result from détente, but
perhaps its scope and potential are more limited than they
appeared in the initial intoxication of success. The central issue for both the United States and the Soviet Union
is their common interest in avoiding a direct confrontation
with each other. Whether this common interest will result
in agreement to limit the further development of strategic
weapons and stabilize mutual deterrence at lower levels,
however, remains to be seen. The basic prerequisite for
success is mutual trust, and the necessary degree of trust
does not exist at present.

The real chances for permanent reduction of international tensions will depend upon evolution of the Soviet
political system. Although détente may encourage certain
trends in this direction, the effect will most probably
be limited. Any agreements about human contacts will be
narrow, and the Soviet Union will interpret them in a still
more circumscribed fashion. Expanding economic relations
will introduce influences for change into Soviet society,
at least among some of the technocracy, but the impact will
be deliberately and probably successfully limited. Cooperation among businessmen, astronauts, and sociologists, no
matter how cordial their relations, is unlikely to affect
political developments in any decisive fashion. Under
these circumstances, the effect of détente on Eastern Europe may also be limited. Despite these considerations,
however, the present period is one of readjustment and
adaption for European states, both East and West. Although
the parameters may be circumscribed, the momentum of change
may carry developments beyond the anticipated limits.

NOTES

1. Political Order in Changing Societies (New Haven,
Conn.: Yale University Press, 1968), p. 5.
2. For a discussion of the problems behind Eastern
Europe's difficulty in adjusting to changing social and
economic conditions, see Zvi Gitelman, "Beyond Leninism:
Political Development in Eastern Europe," Newsletter on
Comparative Studies of Communism, Buffalo, N.Y., May 1972,
pp. 18-43.
3. "The CSCE and Eastern Europe," The World Today,
London, May 1973.
4. For a discussion of this issue, see Fritz Ermarth,
Internationalism, Security, and Legitimacy: The Challenge

to Soviet Interests in East Europe, 1964-1968 (Santa Monica: The Rand Corporation, 1969), pp. 18-23.

5.   See Charles Andras, "The New Left in Hungary," Hungarian Background Report/1, RFER (EERA), 16 January 1974.

6.   Berliner Zeitung, East Berlin, 20 August 1971.

7.   For a discussion of China's relations with the EEC, see Dick Wilson, "China and the European Community," The China Quarterly, no. 56 (London, October-December 1973).

8.   Hsinhua/United Nations, 3 October 1972.

9.   Hsinhua/Helsinki, 13 July 1973.   See also Hsinhua/Geneva, 15 December 1973.

10.   Ernst Kux, "China and Europe," Swiss Review of World Affairs, Zurich, January 1973.

11.   Neues Deutschland, East Berlin, 11 July 1973.

12.   Radio Prague, 31 March 1973.

13.   Sekai Shuho, Tokyo, 11 August 1964; see also Pravda, Moscow, 2 September 1964.

14.   Radio Sofia, 8 January 1973.

15.   In a speech to the 15th Congress of Soviet Trade Unions, Pravda, 21 March 1972.

Chnoupek, Bohuslav, 137, 143, 147

Chou En-lai, 170, 212, 230, 240

Comecon: Khrushchev's attitude toward, 2; and economic integration, 6-7, 25-36, 60, 65, 66, 67-68; and trade with West, 50-51, 242-244; April 1969 summit meeting, 58; and GDR, 106-107; International Bank for Economic Cooperation, 130; and Rumania, 60, 171; and EEC, 242-244

Common Market (see European Community)

Conference on Security and Cooperation in Europe: and USSR, 54-57, 65-66, 75, 76; Helsinki preparatory talks, 66-67; agenda, 44, 183, 236; and military force reduction talks, 72-100; as achievement of policy of peaceful coexistence, 24; as part of détente strategy, 54; East European attitude toward, 60-61, 65; Ulbricht on, 105; impact of on GDR, 109; Polish attitude toward, 120, 127, 132-133; Hungarian attitude toward, 65, 153-154, 156; and Hungary as liaison with West, 162; probable effect of on Danube Basin, 166; Rumanian attitude toward, 168-169; Yugoslav attitude toward, 191-195; probable effect of on Balkans, 227; attitude of People's Republic of China toward, 239-242

Council for Mutual Economic Assistance (see Comecon)

CSCE (see Conference on Security and Cooperation in Europe)

Czechoslovakia: 1968 invasion of, 6, 26, 80, 88, 98, 140, 155, 197; and contact with West, 64, 142-143, 146-147; and national autonomy, 3, 4, 5; and economic reform, 4, 51, 64; and ideological campaign, 18, 40, 41, 99; and CSCE, 65; and MFR talks, 76-78, 86; attitude toward presence of Soviet troops, 97, 98; and FRG, 118-119, 136-139, 143-147; and USSR, 136; and Warsaw Pact, 140; and Danubian cooperation, 164-167; Yugoslav attitude toward invasion of, 196, 197, 199, 200; effect of invasion on Albania, 221

Cyprus, 210, 212, 213, 214, 215, 228, 230

Danube River Commission, 166

Danubian cooperation, 164-167

Davis, Richard T., 154

Debré, Michel, 140

de Gaulle, Charles, 61

Denmark, 127, 176

Dent, Frederick B., 155

Djilas, Milovan, 203

Dolanc, Stane, 197, 199, 207, 227

Douglas-Home, Sir Alec, 239

Dubcek, Alexander, 5

East Germany (see German Democratic Republic)

economic cooperation and trade, 50, 69-70, 236, 242-245, 246

EEC (see European Economic Community)

Engels, Friedrich, 174
Ermarth, Fritz, 216-217
European Economic Community:
and People's Republic of
China, 34, 239; and USSR,
53, 56, 58; and GDR, 104,
106, 107; Poland's attitude
toward, 135, 136; and Ru-
mania, 185, 243; East European attitude toward, 242-
245

Fadeev, Nikolai, 161
Falin, V. M., 105
Federal Republic of Germany:
and Rumania, 54-56, 96-97,
216; and Poland, 73, 118,
119, 128, 129, 133, 136;
and GDR, 18, 55, 108, 109;
and ideological campaign,
21; and USSR, 53, 54, 57-58,
63, 73, 74; defense expenditures of, 77; military
strength of, 86; and MFR,
87, 95; and Czechoslovakia,
118-119, 136-140, 143-147;
and West European cooperation, 135; and Hungary, 151-
153, 154, 156-159, 160; and
EEC, 243; and trade with
East, 245
Finland, 176, 241
Fock, Jeno, 158
France: and military force
reductions, 86; and trade
with East, 53, 244; and
USSR, 53, 54, 61, 63; de-
fense expenditures of, 77;
attitude toward West European cooperation, 135; and
EEC, 243
"free flow" of people and information: and CSCE agenda,
44, 236, 246; East European
attitude toward, 13, 14, 49,

61; and East European
ideological coordination,
21, 22, 23; East German
attitude toward, 109-117;
Czechoslovak attitude to-
ward, 140, 141; Hungarian
attitude toward, 154; Ru-
manian attitude toward, 186;
and economic development,
236
FRG (see Federal Republic of
Germany)

Garai, Robert, 155
GATT, 50, 160
GDR (see German Democratic
Republic)
General Agreement on Tariffs
and Trade (see GATT)
German Democratic Republic:
and FRG, 18, 54, 102, 108-
109; economic policy of,
4-12, 51, 65, 66; and USSR,
18, 97, 132, 237; recognition of, 73, 74-75; and MFR
talks, 76-77, 79-80, 86;
defense expenditures of,
77; bilateral defense treaties of, 96; special relationship with Common Market,
104, 106, 191; unique position within Comecon, 106-
107; relations with Poland,
131-132; relations with
People's Republic of China,
240-241
Gheorghiu-Dej, Gheorghe, 188,
226
Gierek, Edward, 7, 11, 119,
120, 126, 130, 131
Gomulka Plan, 127
Gomulka, Wladyslaw, 128
Goodpaster, General Andrew,
85
Great Britain, 61, 63, 86, 87

Middle East, 193-194, 197, 211, 231-232, 243, 244
Military Force Reductions: and CSCE, 72-100; and U.S., 72, 75-76, 79, 81-95; and Czechoslovakia, 76-77, 86; and GDR, 77-78, 79-80, 86; and Hungary, 77-78, 87, 88, 162-163, 183; and Rumania, 76, 86, 87, 90-91, 179-183; and Yugoslavia, 87; and USSR, 162-163
Mindszenty, Jozsef Cardinal, 154
Minic, Milos, 192
Molotov, Vyacheslav, 102
Munich Agreement, 118, 137, 138, 139, 144-145, 158

Nagy, Janos, 158
NATO (see North Atlantic Treaty Organization)
Nixon, Richard M., 24, 84-85, 89, 90, 170, 229
North Atlantic Treaty Organization: dissolution of urged at Karlovy Vary conference, 180; and military force reductions, 73; and People's Republic of China, 34, 239; Soviet attitude toward, 58, 85; military capacity of, 82-83, 84, 89; and Rapacki Plan, 126; and Greece, 229

Olszowski, Stefan, 120, 136, 181

Palme, Olaf, 115
Papadopoulos, Georgios, 219
peaceful coexistence, 23-26, 43, 44, 45, 46, 75-76, 141, 155
Peter, Janos, 151, 157, 158, 164, 165

Pipinelis, Panayiotis, 220
Poland: and FRG, 73, 118, 120, 128, 129, 132-133, 136; and USSR, 3, 7, 97, 125, 131-132; 1956 upheaval in, 2; and economic reform, 3, 64; 1970 riots in, 9, 11, 119; and ideological campaign, 18, 99; and MFR, 76-77, 86; and GDR, 131-132; and EEC, 135, 136; and People's Republic of China, 238
Pompidou, Georges, 185, 239
Portugal, 239
Prague Declaration, 58
Prague Spring, 3, 5, 30, 56
Prchlik, General Vaclav, 98
Puja, Frigyes, 155

Quarles, Bryan, 88

Ranki, Gyorgy, 165
Rankovic, Aleksandar, 207, 215
Rapacki, Adam, 127
Rapacki Plan, 126, 127
Rumania: and FRG, 54-55, 97, 216; and USSR, 3, 4, 5, 6, 7, 8, 34, 212, 220; and national autonomy, 3, 4, 5, 8, 34, 174-175; and economic reform, 3; and People's Republic of China, 8, 12-13, 239; and ideological campaign, 13, 18, 23, 28, 29, 45, 185-186; and Comecon, 60-61, 171; and economic cooperation with West, 64-65, 184-185; and CSCE, 168-169, 177-179; and MFR, 76-77, 86, 87, 90-91, 179-184; defense expenditures of, 77; and Danubian cooperation, 164-167; foreign policy of, 169-172, 216-217; and Yugoslavia,

CHARLES ANDRAS is deputy director of the Research and Analysis Department of Radio Free Europe. His articles on Eastern Europe have appeared in a number of American and West German journals.

J. F. BROWN is director of Radio Free Europe's Research and Analysis Department. He is the author of The New Eastern Europe (Praeger, 1966) and Bulgaria Under Communist Rule (Praeger, 1970), and has written articles on East European affairs.

ROBERT W. DEAN is a former senior analyst for Poland and Czechoslovakia in RFE's Research and Analysis Department. His publications include West German Trade with the East: The Political Dimension (Praeger, 1974) and articles for such journals as Survey and The World Today.

JOHN DORNBERG is a free-lance journalist and writer based in Munich who specializes in communist affairs. From 1965 to 1972 he worked for Newsweek as Bonn correspondent, then as East European correspondent based in Vienna, and finally as Moscow bureau chief. His publications include Schizophrenic Germany (Macmillan, 1961); The Other Germany (Doubleday, 1968); The New Tsars: Russia Under Stalin's Heirs (Doubleday, 1972); and Brezhnev: The Masks of Power (Praeger, 1973; and Basic Books, 1974).

ROBERT R. KING is currently senior analyst for Rumania and Bulgaria in Radio Free Europe's Research and Analysis Department. He is the author of Minorities Under Communism: Nationalities as a Source of Tension Among Balkan Communist States (Harvard University Press, 1973) and coauthor of Yugoslav Communism and the Macedonian Question (Archon, 1971), and has written articles for several American and West German journals.

F. STEPHEN LARRABEE is a former analyst for Radio Free Europe in Munich, Germany. He has published a number of articles on Balkan affairs in Europa Archiv, Osteuropa, Survey, Orbis, and Problems of Communism, and is presently at work on a study of Soviet policy vis-à-vis the Federal Republic of Germany between 1966 and 1969.

WILLIAM F. ROBINSON is senior analyst for Hungary in Radio Free Europe's Research and Analysis Department. His articles have appeared in both American and European professional journals, and he is the author of The Pattern of Reform in Hungary (Praeger, 1973).

HENRY SCHAEFER is a specialist in communist international economic relations. He has written a number of articles on Soviet and East European affairs and is the author of Comecon and the Politics of Integration (Praeger, 1972).

SLOBODAN STANKOVIC is senior research analyst for Yugoslavia in RFE's Research and Analysis Department. He has written extensively on Yugoslav affairs for Swiss, West German, British, French, Italian, and American publications.

LAWRENCE L. WHETTEN is resident director of the German Graduate Program, School of International Relations, of the University of Southern California. He is the author of Ostpolitik: The Federal Republic's Relations with the Warsaw Pact (Oxford University Press, 1971) and has published in such journals as The World Today, Orbis, Survival, Survey, and Revue de Droit International. He is a member of the editorial board of Studies in Comparative Communism.

THE POLITICS OF MODERNIZATION IN EASTERN EUROPE: Testing
the Soviet Model
            edited by Charles Gati

EAST GERMAN CIVIL-MILITARY RELATIONS: The Impact of
Technology, 1949-72
            Dale R. Herspring
            foreword by Peter C. Ludz

SINO-AMERICAN DÉTENTE AND ITS POLICY IMPLICATIONS
            edited by Gene T. Hsiao

THE FUTURE OF INTER-BLOC RELATIONS IN EUROPE
            edited by Louis J. Mensonides
            and James A. Kuhlman